Life Through the

Rearview Mirror

Enjoy!

Ed Lincoln

Edward Lincoln

BOOK PUBLISHERS NETWORK

Book Publishers Network
P.O. Box 2256
Bothell • WA • 98041
PH • 425-483-3040
www.bookpublishersnetwork.com

10 9 8 7 6 5 4 3 2 1
Printed in the United States of America

LCCN 2010934497

Soft Cover
    ISBN10 1-935359-54-1
    ISBN13 978-1-935359-54-8

Hard Cover
    ISBN10 1-935359-63-0
    ISBN13 978-1-935359-63-0

Although this book is based on real life experiences, a few names, places and dates have been changed due to faulty recollection or for anonymity's sake.

Photo Credits
Matthew Weston, Fowler Portraits, cover photograph of Pink Toe Truck
Gene R. Doven, Fun Meters, page 260
Yuen Lui, page 295

Editors: Lori Zue and Katrina Hayrynen
Cover Designer: Laura Zugzda
Typographer: Stephanie Martindale

I dedicate this book to my dad and mom, Ed and Susie Lincoln, who lovingly taught me the skills and work ethic that have helped me achieve success throughout my life.

To Connie, my wife of forty-six years, you are the love of my life.

To Wendy and Katrina, you make me proud to be your dad.

To Keith and Mark, you will always be genuine sons to me.

To Marcia, Craig and Shawn, you hold a special place in my heart.

To Isaac, Luke, Grace, Cole, Jonah, Eli and Brooke, you all are the joy of my life.

To our hundreds of employees, without you, we would never have succeeded.

Contents

Acknowledgments

I wish to thank my wife, Connie, for giving me the best years of my life. She is my closest friend and confidante. She has kept me focused during the times I was fading underneath a heavy load.

There are many others without whom this dream would not have been realized. I would like to thank my writing teacher, Francis Dayee, for all of her advice and inspiration. I would like to thank my publisher, Sheryn Hara, who believed in my project and encouraged me along the way. My seasoned editor, Lori Zue, whose sense of humor and dedication kept me on track.

My deepest thanks go out to Ichabod Caine for taking the time to read and review my book. Thanks for your generous praise.

A very special thank you to Matthew Weston, our friend and the owner of Fowler Protraits, who allowed us to use his photograph of the Pink Toe Truck for the front cover of the book.

Others who contributed countless hours to the ongoing editing phase include my wife, Connie, who helped me through every step of this writing journey; my daughter Katrina, who worked tirelessly to fine tune my writing and get me to the finish line; my daughter Wendy and her husband, Keith, who helped along the way with editing and during the final read-through; and our son-in-law Mark, who sacrificed his wife for an extended period so she could finish this project.

I want to thank our grandchildren, who were also involved. They read some of my stories and gave me pointers and feedback along the way.

And, finally, I want to thank my beloved parents, whose influence is scattered throughout the pages of this book.

Foreword

I first met Ed Lincoln back in the early 1980s through our mutual friend, George Toles, the Seattle SuperSonics' longtime PA announcer. Back in those days, we were both involved in the same business organization and we also joined forces in a number of advertising pursuits. I've always thoroughly enjoyed Ed's humor and wit, and I know him to be a man of great character and faith.

If you grew up in Seattle or lived here for any length of time, a certain icon stood out to us all. Standing in the shadow of the Space Needle was the Pink Toe Truck, the funny-looking truck with giant toes. We loved it; it made us smile and it became a part of us and Seattle.

The story you're about to read is the story of the man behind the toe. It's an American story of family, love, hard work, heartbreak and a lot of humor. It's proof that if you follow your heart, are a person of your word and listen to God, dreams do come true . . . even if you stub your toe along the way.

Ichabod Caine
Seattle radio personality
www.wildboarradio.com

Ed's sister Barbara and Ed

Chapter 1

Early Lessons in Salesmanship

I started learning to be a salesman in the training ground of our Ballard neighborhood in north Seattle when I was six.

My mom was the catalyst for my newfound career. Well, Mom and the single large holly tree crowding our front sidewalk. Taller than my dad and fatter than our kitchen table, it sported thousands of stiff, sharp-pointed green leaves and clusters of bright red berries.

When I arrived home from school one winter day, Mom called me into the kitchen. She looked kind of serious, and I wondered what she was going to say.

She motioned for me to follow her outside. "I've got an idea," she said. "If you'll help me cut these holly branches, I'll make some Christmas wreaths. You can sell them to our neighbors. Do you think you could do that?" Enthusiasm had replaced her seriousness. "You can use your red wagon to carry them around the block."

"Really? That sounds like a great idea!" I was so proud that my mom was giving me a responsibility like this.

"I'll let you keep all the money you get so you can buy Christmas gifts. If you sell enough, you might even be able to put some money into your own savings account at the bank. Does that sound good to you?"

Ed sizing up the holly tree

I nodded vigorously. I wasn't really sure about the bank account suggestion, but I loved the idea of being able to buy Christmas presents for my family all on my own.

"I can hardly wait. When can we start?" I asked.

"If you'll get the stepladder from the shed out back, I'll get the clippers from the garage. We'll see how much we can accomplish before dark."

I raced into the shed and dragged the four-foot stepladder to the front of the house. We both donned our work gloves; mine were way too big, but that didn't matter to me. Mom climbed the ladder, and soon I could hear the clippers at work. She looked down towards me and held out the first fruits of our labor.

I stacked each bunch on the grass. Mom worked her way down the holly tree, and my red and green collection on the ground grew with each armload. She stepped off the ladder and surprised me by handing me the clippers. I'd never used the sharp, pointed tool before.

"Unhook the safety clip, and take your time. Be sure to keep your fingers away from the blade."

I started cutting the lower branches she pointed out. Several times I cut the wrong ones, but Mom said that was okay. It felt good to be in charge of such a grown-up tool.

Then Mom said, "I think we have cut enough for one day. Let's pick everything up, and we can start making the wreaths."

It took three trips to carry our bundles into the garage. I wrapped the wire for Mom while she shaped the holly into circles. The sharp leaves often poked my hand and left red scrapes, but I didn't complain.

After several hours of hard work, we had a large stack of arrangements finished. The garage floor was a mess of clipped-off leaves and berries. My fingers hurt from tying the wire and I was tired, but the experience of doing something new made me feel a bit older. I was proud of that.

"These are beautiful. I think this was a swell idea, Mom."

After Mom pulled off her gloves and closed the garage door, she said, "I think you should wait until ten o'clock tomorrow morning before you start showing our neighbors what you have to sell. Saturday is a good day to catch a lot of people at home, but most people want to sleep in and have a leisurely breakfast. After that, they might be in a better mood to buy."

"Can I load up my wagon right after dinner?" I couldn't wait to get started.

"Okay. But be sure to double-tie some string around your load. After that, you might want to think about going to bed early. It's going to be a busy day tomorrow."

I sighed but gave in with a smile. After finishing my meal and tying my load, I said goodnight and headed to bed earlier than I usually did on a Friday night.

The next morning, I trotted downstairs at eight o'clock and went directly to the garage to stare at my load of ten wreaths. The prickly green leaves and red berries were all tucked into my Radio Flyer wagon, just as I had left them.

As ten o'clock approached, the reality of going door-to-door on my own began to sink in. Suddenly, it felt as if there were a swarm of butterflies in my stomach. Mom appeared out of nowhere and asked, "Are you ready to head out?"

I nodded, since my throat was too tight to talk. I must have looked scared because she knelt down, held my shoulders and looked me in the eye. "You can do this, Eddie. I'll tag along and keep watch from the sidewalk. I'll stay just one house behind you." After her encouragement, I felt better and started on my way.

When I reached the front porch of the first house, I hesitated and glanced back at my mom. Then, I took a deep breath and knocked as firmly as I could. I was greeted by a friendly lady who was very enthusiastic about my wares. She happily paid the two-dollar price to buy one of the Christmas wreaths. As I towed the wagon back to the sidewalk, Mom gave me a huge smile. I sure felt good about my first sale.

I whispered, "That wasn't so hard. I think the lady liked me."

In a little over an hour, Mom and I danced home with an empty wagon. The success of selling every wreath so easily filled me with boundless excitement. I never wanted to stop.

Recognizing my enthusiasm and her own limits, Mom pronounced, "We'll make some more, but tomorrow will be the last day for selling. I still need to make cookies with Barbara and get our house decorated for Christmas." My sister, Barbara, was just over a year older than me. She was born with a heart defect and couldn't do any of the heavier work I did.

"Do you think Sunday's sales will be as good as they were today?"

"I sure hope so," Mom smiled.

"Don't worry, Mom. I can sell." I showed off my best ear-to-ear grin. "It's too bad we can't make a hundred wreaths, because then we could use Dad's truck."

"Don't go overboard on your dreams," she warned.

After lunch that day, I picked up my gloves and the clippers. Again Mom let me clip the lower branches myself. I went to work trimming the limbs I could reach while Mom gave me specific instructions. My stack of green holly branches grew and grew. I just knew that tomorrow was going to be the biggest sales day of my life. I could hardly wait to see what the new day would bring.

That night, as promised, Mom finished making the Christmas wreaths. I again tied the wire for each bundle and carefully stacked the first half in my wagon. The next morning, I headed out on my own, armed with a load of confidence from the previous day's success. I expanded my territory to a block north of where we lived. Nobody knew me there, so I realized it might be a little harder to make a sale.

Right away, I was wary of houses with fences because I noticed that some of them had dogs inside. If I entered a dog's yard through a gate, I risked getting bitten. So, instead, I'd shake the gate and, if a barking dog appeared, I'd skip the sales call to avoid any trouble.

When I reached the house on the corner, a friendly lady surprised me by saying, "I'll take two of them."

"What are you going to do with two?" I asked, after I ran to my wagon to grab a second wreath.

"I'm going to surprise my sister with one. I'll see her tomorrow, and I'm sure she'll love it."

By noon, I was down to my final wreath. I knocked at the door of the last house on the block. A weathered grandma, holding a cane, opened the door and smiled at me. I gave her my sales talk, and she listened politely.

She asked, "Who made the wreath?"

"My mom and I made it in our garage. We actually made twenty-four, and this is my last one," I said proudly.

Then she quietly said, "You did a great job. I would love to buy your wreath, but I don't have any extra spending money right now."

She seemed kind, and she reminded me of my own grandmother so I said, "Actually, this one's free if you would like it."

The surprise and gratefulness that lit up her face made my heart feel full. I immediately knew that I'd made a great decision. In one brief moment, I had learned that giving can be even more fun than making money. It was the right thing to do.

I have never forgotten my first weekend as a salesman from that Christmas long ago. I learned not to be disappointed by an unopened door and, instead, to move on and keep knocking. I've been selling ever since. I also learned to share my blessings with others less fortunate, and it has been deeply rewarding.

―――――

The next year we moved a few blocks north and no longer had a holly tree in our yard. At dinner one evening, my dad mentioned he had a new business idea.

"How would you like to sell Christmas trees this year?" he asked.

"Sure!" I responded, jumping at the idea. "Where do we get the trees? Do we have to go to the forest and cut them down?"

"I've seen commercial Christmas tree farms out in the country, less than an hour from here," Mom said. "You just tell them how many you want, and they cut them."

I wriggled in my chair, eager to ask my next question. "Is it that easy?"

Dad nodded and smiled at my enthusiasm. "So, now you can try your hand at selling again. I'll look for a vacant lot to rent for the first two weeks in December."

That year and the next, I sold Christmas trees with my dad.

Selling trees was a lot harder than selling wreaths. On many nights, it was bitter cold, and my fingers tingled painfully despite my leather gloves. After the first really cold night, Dad brought a camp stove to warm us. During the second year, I helped Dad build some tree stands so the trees weren't squashed. Our first year's customers returned and new ones showed up. Our sales increased. I liked the action. The busier we were, the faster time passed. More customers made the long hours and cold nights worth it.

At that time, Dad was a commercial fisherman and gone to Alaska for six months of each year. So, to me, the biggest benefit of the tree business was the time spent working alongside my dad. When business was slow, he would tell tall tales and then challenge me to make up my own taller ones. Other times he would tell riddles that were difficult to remember. My job was to repeat the riddle perfectly or else start over. On some nights, we would play tag among the trees to keep warm. It was always great fun to be with Dad.

At the end of those first two weeks, we had ten trees left over. Dad made a cardboard sign that said FREE TREES. I helped clean up the rest of the lot, and we took our tools home. Dad opened up the money box for me to look inside. I'd never seen such a pile of cash.

"Don't forget, I haven't been paid back for the cost of the trees or the lot rental," he cautioned. "Let me show you the paperwork."

I looked down at the invoices and then watched Dad take out his one hundred and fifty dollars. The pile of money was reduced by half. I knew my 20 percent share had just shrunk. Dad began to count the leftover money.

"Dad, how much will I get?"

He handed me the money as he answered, "Thirty dollars."

I was thrilled. That was a lot of money. I gave him a big smile and a bear hug. I put some of the profit aside for Christmas presents and deposited almost all of the rest of it into my bank account. With the bank's added interest, my savings were growing faster than I had imagined.

My aptitude for salesmanship found opportunities to make money in the strangest places. If there was something to sell, I didn't hesitate to get involved.

When I was eight, my friend Buddy introduced me to frog hunting. He and his younger brother, Billy, had discovered a frog haven near the Ballard Locks.

Buddy made me a simple offer. "If you come with me to the frog pond, I'll show you how to catch some fast frogs."

"That would be great! When are you going next?"

"How 'bout this Thursday? It has to be near dark for the frogs to come out. Bring your flashlight and, if you want to take a few home, bring a jar with a lid that has holes punched through it for air."

I waited until Thursday morning to ask permission. "Mom, can I go frog hunting with Buddy after dinner? He knows where to find them."

"Sure, but you'll need to be careful since it will be getting dark by then. How long will you be gone?"

Excited that she had agreed, I answered, "Probably an hour, but we have to wait until it's almost dark so the frogs will show themselves."

It seemed a long wait until after dinner, but finally Buddy knocked loudly at my door. I grinned as we raced down the steps towards our bikes.

"How much time did your mother give you?"

"She said an hour or so."

"That's not much time. It'll take ten minutes just to get there if we pedal full speed."

"Boys, don't forget to turn on your headlights," Mom shouted from the porch.

We finally reached the water-filled ditch near the Ballard Locks, after pedaling for nearly a mile.

Buddy whispered some advice, "If we stay quiet, they'll swim to the surface and start singing their frog songs. Listen, they're just starting to croak."

When a minute had passed, with a flick of his wrist, he sailed a small rock into the middle of the pond. There were little splashes everywhere as the frogs dove for cover. All hints of frog songs were gone.

"After they start croaking again, look for the closest frog. When you see one, aim your flashlight right at him. He'll freeze for a second because it blinds him. Then, if you're fast enough, you can make a grab for him."

I watched Buddy for a few minutes. On his third try, he captured a frog and put it in his jar. After a few empty grabs and a near fall, I wasn't sure I'd be catching anything. The slime and slippery muck had me stumbling all over the place. Finally, I got really close to a frog. It was no bigger than a prune. I was standing in a foot of water when I bent down and faced the frog eye to eye. In one quick swinging motion with my right arm, I scooped him up and plopped him into the jar. My head spun with excitement. Twelve more tries yielded seven more frogs. Even in a foot of water, I felt ten feet tall.

"You're doing great," Buddy exclaimed.

Suddenly, I looked at my watch and panicked. "It's getting late."

"How many frogs do you have?"

"I've got eight," I said proudly.

"I've got ten in my jar," Buddy bragged.

When we got back home, Mom was surprised how soaked I was, but she didn't complain.

"It looks like you're a good frog hunter. How many did you catch?"

"I got eight, and Buddy got ten. It sure was fun."

"What are you going to do with them?" she questioned. "They're too small to fry."

"I haven't decided."

"Well, don't let them get loose in the house, and be sure to let them out of the jar before too long or they'll die."

After breakfast the next morning, I walked to the garage to check on my sleeping frogs. They looked hungry so I added a cracker and a small clump of grass. As I looked at all of them in my jar, I realized that it might be fun to show off my new pets at school.

Ed and his sister, Barbara, walking to school

My frogs drew a crowd as I walked down the road. Some of the kids wanted one. Not wanting to give away my treasures, I decided that five cents, the amount most kids carried for milk money, was a good price. Since I had just the one jar, my customers stuck their frogs in whatever spot seemed most convenient and secure: a pocket, a bag or wrapped up in a coat. When I arrived at school, I had only four left in my jar. It was ten minutes before I had to worry about the bell, so I stood next to the swings and sold them all before school started.

I had been in my classroom for an hour or so when my teacher handed me a note. "The principal wants to see you in his office," it read.

I had no idea why he wanted to see me. Maybe he found the hat I had lost last week. I strolled down the long hall and turned into the school office.

Mr. Carpenter was waiting. He stared down at me and said in a deep voice, "Edward Lincoln?"

"Yes, sir."

"Come into my office," he commanded.

He didn't look very friendly. He didn't sit down nor waste any time.

"Don't ever bring frogs to school again! Do you understand me?"

I hung my head low and made no excuses. I had known in the back of my mind there might be some reason not to bring them to school, mainly because I didn't have permission from Mom. Plus, it wasn't the right day for show and tell. I had only planned to show off my frogs. The selling idea was mostly an afterthought.

"Young man, answer me!"

My face felt red, like it was sunburned. "Yes, sir," I mumbled. I was embarrassed that he had yelled at me, but I was very happy that he didn't make me stay after school. Actually, as I remember it, the meeting was over almost before it started. I'd learned at home that it generally worked out best if I didn't make excuses for my mistakes.

At recess, a friend told me that two of the frogs had gotten loose in his classroom. The kids burst out laughing while the surprised and perturbed teacher sent for the principal. After several minutes of chasing the frogs on his hands and knees, he finally captured them. With a frog in each hand, he had stormed out of the room while the teacher tried to bring her chaotic class back to order.

As I sat at my desk that afternoon, I couldn't get the principal's voice out of my mind. I had no plans to get him angry ever again.

On the way home, no one asked for any refunds, so at least I got to keep all the profits. I didn't know who squealed on me, but it didn't matter.

When I got home, I confessed to my mom. "My frog days are over. I got busted by the principal. I don't think he knew I sold the frogs for five cents each or he might've made me give the money back. By the way, do you have any good ideas on what I can sell next?"

She smiled and said, "You're just like your dad."

———••———

No matter what I sold, the challenge of selling and the rewards for success stirred something within me. Early on I discovered I had a natural drive to work that exceeded that of most of my peers.

These two years of my childhood, which included lots of business dealings, helped shape my personality and my ambitions. In that short time, selling had become nearly as natural to me as breathing.

Chapter 2

Growing In Responsibility

Our next family move landed us out in the country in south Everett, right next to a busy highway. The house had a small barn out back where I played when it rained. I liked to roam the trails in the woods beyond the barn.

One day, Dad came home with a black and white "Heinz 57" midsized dog. "Here's a friend for you."

It was love at first sight.

"My own dog! Thank you, Dad. I'll take good care of her."

She immediately became my best friend. As soon as I came home from school, she greeted me with her wagging tail and wide smile. On the weekends, we explored the trails. Sometimes she ran off chasing squirrels or rabbits, but she always returned to me.

When springtime came, my dog, who I'd named Blackie, was going to have puppies. I created a spot in the garage to make her comfortable by putting some old towels in a basket.

"I'm sure Blackie appreciates her new bed," Mom quietly whispered.

The first puppy arrived, followed by seven more. They were softer than a bearskin rug. Blackie cleaned them all with her tongue, one by one. I held one in my hand, and all it wanted to do was suck: my fingers, my thumb, even the buttons on my shirt. Blackie was a good mom, sometimes feeding all eight puppies at one time.

Barbara and Ed holding some of the puppies

Before the puppies were two weeks old, tragedy struck. Dad was having coffee in the kitchen on a Sunday morning, when a stranger knocked on the front door.

"Do you own a black dog?" asked a sad-looking man.

"Yes, my son does."

"I'm so sorry, but your dog tried to cross the highway. I swerved, but not enough, and there was a thud. I carried her out of the road and put her in the grass. She didn't make it."

Dad told me as soon as I got up. I rushed outside and found her in the weeds. There was no hope: Blackie was dead. Dad and I carried her out to the edge of the woods. I got my shovel, dug a deep hole to protect her from other animals and laid her to rest. Later that week, Dad helped me make a grave marker, and I placed it next to the grave to remember her.

I couldn't believe Blackie was gone. It was a very sad time for me. The puppies helped, but it took a long while before the hurt began to fade.

———≫≪———

Fortunately, the next few weeks were busy ones. My mom and sister offered to help feed the puppies so they wouldn't starve to death. We took turns using baby bottles. By the end of the month, Mom found homes for seven puppies. I got to keep number eight, the pick of the litter. He was a cuddly, very active black and white puppy.

With summer arriving, I hoped to find a job to keep busy. I had a lot of free time because I didn't have any friends who lived close by. After my dad inquired at the fruit stand five minutes from our house, I was hired by the owner to sweep up and sort spoiled produce. It wasn't very hard work, and it only took me a few hours, three days a week

A month later, I landed a second job directly across the highway at a hamburger spot called The Handout. My job was to pick up, by hand, all the hamburger wrappers and paper cups scattered across the one-acre lot. I received a flat rate of one dollar and twenty-five cents for each Saturday morning and one dollar and fifty cents for the same project on Sunday. I thought the money was fair considering I was only nine, and I could finish in a little over an hour. The eight o'clock start time could be very chilly, but I kept warm by working fast.

The best part of the jobs was earning money, so I did them for several summers. I liked saving money and watching it grow. One time I bought a new Sears bike. Another time I saved enough for a mitt and a board game. There wasn't much I needed in those days.

One Saturday, Dad took me to the local feed store to get a big bag of dog food. I looked over to the far corner of the store where I heard some chirping.

"Dad, can we go see what's making that noise?"

"I can tell you from here," he said as we headed in that direction, "that's a batch of newly hatched chicks."

A heat lamp warmed a large square box, which was wider than I was tall. Then I saw fluffy yellow chicks everywhere—there must have been a hundred.

I reached down to pick one up, but it ran through my fingers and scurried away. I picked some feed up off the floor and held it out to the chicks. They went wild, jumping over each other to get to my hand. Dad reached in with his big hand and caught one on his first grab. He handed it to me to pet, and, when it was time to go, I didn't want to put it back.

"Dad, I really like these baby chicks." I was in love again.

"It's time to grab the dog food," he said, trying to distract me.

"Can we get some chickens?"

"Let's hear what Mom says."

When we got home, Dad brought up the subject with Mom.

"You'd have to take care of the chickens," she said. "And you and Dad would need to build a henhouse next to the barn to protect them."

"If you followed through on tending the chickens," Dad added, "I'd let you share in the profits, but that won't happen until next year when we start selling the eggs. We could start with four dozen and see how you do. You'd need to feed and water them daily, as well as rake out the chicken droppings from the henhouse. Remember, these little chicks will become big chickens in no time."

"Okay, I'll do it. I think raising chickens is going to be fun."

Dad smiled at me and held out his right hand. "Let's shake on it."

I felt so grown-up and proud. It would be good to be in a selling business again.

I enjoyed the job of caring for the chicks. They were always happy to see me and always hungry. Dad was right; the chicks became chickens almost overnight. We had a few roosters, but most of the birds were laying hens. In time, we sold dozens of eggs to the fruit stand where I worked.

Ed and the baby chicks

The roosters were more of a challenge since they would start fights for no reason. Sometimes even the hens would be aggressive.

On occasion, the chickens hemmed a weaker one into a corner of the fence and pecked it enough to draw blood. When that happened, the squawking increased and the whole henhouse would turn against the wounded chicken until they killed it. It was my job to take the dead chicken out before it started another chicken riot.

Some of the chickens became my friends. I especially liked two of the older, more mature laying hens. On the weekends, I would give each an extra handful of chicken feed and pet them while they were sitting in their straw nests. Every now and then, I was lucky enough to be standing at their side, talking to them and stroking their feathers, when a gift plopped out. The eggs were always brown and very warm. Occasionally, my two special chickens gave me somewhat larger eggs than all the other birds. I would gather up these treasures, carefully carry them to the house and present them to my mom. She loved to cook fresh eggs for breakfast.

One morning Mom called me to the kitchen to see a surprise. "Look in the frying pan. Two of the eggs you just brought in were double-yolkers."

When I saw the eggs, I was amazed; I had never seen double-yolks before. "I don't know how those two hens did it," I said, feeling a sense of pride.

Late in the fall, we expanded the size of our chicken coop. My dad found more customers for next year's eggs. Mom and Dad went to the local feed store and bought four dozen more baby chicks.

Dad said, "You're eleven years old now. Do you think you can take care of all the chickens? If you think it's too much work for you, your mother can take over the job."

"I'd love to try," I said.

Two months later, early winter temperatures dropped quickly and hovered somewhere near twenty-five degrees. The heat lamps in the henhouse could not keep out the chill. In the morning, I went into the coop to feed chickens; to my horror, all of the baby chicks were dead. Four dozen dead chicks were scattered around. The largest group of frozen chicks was in a big pile in the corner of the coop. I think they were trying to get warmth from each other, but Mother Nature's cold night got to them all. I was sad for weeks.

———

My parents allowed me, at an early age, to shoulder a generous load of responsibility. I will forever be thankful to them for developing my character and maturity by trusting me to be equal to life's challenges.

Chapter 3

Like Father, Like Son

Even before I became a teenager, I learned to be on guard for my dad's tricks. He had what you'd call a dry sense of humor, and many of my friends never knew for sure if he was kidding. Dad got a kick out of pulling a person's leg, and he'd perfected the art of the blindside. His creativity and timing were unmatched. Every other week or so, he got me good. A few of those pranks still make me chuckle, even today.

One hot summer day, when I was eleven, I was out in the street playing ball with four friends. I noticed Dad drive up in his old Ford. He jumped out and waved and then disappeared into the house. Ten minutes later, he called me over to the front porch.

"Why don't you round up your friends and meet me in the backyard for a Coke party?"

"Sure, that's a great idea. We're all hot and thirsty, and we were just talking about looking for something else to do. They're gonna flip!"

I ran over to my friends and pitched the idea. "My dad has invented a game for us to play. It involves drinking some Coke. Want to give it a try?"

Soon my friends were marching behind me through the side gate. When I looked up, I saw my sister in the kitchen window. She had a knowing smile on her face and a concealed front-row seat for the action.

We all gathered expectantly in our tiny backyard as Dad finished lining up two picnic benches, side by side. He walked over and handed me five blindfolds. I knew the drill. It was the second time I'd seen this trick but the first time I'd been asked to take part in the shenanigan.

"Dad has some Coke for each one of you to drink, but only if you put on one of these blindfolds."

Quickly and unquestioningly each friend complied.

Then Dad took over. "Each of you needs to sit down on the bench that's just behind you."

All of us followed the instructions. Dad came down the line and placed a towel on each of our laps. Then he asked the first boy, Mike, if he preferred a glass of water or a Coke.

He answered, "Coke."

The next thing that happened would have totally shocked all of the boys' mothers. I heard the cap pop off the hefty twenty-six-ounce Coke bottle. I couldn't resist the urge to peek over the top of my blindfold just in time to see Dad shaking the bottle like crazy.

Mike whispered to the kid next to him, "This is going to be fun." At that moment, he took the first blast as my dad awkwardly slid his thumb partially off the top of the bottle. He tried to control the warm spray, but the pressure was so strong it knocked Mike backwards off of the bench. He landed in the flower bed. He was completely stunned. Soda pop covered him from head to toe, and foam was spilling out of his mouth. Then, suddenly, he burst into laughter.

Dad knew he had to move quickly, before all of the boys scattered. Without a moment's delay, he gave the next kid in line a free taste of Coke. As each friend took a turn at the outdoor "soda fountain," the screams of surprise and delight grew louder. We all doubled over with laughter as we removed our blindfolds and took in the foamy mess that covered us all. From that day on, my friends loved my dad—but, of course, not nearly as much as I did!

At our home, practical jokes had a way of escalating. I vividly remember another event that took place at a different house and backyard. I was twelve, and, by that time, my family had moved to a house in north Seattle.

It was the beginning of summer break, and I had two friends over for an outdoor sleepover. We set up my family's tent on Thursday evening and proceeded to goof off until bedtime. Around ten o'clock, we made our way outside where we stayed up late, telling jokes and stories, including some about my dad's past pranks.

"He can't be trusted," I reminded my friends.

We finally fell asleep around midnight.

At close to seven in the morning, I heard a strange noise that I chose to ignore because I was so exhausted. It sounded like someone was messing with our tent, but then the sound disappeared and everything was completely still. A few minutes later, out of nowhere, a blast of cold water sprayed me in the face. I joined the chorus of my friends' screams as I opened my eyes to see water spraying in every direction. I leaped out of my sleeping bag and I tried to unzip the tent door. It was stuck! I frantically jerked on it until it gave way. As soon as the door was partially opened, the three of us fell out together in a tangled mess.

Once out on the lawn, I immediately saw the problem. A green garden hose was threaded into our tent. Inside, a lawn sprinkler still twirled at full speed. I quickly ran to the faucet and cranked it off.

Dad, the King of Pranks, was nowhere in sight. We all knew, immediately, that he was the culprit.

Right then and there, I planned to exact revenge and save face. I didn't discuss any payback ideas with my buddies because I didn't want to give any warning to my victim. Dad was headed to work soon, so I needed to think fast.

His work boots were always located in the utility room next to the back door, so I knew his exit path to his Ford pickup truck. After thinking for a moment, a brilliant idea formed in my mind. I was going to fight water with water!

I grabbed an empty bucket from the garden and headed over to the nearby faucet. I turned it on and then ran to the end of the hose. I didn't have time to unscrew the sprinkler, but it didn't matter. I was already soaked to the bone. I jammed the swirling spray into the five-gallon container and anxiously watched it fill up.

I worked alone as my two buddies stood back in wonder. I whispered, "Signal me as soon as you see my dad coming out the screen door."

Both of my friends gave me a thumb's up.

I knew there was an old ten-foot ladder behind the shrubs because I had used it a few weeks earlier to clean the gutters of our single-story rambler. I looked around for my dad; I knew my preparation time was almost up. I found the ladder and tilted it upward to touch the roof. With a sloshing, nearly full bucket in hand, I quickly climbed the ladder to the roof. To protect myself from a possible counterattack, I carefully pulled the old ladder up next to me.

Stepping very lightly, I stealthily made my way to a position just above the utility room's back door. I stood poised and ready and shaking with adrenalin. *This is a perfect opportunity to get even, so aim well.* Then to calm myself, I waved to my anxious buddies standing thirty feet away.

As minutes passed, I considered the wisdom of my plan. Dad's payback could be swift and brutal. Did I really want to risk it? Still, this was my big chance to impress my friends and, at the same time, get my revenge. Should I go through with it or would it be wiser to chicken out and avoid the consequences? It was a high-stakes decision.

I could see my two drenched pals pacing nervously near the tent with both sets of eyes staring at the back door. With bated breath, they awaited my retaliation. At that moment, I made my choice.

Now, all I needed was the victim. *What was taking so long?*

Maybe it was the luck of the draw or just the way it worked out, but as soon as I'd made up my mind, dear old Dad stuck his head out the door. Because of the roof overhang, he was not yet in my line of fire.

He must have thought it was safe because he took a step onto the small patio and then paused as he said something to my friends. One of them had tried to send me a signal with a short wave of his hand. Dad must have thought the wave was for him. The moment was right, and my target was in full view. I was perfectly aligned so I immediately dumped my entire load of ammunition out of the bucket. At that instant, I was fully committed—there was no stopping the force of gravity. Five gallons of ice cold water rushed towards my dad's head. He let out a loud yelp like a wounded dog and quickly disappeared into the utility room.

(My dad later admitted, "I was so shocked by the blast of cold water that, for a few seconds, I wasn't sure where it came from.")

I was triumphant! I knew this win was a big one. I felt a little giddy inside.

As soon as he composed himself, Dad burst back out of the screen door like a Doberman Pinscher. He looked up and our eyes met. It was obvious he was hoping to find a way to counterattack.

He grabbed the loose hose and spun off the still-active sprinkler. In an instant, I was no longer the hunter but the hunted.

"Boys, where's the ladder?" he demanded.

Receiving no answer, Dad attempted to blast me with the hose. Fortunately, I was out of range and getting farther away every second as I ran to the other side of the sloped roof.

Dad tried running around the front of the house, but he ran out of hose; as he came around the corner it jerked itself right out of his hand. I stayed on the move, traveling from one side of the roof to the other. I refused to be taken captive.

Time was on my side because Dad needed to change all of his clothes and get to work. As soon as my friends gave me the "all clear" sign, I snuck off the roof by climbing down the ladder I lowered to the front of the house.

"That was one cool water fight with a great ending," my friend said.

"Let's talk later," I urged. "We need to get out of here fast!"

My buddies and I sprinted down the street and were three blocks away when Dad, driving his Ford truck, found us. He stopped and slowly rolled down his passenger window. With his stony face protruding halfway out, he looked directly at me and loudly barked five words I'd never heard before.

"EVERY DOG HAS HIS DAY!"

Ed and his dad

Chapter 4

Cushman Caper

By the time I was eleven, my dad owned and operated Lincoln Auto Wrecking on Aurora Avenue in Seattle. In the summer months, I usually worked five days a week doing odd jobs, mostly cleanup work. During the school year, I only worked on Saturdays. I loved going to my dad's car yard. I can't remember a time when I wasn't learning about car engines. There was so much to know about so many different types of engines. As I got older, my dad started giving me a variety of projects to work on so I could expand my knowledge. Sometimes Dad let me do things that should have been reserved for older boys.

Ed's dad and mom in front of their office

One memorable escapade, in 1955, could have put me in juvenile detention at the ripe old age of fourteen. My adventure involved a step-through-style 1948 Cushman scooter. The stage was set for this incident on a Friday in March, one year earlier. That evening Dad pulled his truck into the carport and motioned for me to come outside. I eagerly responded, but I was cautious in case he had a trick up his sleeve.

"Help me unload this scooter. I just bought it at the Seattle Police Department auction. I thought it might make a good gift for your thirteenth birthday."

"This is mine? You're not just joshing me?"

He shook his head and smiled, "It's all yours."

"Wow! Thanks, Dad!"

"It must've been abandoned for some time because the license plates are two years old. I'm sure it will take some extra work to get it running," he explained as I tried out the worn seat. "You might need to charge the battery and add fresh fuel, and don't forget to check the air pressure in the tires."

I nodded as I looked over my birthday present. The scooter looked like a baby motorcycle. Even with its bulky body and fat tires, I loved what I saw, mainly because it was motorized. Sure, there were a few dents and the mirror was broken, but everything else seemed to be in place. I couldn't wait to show my scooter to my friend and neighbor, Victor.

Mother poked her head outside and announced, "Dinner in fifteen minutes."

I eagerly said, "Hey, Mom, check out what Dad just gave me for my birthday!"

She stepped outside, and I thought I caught a flash of disapproval in her eyes as she looked from the scooter to Dad to me. "It looks like fun, but you'll need to be very careful on that thing."

As soon as she went back into the house to finish getting dinner ready, I grabbed the gas can and added fresh lawnmower gas to the fuel tank. After that, I hooked up the battery charger. I wished I could tell Mom I'd like to eat later, but that wouldn't go over well with Dad. Eating together was important to my folks.

Ed on his birthday scooter

I ate as quickly as I dared and then asked to be excused to go outside. I immediately tried to start the engine. It made some noises and slowly turned, but I still couldn't get it to run. It was time to ask the expert.

I walked over to house and called out to get my dad's attention. "I put in gas and charged the battery for half an hour, but it still won't start. Will you help me get it running?"

"Try disconnecting the gas line and draining out the old gas," he answered from the kitchen window. "While you're at it, try blowing through the line to clear it out. You'll know if the fuel is not good because it will stink like rotten eggs. It might be a good idea to leave the scooter connected to the charger while you work on the gas line."

"What if I do all that and it still doesn't start?"

"Then you'll need to change the spark plugs. We have some spare lawn mower plugs in the garage. I'll help you tomorrow if that's needed. But, it's good for you to learn how to work on the scooter by yourself."

My heart sank with disappointment. I might not get this scooter going until tomorrow. In the past, Dad usually helped me when I asked. He seemed more confident in me than I felt at that moment.

Dad was a magician with engines. If one thing didn't work, he always had other possible solutions. I'd seen him start car engines at the auto wrecking yard even if the motor was already removed from a car and placed on a motor stand. With a surprised customer looking on, Dad would grab a spare battery, a small can of gas and an electrical wire with clips on both ends. Without fail, the engine would roar to life. I wished Dad was helping me right now.

Thirty minutes passed as I completed the stinking gas line trick, followed by adding fresh gas. I tried, once again, to fire up the air-cooled engine. On the fourth try, with the battery wearing down, the machine sprang to life, its little muffler spouting smoke and making a loud, raspy sound. Worse, though, was the smell of something dead and simmering in the exhaust pipe. I wondered if it could be a dead rat. *No, the pipe wasn't big enough.* Just then, out popped what looked like the remains of a half-decayed mouse. At that moment, the engine perked up and smoothed out.

The engine noise alerted my father to my success, and he burst out of the house.

"It's running. But it sure stinks." I added, "The problem was a combination of a dead battery, old gas and a dead mouse plugging up the exhaust."

"Good job!" he said. "I knew you could do it."

Excitedly, I asked, "Can I go for a ride?"

"Let me check it out first. If all goes well, I'll swing back and pick you up."

Dad was a bit oversized for the little scooter; he looked like a gorilla trying to ride a tricycle. Both Dad and the scooter wobbled as they were trying to get used to each other.

When he returned, he gave his report. "The clutch is a little sticky; it needs a minor adjustment. But, the brakes responded as they should. Jump on behind me, and I'll show you how it feels."

Like a racehorse out of the starting gate, I leaped onto the back of the scooter. Dad steered the Cushman down the block with me wedged in behind him. I was desperately hanging on to the front of his belt with my thumbs digging in for traction. As Dad picked up speed, I could feel the engine's vibrations and hear the leaky muffler noise, but I couldn't see around my dad. It was like riding a roller coaster in the dark. Fear and excitement were tussling in my belly, but fright had the upper hand. At every turn, I felt like the scooter was leaning one way, and I'd forgotten to do the same. After going around the block, I was relieved to be back home.

Dad announced, "It's your turn. Take it down to the end of the block, stop and get off. Then turn it around and head back, but GO SLOW." His eyebrows rose and he talked louder—sure signs he was having doubts as well.

"I think I got it, Dad." I hopped back on, trying to appear braver than I felt. *I can do this.* Then I noticed the goose bumps on my arms.

Dad offered some encouragement, "It's a little like riding a bike, except it's much heavier—about twenty times the weight of your bike." He continued, "Lean into your turns or the scooter will be riding you instead of you riding it. Remember, the brake lever is on the left, and the gas control is on the right."

The scooter felt like a lead weight compared to my Sears bike. Dad must have given me too much input because I was confused about what he'd said. Driving ever so slowly—maybe too slowly—I didn't get but halfway down the street before the Cushman swung to the left and then to the right. I squeezed the brake lever too late as it wobbled into the shallow drainage ditch and slid to a sudden stop in the soft wet dirt. To avoid total embarrassment, I quickly grabbed the handlebars and jerked the scooter around. It resisted so I jerked harder and broke it free of the mud. I was determined to keep going. I hit the starter button, and it roared to life once again.

I drove it out of the muck and back onto the street. I completed my trip with no damage done to me or the motor scooter. Dad watched me with a wide smile that reached his eyes as I came to a stop in our driveway.

"You made a quick recovery from that ditch. I think you were going too slowly to keep your balance." Then he motioned for me to circle around again.

By the third try, I was able to navigate the motorbike all the way down the street and back. All fear and embarrassment left me as the number of laps increased. I felt a wonderful sense of accomplishment as the scooter responded to my touch. When I leaned, the scooter leaned. When I squeezed the brake with my left hand or the throttle with my right hand, the bike responded perfectly. Driving this scooter was nothing like riding my bike. Everything felt different and better.

I was thrilled. I had learned to work on my first motorized bike and drive it in the same evening. Dad showed me the spot in the garage where I could park the scooter. I would have gladly spent the night sleeping next to my new friend.

Before I went to bed, I thanked Dad again for the great gift. I could hardly sleep that first night. My dreams were all about my new machine locked in the garage. I was imagining myself zooming over dirt trails and racing past my friends on their bicycles. That dream became my new secret goal.

After school the next day, I couldn't wait to grab a snack and start practicing on our street. Once word got out, it didn't take very long before I became the most popular kid in the neighborhood. Most of my friends had never even seen a motor scooter.

We lived only four blocks from a wooded five-acre tract of land where I had been riding my three-speed bicycle for the past two years. It seemed like the ideal place to take my new toy if I could get permission from Mom or Dad.

After a few days of practicing up and down our block, I approached Mom. "I've had a lot of practice on my scooter this week. Can I ride it to the bike trails?"

Mother looked concerned as she stated, "Driving on city streets is illegal, even in front of our house. If you are going to take it to the trails, you'll need to push it all the way there. Remember, the scooter is not licensed for the road and neither are you. I'll let you go because you'll be on private property where no driver's license is required . . . but you've got to promise me you'll obey my rules, be careful on the trails and be home in time for dinner."

I heard most of what Mom said, and my head was spinning with delight. Now that I had her permission, I couldn't wait to get to the wooded area to make my dream come true.

I phoned my schoolmate Victor, "I'm taking my scooter on a trip to the trails—want to come along?"

Victor was over in a flash, and we alternately pushed and guided the motorized machine down the street towards our "Dirt Disneyland."

"Wow, this thing is sure heavy," Victor complained, "and we still have two more blocks. I can hardly breathe."

Finally, we reached the target area in the woods and pushed the scooter across the last street. My shirt was soaking wet, but I didn't care. I pressed the start button and held my breath. The little engine came alive, and a smoke puff settled towards the ground. My inaugural lap was about to begin.

"Climb aboard, Vic, and hang on; this is going to be fun."

We cautiously took a spin around the existing bike trails and small jumps.

"What a gas!" Victor exclaimed.

On the final turn, we had to pass through a narrow section of brush. A boulder stuck out on the left and a large bush on the right. For the past two years, my three-speed bike easily maneuvered through this narrow place. I slowed to a crawl as I passed through, but, at the last minute, a branch grabbed my throttle hand, forcing the bike to lurch forward and veer off the trail. The scooter snapped off a large branch, and it struck Vic, throwing him to the ground. I stopped, jumped off and ran back to check on my friend.

"That was a quick way to widen the trail," Vic remarked as he stood up and brushed himself off. "I'm okay," he assured me as he climbed aboard for our second loop.

That evening Dad asked, "How did the scooter perform on the dirt trails?"

"Vic and I had so much fun. We must have done twenty laps."

Victor and Ed

During the next few weeks, Victor and I decided to use Dad's shovels to add additional scooter routes through the wooded lot. In time, the entire area became a patchwork of trails. Our friends showed up to race their bikes against my scooter. I usually ended up in front of the pack, even if I gave my friends a head start.

I always offered free rides to whoever showed up at the trails. As it turned out, the Cushman was also popular with the girls. Even some cute girls stood around waiting for me to take them for a ride. Girls I hardly knew were squeezing my hips to keep from falling off. My machine made me feel more confident and mature. By summertime, I had accumulated more friends than I could count. A few of my guy friends asked to drive my scooter, but I never handed it off to anyone because my dad had said it wasn't allowed.

No one offered to pay for gas, but, back then, it wasn't a financial drain because the price of gas was only twenty-five cents a gallon. The scooter could run for two weeks on a three-gallon tank of gas.

We spent as many afternoons as possible at the bike trails that summer and fall, and we were back out on the course nearly every day as soon as spring weather arrived. Then one day, I noticed two bulldozers parked near our bike and scooter racetrack. A sign, which had been posted there for a few months, indicated twenty-five houses were to be built.

I called Victor with the bad news. "I think our good times are coming to an end. It looks like they are going to bulldoze our riding trails soon."

"I want to go see for myself. Let's take one last ride around the track tomorrow afternoon."

The next day, we slowly pushed that old worn-out scooter four blocks to the track. We weren't in a hurry this time and pushing the scooter had gotten easier since we were bigger and stronger. We talked about the good times, the races, the bumps, the jumps, the crashes and the girls. Where else could thirteen-years-olds have had more fun?

When we arrived, we were shocked to see that, overnight, the racetrack had been wiped out. The trails were smoothed over, the trees and brush were gone and there was not going to be one last ride.

With no place to ride my scooter, it sat in the garage gathering dust.

On a sunny Saturday morning in late April, Victor knocked on my front door. With a smile and a dose of optimism, he said, "Don't you think it's time to knock the dust off your scooter? I've got an idea for today if you don't have any plans. Let's go outside so we can talk privately."

"What crazy idea do you have this time?" I asked.

"You've talked about selling your scooter soon. Let's take one last ride. How about going to the golf course for a fun adventure? It's only a mile away."

"It sounds risky—but fun."

"Come on, let's do it," Vic urged.

It's probably my last ride. I shrugged, "Okay, let's go check the scooter's gas gauge."

We decided to leave after lunch while my mom was busy cleaning. With excitement fueling our energy, we pushed the scooter down the street. It was a hot day, and before long we had to stop to rest.

"I think we're far enough away from your house. Let's fire it up and drive it the rest of the way," Victor proposed. "We could be at the golf course in five minutes."

I hesitated before answering because I could picture Mom pointing her finger at me, reminding me of her rules. I was tired, however, and I knew that riding the scooter would make our trip so quick and easy and much more exciting. "Okay, let's do it," I said as I mounted the motorbike, turned the key and hit the starter button. Victor jumped on behind me.

I tried to block out the negative thoughts tumbling through my mind as I merged into traffic. I crossed a busy road and drove a half mile further on side streets. As we neared the golf course, I pulled over to a view area. We had arrived at our destination, unlicensed and a mile from home.

We watched several golfers driving around in their carts. This was a great spot to hang out, but I knew we didn't belong here.

"I think it's time we head back. We've been gone awhile." Guilt was seeping out of my pores. "Let's turn this bike around and head home."

I started the engine and swung the scooter around towards the street. Victor climbed on without arguing. We were on our way and making good time. I started to relax and enjoy the ride. We were eight blocks from my home when a police car sped by in the opposite direction. The officer must have noticed our youthfulness as he glanced back in our direction.

Looking over his shoulder, Victor announced his version of the play-by-play. "Oh no, he turned on his red lights! He's pulling off to the side of the road. Now he's trying to turn around, but traffic is holding him up. I think he's coming after us!"

I didn't know what I should do, especially with my friend shouting non-stop in my ear, "Come on—go as fast as you can!"

As long as we had a chance to get away, I wouldn't have to explain my disobedience to my parents. Plus, I'd never been in trouble with the law, and I didn't want to start now. With no better plan, I decided to listen to Victor's prodding.

In addition to the officer chasing me, I knew I had another big problem. There was a steep hill just around the next corner that we had to climb, and the scooter didn't have much more power than a riding lawn mower. Eighteen horsepower on level ground scooted us along; on a steep hill, however, we couldn't drive much faster than we could walk. As we turned into the corner, I squeezed the throttle to full power. I stared up "killer hill," and my panic intensified. Just as I feared, we lost speed quickly. Victor must have realized the situation was deteriorating because he was no longer giving advice. I knew then that I should have told him to jump off before I started up the incline. Our chances of success would've been greater without his extra weight. If that policeman was after us, I had only seconds to decide whether to give up or try to find some way to disappear.

During the next few moments, I considered all my options and realized I had none. I knew my goose was about to be cooked. I needed a big break. I glanced to my right and noticed that the house we were about to pass had a narrow, tree-lined driveway which disappeared alongside it.

"Victor, hang on!" I yelled over my shoulder.

I was in survival mode; I could feel the adrenalin coursing through my body. I cranked a hard right and barreled down the stranger's long driveway. At the rear of the house, where the driveway ended, stood a single-car garage. Lucky for me, the garage door was wide open, and the spot where there could have been a car was empty. I braked hard and eased a few feet into the garage. It was gutsy, but, if everything worked as planned, it would be a great place to hide out. I felt my body go limp with relief.

Losing my scooter and taking a trip to jail in a paddy wagon were not in my plans for the day. I was so thankful that we had outwitted the cop. I turned off the ignition switch and watched to see if the police car raced by. My heart was beating so hard I thought it might try to jump out of my ribcage.

Just then, the police car, with its flashing lights, zoomed past our hiding place. The squad car seemed to be headed over the top of the hill. I knew we were only temporarily out of danger because the policeman could turn around and backtrack or stop at the top of the hill and wait us out.

"That squad car *was* after us. We're lucky he didn't look down this driveway." Victor whispered to me. "What are we going to—"

His question was interrupted by the slamming of a screen door. We both looked up to see a tall man standing on the nearby back porch, arms folded, staring at us.

With my heart pounding in my throat, my mind raced, searching for a way out of this new predicament. What was I going to say? We were two strange kids trespassing on his property with a motorbike parked in his garage. The man's scowl was severe enough to wrinkle his forehead for life. He looked as unpleasantly surprised to see us as we were to see him. The stew instantly thickened as the homeowner stared us down.

During my entire young life, I had been taught to never lie. So, what did I do? I lied.

"Is Jimmy home?" I asked.

His answer was quick and gruff. "No, he does not live here."

"I'm really sorry. We must have the wrong house. Victor, let's go."

I took one step forward, grabbed the handle bars and swung the scooter around. Vic and I pushed it very quickly up the driveway. We'd escaped, for now.

"Vic, we have to go up this hill. I think it's safest to stay on the side streets, and it's the shortest way home. The police have already searched this street, and we just have to hope that they won't come back."

"Okay, let's get out of here."

We turned right onto the hill, and we both pushed with all our might. By the time we reached the top of the hill, my legs were burning and my lungs were ready to explode. We were both dripping with sweat from head to toe. I was still terrified that we were walking into a police trap.

Victor, also tired of straining, complained bitterly. "I can't go any further. Let's drive it home."

"Just keep pushing. We can't get caught riding it a second time."

A half hour later, we arrived at my house, relieved and exhausted.

During the next week, I talked to Dad about selling my toy.

"Whenever you're ready," he said.

"I think I'll be ready in a week or so. I just want to clean and polish it."

A few days later, after school, I decided to take the scooter down our block for my final ride. When I got to the corner, I decide to go one more block. Unfortunately, the police were about to get their revenge.

I was reminiscing about all of the fun times with my Cushman scooter, so I didn't notice the danger ahead. Halfway down the second block, I passed an unmarked patrol car parked in an unused driveway. As I passed, the officer flipped on a red light mounted on his dash. The car zoomed past me and cut me off. I brought my scooter to a stop on the side of the road. A husky man in a police uniform stepped out of the car.

He asked, "Can I see your driver's license and your registration?"

"I don't have any," I admitted with a shaky voice.

"Wait here. I'm going to call my sergeant."

That doesn't sound good.

Five minutes later, a blue and white cruiser arrived with its beacon flashing. In big bold print, the car's lettering on the side read SEATTLE POLICE. I was terrified.

The second policeman asked for my name and address and then directed me to get in the backseat of his patrol car. Once the door slammed, I quickly discovered there were no inside door or window handles. I immediately felt the confinement of the thick fencing material that separated me from the front area of the car. I felt like a caged animal. *This is all wrong; I'm not a criminal.*

I knew I could have avoided all of this if only I hadn't taken my one last ride. *This is the worst day of my life.* The reality of the situation sank in. I didn't know what to expect next, but it didn't take long for me to find out.

A tow truck soon arrived, and, after the driver had some words with the policeman, he wheeled my scooter over to the back of his big tow truck. I peered out the tinted side window and wondered why the truck needed to be so big. It was certainly overkill. The men exchanged paperwork, and then the tow truck driver wrapped a cable around my motorbike. When my scooter was two feet off the ground, he jumped into his truck and sped off, my scooter swinging back and forth.

I had a very sick feeling in my stomach. *What will my parents say? Will I be grounded for life? I'm in so much trouble.*

After my Cushman was out of sight, one of the officers interrupted my thoughts when he opened the front door and slid his lanky body into the driver's seat. Through the wire mesh, he handed me the tow company's business card.

He started up his squad car and then looked over his shoulder. He stared me in the eye. "I'm taking you home and I want to talk to your parents. Your scooter has been impounded by Aurora Towing. The information is on the business card."

I nodded but kept silent. The police officer drove slowly in the direction of my house, and I soon found out why he drove at a snail's pace. In those two short blocks, I collected a private scolding. When the police car turned into my driveway, I felt panic rising in me.

"Is this your house?"

"Yes, sir."

He opened the driver's door and stood tall next to the police car. Ten steps later, he was knocking on our front door. His knock was so loud I could even hear it from inside the car with the windows rolled up tight.

We had see-through curtains in the living room, and I figured Mom probably guessed what had happened even before she opened the door. The officer spoke to her for a few minutes. I couldn't hear the conversation, but I knew the words wouldn't be in my favor.

After the exchange ended, Mom stood by the front door, as if she were expecting something to happen. The officer walked over to the squad car, unlocked my door and opened it wide.

"Watch your head. You're free to go. Just don't repeat your bad judgment."

Once I was released from what felt like a miniature jail, Mom said firmly, "Go to your room and wait for your dad to come home."

An hour later, I saw Dad's truck drive up, and then I heard my parents speaking in hushed voices. I braced myself for the consequences because I knew my dad was a man of action. Immediately, he opened my door and released me from my room. I didn't know what was to follow, but my mind conjured up all kinds of punishment: grounding for life, a trip to the woodshed, five hundred pushups, a good scolding or all of the above.

Instead, he said, "It's time for dinner."

"Can I be excused? I'm not very hungry right now."

"No, you cannot," he said gruffly.

It was a strangely quiet dinner. Even my usually chatty sister was silent. The few words exchanged were between Mom and Dad. From the lines in his forehead, it seemed to me that Dad was doing some deep thinking.

Immediately after dinner, Dad abruptly said, "Get your coat. I want you to go with me to retrieve the scooter from the towing company."

It was a quiet and uncomfortable four-mile drive to the tow yard. Once we arrived, Dad growled, "Stay in the truck."

After Dad paid the bail-out fee, he rolled the scooter out the gate and to the back of his truck.

He knocked on my window. "Give me a hand."

I got out, and we both loaded the Cushman into the truck.

I needed to break the ice and accept responsibility for my mistake. "Dad, I'm awful sorry for all the trouble I caused."

He still wasn't saying anything to me and my nerves were straining. At any moment, I knew he was going to give me a speech or something worse. It was torture waiting for the other shoe to drop.

He turned to me after we closed the truck's tailgate. "You've had the scooter long enough. It's going to stay in this truck until it is sold. Do you understand?"

I didn't argue. I looked him in the eye and said, "I understand."

Two weeks later, Dad came home with an announcement. "I sold your scooter for forty-five dollars. You can have what's left after I pay myself back for the tow bill and your ticket."

I felt lucky to get off so easily. That extra money went straight into my bank account to increase my stash for my first car whenever opportunity came knocking. I was officially less than two years away.

Today, looking back, I can say I had more than a year of outstanding fun with my Cushman. The fun parts made great memories for life. But, the rough ending taught me a valuable life lesson about laws and rules that I also never forgot.

Chapter 5

My First Car

By the ninth grade my life centered on school and work. For me, it was fun to work, especially when I could hang around all of Dad's old cars. If I didn't have homework, I would bike down to Dad's auto wrecking business after school. When I arrived, the office blackboard usually had a list of jobs for me to do. Whether it was sweeping, dismounting tires from wheels or digging fence postholes, I was ready and willing.

It was not uncommon for one of Dad's employees to tell me, "Slow down, you're going to hurt yourself."

I had an internal drive to work, but I also loved to make my dad proud of me. If the block-long driveway needed sweeping, the dust and rocks would fly as the push broom and I worked in harmony. When Dad came around to inspect my work, he would frequently say, "Nice job!" I craved that kind of approval from my dad.

I knew that the raises I received were a just reward for my efforts on the job. My savings account was always in the back of my mind. Everyone who knew me understood that I was serious about saving for a car. During the summer of 1955, I worked all the hours I could, averaging nearly forty hours per week.

I leaned on Dad's soft side once or twice a month. "Can I go to Haller Lake with Gerry tomorrow?"

Dad never turned me down, but he did remind me, "You will be missing out on some pay."

By the first week of February in 1956, the month before I turned fifteen, Dad completely surprised me by saying, "I think you are old enough to start looking for a project car. You'll need to allow enough time to get a car finished by the time you turn sixteen."

Mom, who was sitting directly across from me, wrinkled her brow. "I'm not comfortable with the idea of you having your own car at fifteen. It seems irresponsible. You might be tempted to illegally drive your car up and down the block like you did with your Cushman."

Dad argued, "It'll take him at least a year, or longer, to rebuild a car. I'm sure he'll learn a lot."

Mom glanced at me and spoke again, her voice beginning to soften. "I think I'll let your Dad take responsibility for any trouble that might result from this decision."

I was proud of Dad for taking a stand for me. It was the first time I'd seen him back Mom down in front of me. *We men have to stick together.*

I looked at Dad and Mom, "Is that a yes?"

"It's a yes from me," Dad answered.

Mom replied, "I'm not convinced, but I'll go along with it."

I thanked them both with a hug. "I can hardly wait to get started looking for a car." The words stuck in my throat; I hoped they didn't notice. I was so excited; my vocal cords seemed to wrap around each other. I could feel myself getting older with the hope of soon owning my own car. After I went to bed, I thought of some important questions I needed to ask Dad. I saved them for breakfast.

I joined Dad at the table the next morning and immediately asked, "What kind of a car would you recommend? Where should I start looking?"

Dad answered, "I have always liked Ford's Model A. It's not a complicated car, and it's cheap to repair. Older cars can be fun to own because not many people have them. Actually, a few days ago,

I bought a 1931 Model A from an older man who had it in storage for a long time. It's nearly twenty-five years old, which qualifies it as a true classic. If you come by work after school, I'll show it to you. If you're interested and want to buy it, it will cost you exactly what I paid for it—seventy-five bucks. But, remember, you don't have to buy the first car you look at."

"I can certainly afford that," I responded, as I wolfed down my breakfast. "I can't wait to see it."

"Let me tell you a little more about it first. There's no engine. It was removed by the previous owner, but I have others in the motor pile. I'd be willing to throw in an original four-cylinder engine, but you'll need to rebuild it. The car needs a lot of work, but I think it could be a worthy project. It's not a problem if you decide this car is not for you. We buy five or six cars every week."

At school that day, I felt like a water drop on a red-hot skillet. I could hardly sit still, and I couldn't concentrate on anything. Instead of focusing on my school assignments, I was already imagining myself driving a Model A all over town. I knew I needed to settle down. After all, Dad said it was going to be a year-long project.

At lunch, I finally saw my friend Gerry, and I couldn't wait to share my exciting news. "My dad told me I can start looking for a project car, isn't that swell? Today I am going to look at a 1931 Model A coupe. It's at Dad's wrecking yard. He just towed it in. The best part is I can buy it for seventy-five dollars."

"I wish my parents would let me buy a car before I turn sixteen," said Gerry, showing a long face.

"Dad said it doesn't have an engine, and it needs a lot of work. But I'll have plenty of time to fix it up."

"When can I see the car? Can I have the first ride?"

"Whoa, don't rush me! I haven't even bought it yet. I'll let you know if I get it. Will you help me work on it?"

"Of course I will. You're lucky to have such a great dad, with a wrecking yard to boot."

After I got home from school, I was going to ask Mom if she would take me to the bank to get money for the car. But then reality hit; I hadn't even seen it yet. Instead, I asked my mom if I could bike down to the wrecking yard to check it out.

"Sure. If you stay 'til closing, you can throw your bike in the back of Dad's truck and catch a ride home with him."

Soon I was on my three-speed bike headed to see the classic car. I was so eager that I covered the mile and a half to Dad's business in record time. My heart was racing, and I was out of breath so I took a minute to get a drink out of the hose next to the office. Seeing no sign of Dad, I entered the security gate and started searching for the classic Ford.

After I scanned the upper lot, I finally spotted it in the distance, parked along the lower driveway. As I pedaled down the hill, I saw Dad through the open door of the nearby tire shop. He waved, and I returned the gesture. *This might be one of the most important days in my life.*

Dad walked down to join me and said, "You sure got here quick today. I see it didn't take long for you to find the car." Then, together, we walked around the car, stopping at the driver's door.

Dad opened it. "Go ahead and climb in."

Eagerly, I put one foot on the running board, ducked my head low and swung into the driver's seat. I sat there holding the rather large steering wheel. As I turned it back and forth, excitement flooded over me. I closed my eyes and imagined cruising down a country road all by myself.

Dad's voice snapped me back to reality. "Like I told you, this car was built back in '31. Next to your right leg is the Model A's transmission shifter; it has three speeds and works with the manual clutch by your left foot. It doesn't operate any different than my old truck you've been driving around the wrecking yard this past year."

I eagerly replied, "I think it's easy to drive a stick shift. In fact, I'd take one over an automatic anytime."

"The gas float gauge, in the center of the dash, is actually built into the gas tank. Even though you can't see it, the gas tank is behind the dash. You put the gas in right by the windshield, and the tank holds about twelve gallons. I'm not sure why the factory put it in such an awkward spot. There is no room for a radio because it takes up so much space. Does that bother you?"

I thought about it and quickly decided, "Who needs a radio? Just listening to the purring of the engine will be enough for me."

As we walked to the back of the car, Dad said, "Look here, this car came with a rumble seat." Then he twisted the handle and pulled the trunk lid back, exposing a small seat.

"Wow! That whole seat is hidden. It's pretty small; it looks like it would barely fit two people."

"In my day, some people called it a love seat," Dad laughingly remarked.

"I've never heard of a seat outside of a car. I bet it would be tons of fun for my friends. On a warm day, they would feel like they were riding in a convertible. Can I try out the rumble seat?"

"Sure, climb up."

I stepped on the bumper and swung my body onto the tattered seat. It was as stiff as a board, and I could feel a spring giving me a slight poke. But I didn't care because I was completely enamored with the open-air feeling.

"Riding back here might be almost as much fun as driving," I remarked.

"That's true. Your friends might fight over who rides in this seat. From my experience, years ago, even the girls liked soaking in the sun and fresh air in the outside seat."

Dad said the magic word: girls. I hadn't even factored in their possible interest in my car. Because this car was a classic, it was possible that a few girls might want to ride in the front seat with me.

My enthusiasm was building as Dad pointed out more features. "In the old days, if you had more friends than could fit in the car, they could stand on the running boards for short rides."

"Is it legal to ride down the street with people hanging on?"

"No, not these days, but it gives it the old, classic car look."

Then Dad pointed to the headlights mounted on a metal bar in front of the radiator.

"You'll want to change out those old-fashioned, oversized headlights. You can replace them with smaller seal beam units that are much brighter and safer. It will require some rewiring, but it's worth it. You should be able to convert them in one afternoon."

"Dad, I love this car! I bet no one at the high school will have one like it."

The best part of the car, of course, was that it could be all mine for seventy-five dollars just by saying, "I want it." And I wanted it! But I knew I shouldn't let my heart make the decision alone; I needed to involve my brain. So I resisted the urge to commit to the car before I better understood the work ahead of me.

Upon seeing the magnitude of the project, a lad with less experience might have immediately passed on this car. Even though I knew restoring it would be a huge challenge for me, I felt optimistic about my ability to get the job done.

One of the areas I was still a little nervous about was the serious rust problem in the doors. I could poke my thumb through the holey area all along the bottom.

"Dad, how do you fix the rust problems?"

"You can cut the bad stuff out with a metal saw, overlay a new metal strip and then cut it to the size that needs replacing. You can use rivets or screws to attach the overlay."

"Okay, I think I could do that," I said.

"The interior is shredded—probably from several generations of mice," Dad explained. "Most old cars that have been sitting around awhile have that problem."

"The roof cloth is also sagging," I pointed out.

"The interior and roof will be easy to repair. I did it myself when I had my Model A. You just remove the cloth roof and repair the wooden supports. Then you can cut a piece of sheet metal to fit over the roof, caulk the edges and secure it with sheet metal screws. Your mom might be willing to help you with the upholstery work," he added.

"You sure make the repairs sound easy."

I did some final thinking. It would be a lot of work—that was for sure. Still, it wasn't too bad for a car twenty-five years old. My mind was almost made up. If I took on the car's repairs, one at a time, I would have a nice reward to look forward to: a totally unique car that was all mine. It didn't matter how long it took as long as I finished it before my sixteenth birthday.

"Dad, what exactly comes with the car for seventy-five dollars?" I asked.

"I'll throw in a complete engine for you to rebuild, like I promised, plus parts to upgrade your brakes, and a used radiator. Any other parts you might need, you'll have to pay for. But, of course, you qualify for an employee discount on all the parts you buy, new or used."

As a fifteen-year-old optimist, I recognized that the car had great potential. And Dad was throwing in some major parts for free. Down the road, driving the Model A would offer me a lot of fun and independence. Doubt lifted and clarity settled in. I decided to take the risk.

"If I buy this car tomorrow, will you tow it home after work? I want to get started tearing it apart right away."

"Okay, I'll throw in a free tow," he offered, nodding. "I know you're going to learn a lot!"

I could tell Dad was happy that I was choosing the old Ford. He shook my hand and then gave me a man-sized hug. Buying my first car was a big step towards feeling like an adult. From head to toe, it felt great.

The next day after school, Mom took me to the bank so I could withdraw some of my money. Then we stopped at the wrecking yard to complete the purchase.

After I parted with my money and Dad handed me the invoice, he again shook my hand and congratulated me. With the official paperwork in my hand, I felt like I had accomplished a lot. Schoolwork was waiting so Mom gave me a ride home.

Once on our way, Mom smiled. "I'm happy for you."

As promised, Dad towed my car home after work. I got started with the restoration that night. For two evenings, I did nothing but remove the seats and the glued-in floor mats. The seat bolts were rusted and extremely hard to remove. Mom came out to the garage and watched me for an hour.

"Rather than take your seats to the upholstery shop, I can make patterns and sew covers for them. You just need to decide what color and texture you want."

"Wow! That would be great, Mom. Thanks!"

It was good to know that Mom was willing to help after she had been the reluctant one. We worked great together, tearing the seats apart and laughing and joking about my car. Mom and I made a trip to the upholstery shop and placed my order. The shop owner recommended I buy new foam for the project, and I added that to my order.

The upholstery arrived on April 8, 1956. Mom was home when the mailman dropped off my package. As soon as I came home from school, Mom shared the good news. "Your order came in today. I'll start making the patterns tomorrow, and next week we should be ready to install them on the seat cushions. I'm glad you decided to order some extra material like I recommended because now I can repair the rumble seat too."

"One more thing—would you like me to recover your door panels to match your seats?" She grinned, "I measured, and there is just enough material."

I smiled to myself; some things were turning out better than I had expected. The door panels had just been plywood, but now they would look sharp.

"Thanks, Mom! I'll take the door panels off tonight so you can start on the patterns." A week later, Mom and I completed the upholstery project. It looked terrific!

The next thing Dad suggested I tackle was replacing the current brake parts with a newer-style brake system. The original mechanical brakes would take a long time to stop the car, which wasn't safe. He informed me that he had a newer Ford in the lot that I could cannibalize for parts. Dad towed the car back to his business to make it more convenient to work on.

With his instructions and plenty of spare parts, I set to work on the brake modernization project. Without experience, it was almost more than I could chew. Dad offered free advice, but some of it I didn't fully understand. I felt discouraged by the daunting process. I took off all four wheels and then began to remove the brake drums. I discovered every bolt of the whole brake system was rusted tight and needed to be soaked in oil. I let Dad know how I felt, and I suggested that maybe the old brakes would have been okay to use for awhile.

He replied, "I promise you won't be sorry for upgrading the brakes. I did it to my first Ford when I was twenty."

It took nearly a month to complete the brake system. I installed used hydraulic brake lines, a master cylinder, backing plates, brake shoes and brake drums. I was sure glad Dad had included all the brake conversion parts in the deal. They filled up three apple boxes, and I dared not ask their worth. Almost all of the parts came off the 1940 Ford that Dad had parked inside a dry carport. It was a real advantage for me to have protected space where I could work on rainy afternoons.

The installation of the brake pedal assembly required drilling support holes in the firewall. It was impossible to work inside the car and be outside at the same time to tighten up the bolts. This was where Gerry came in handy. I had already bloodied my knuckles more than once pounding things in place.

"You still have a long way to go," Gerry said. "Do you ever think about giving up?"

"No, quitting is not in my vocabulary. Down the road, I know there is a finish line, and I'm going to cross it with time to spare."

"I honestly thought you were crazy to take on this project in the beginning. But, with the upholstery work finished and now the new brakes done, I just know you're gonna make it. I think restoring your own car is exciting, and I'm really happy to help you."

Ed working on his Model A

"That's great because I want to start rebuilding the engine next week. Do you want to tackle that project with me?"

"I wouldn't miss it," he confirmed with a smile.

I knew he would say that.

"We'll start by completely disassembling the worn-out engine that Dad is giving me," I explained. "Model A's have only four cylinders so that means only four pistons and four connecting rods to work with. The cylinder head is the biggest part we'll have to remove."

The engine project turned out to be a larger challenge than either of us had imagined. Because the prior owner had removed the old engine, there was nothing under the hood; it was just an empty hole. As a result, we needed to round up motor mounts, all of the missing brackets and at least a hundred different sizes of nuts and bolts.

Gerry and I spent nearly a month rebuilding the motor, including adding new rings, pistons and other expensive parts. Finally, the day came for us to install the newly assembled engine. Using the winch truck, we hoisted it into the motor compartment. We spent two days connecting the various parts: the motor mounts, transmission and radiator, for starters. We had to be very careful when we connected the electrical wiring. I used an instruction manual to keep me on track, plus I visited the Model A parts cars in the back lot numerous times to solve the many puzzles we faced.

At last, we were ready to test the engine. I made sure that it was full of oil and the radiator was topped-off with water.

I told Gerry, "Stand back. I'm going to push the start button."

I got in the car, held my breath, turned on the key and pushed the button.

Nothing happened, except for a clicking sound. My shoulders sagged with the weight of the disappointment.

"Maybe it's a bad starter," Gerry guessed. "That happened to my dad's Dodge last year."

I exchanged the starter for another used one, but that didn't help. Then, I swapped the battery with a fresh one. Still no luck.

Frustrated, I told Gerry, "I'm going to borrow one of Dad's trucks with a push bumper. You hop into the car and operate the clutch, and I'll push it with the parts truck. After we both get rolling, when the timing is right, I'll honk my horn and then you pop the clutch. Maybe the engine just has to be forced to cooperate. Sometimes new parts can be stubborn like mules."

I maneuvered the truck behind the little car and lined up the bumpers. Then I gently pressed the accelerator and both vehicles started down the driveway. Once we were moving fast enough, I honked and Gerry released the clutch. Immediately, the little car's back wheels locked up. The tires started skidding down the gravel driveway, and a dirt cloud quickly formed in front of me, covering the truck and its interior.

I hit my brakes and ran up to Gerry's opened window. "Let's try it again. I'll try pushing you a little faster."

He seemed a little shaken. "The moment I let the clutch out, your car started vibrating like it had four flat tires. I hope things go better this time."

On the second try, we were going much faster, and the same thing happened. Only this time, the car started to spin toward a four-foot ditch on the right side of the driveway. Gerry steered like a crazy man as the car slipped partway into the ditch and stopped.

Gerry leapt out of the car and started cussing at me, and I immediately apologized. But, he couldn't quite let it go. "Were you trying to kill me? I lost control of the steering, and you just went faster. The back of the car started to chase the front; I thought I was going to end up in that ditch backwards or upside down."

Dejected, I coasted my project car into the lot alongside the shop.

"We struck out. Let's call it a day. I'll let you know what Dad says."

After all of our troubles, I was eager to get advice from my dad. That night, before dinner, I poured out my frustrations about our unsuccessful attempts get my car running.

I was counting on him so I asked, "Do you have any suggestions?"

Dad always had the answers, and he didn't let me down this time either. He knew exactly what was wrong. "I suspect you might have installed the pistons in the wrong cylinder holes. When you're mixing new parts with used, you need to keep track of how you disassembled the engine. You have to put it back together exactly the same way. If you didn't number the four pistons, you're in trouble. You might as well start over."

"Did you say start over?" The news was such a blow that it felt like someone had just kicked me in the stomach.

"Yes, you will need to pull out your existing engine and start over from scratch with a different motor from the motor pile. Then you'll have to transfer over all of your new parts. There are too many possible combinations when you combine four unmarked pistons; if you use trial and error, you'll waste too much time trying to find the right four cylinders. Don't feel bad. Most men who are learning to turn a wrench have made similar mistakes."

I told Gerry about it the next day at school. "You won't believe what Dad said last night about the engine. He said we have to start over."

He looked stunned and responded with a groan.

"I know. I felt the same way when I heard it, but we've got to trudge ahead. At least he's helping by giving me another engine block for free. Today is a new day," I told him, "and I'll never make that mistake again."

That evening, Gerry and I picked out another engine from the pile. For the second time, we started the difficult task of removing and replacing motor parts. The work party with Gerry lasted a lot longer than either of us could have guessed, but we finally got it right! The purr of that engine was one of the best sounds I'd ever heard in my life. The hard work and huge time commitment made the glory of success so sweet.

I quickly found out that most of the restoration projects took three times longer than my best guess. I was learning endurance and patience right alongside my new car-rebuilding skills.

One of the best exterior improvements I made to my car was replacing the tall, nineteen-inch wire spoke wheels with wide fifteen-inch ones. In my opinion, the appearance was radically improved. The car body dropped by four inches, and I added fat tires to make it corner like an Indy 500 race car. During that first summer, many of my friends biked over to see the progress on my car.

After I lowered it, they agreed. "Your Model A looks great with its new 'low rider' look."

I finally finished my car three months before my sixteenth birthday. I covered it in three coats of gray primer from a case of spray paint cans. It looked amazing!

Dad wanted to get me ready for the road, so he and I spent up to two hours driving around every Sunday. Sometimes we would take his truck, but mostly we practiced in the Model A. During driving practice on a side street, I quickly discovered that parallel parking was a breeze in a short car.

Ed's restored Model A

I passed the driver's license test the day of my sixteenth birthday. What a day of celebration that was! I could hardly wait to show off my car at school.

The next day, Gerry and I drove my pride and joy to Lincoln High School in north Seattle. Most kids who saw us took a second look as we passed by.

My buddies all wanted a ride, and I was happy to oblige. When I first took my friends for a spin, I loved to display the Model A's lightning-quick stopping ability. My updated brakes stopped on a dime and gave change!

With my new passenger buckled into his seat, I would cruise down to a dirt road not far from my house. I always had a set of braking maneuvers on my mind. The first sudden stop was controlled and quick and caught them off guard. For the second stop, I'd drive even faster. Instead of stepping on the brakes, I'd spin the steering wheel and, at the same time, yank on the emergency brake. The resulting spinout left us heading in the opposite direction. It freaked out nearly every unsuspecting friend. If someone was riding in the rumble seat the thrill was tripled. Some of my braver friends asked for more. Others would end up with a pale look on their face, coughing from the rising dust cloud. I'm certain that Mom would not have approved of this maneuver.

When the weather improved, the rumble seat became a huge hit with my friends. On sunny days, just as predicted, my buddies fought for the privilege of riding in the outside seat.

By spring quarter, even the local girls had warmed up to cruising in the rumble seat. "So many cute girls and so little time," I told Dad with a smile. He was right: a fun car sometimes attracts the girls. Gerry and I talked, and we agreed that it was a good time to start double dating.

Chapter 6

Fast Police Cars

When I think of high school, I think of cars. Some kids are crazy about sports; for me and my friends, it was all about cars. On Friday nights, we often headed out to the Monroe Speedway to watch the souped-up cars race. The deafening roar of the engines vibrated the bleachers beneath us. Twenty cars tore around the track simultaneously at breakneck speeds. We all cheered loudly for our favorites. The entire experience was invigorating and kept us coming back for more.

One spring evening, as we drove home from the races, I confided with Gerry about my secret desire. "I'd love to own a fast car someday. I've had a lot of fun driving my Model A, but now it's starting to feel like I'm moving in slow motion. When I hit the accelerator, I want to feel some power behind it."

"You could easily do that. Just sell your car and buy a faster one," Gerry commented.

"That's easier said than done. Dad found the Model A for me, and he's so proud that I restored it. It won't be easy to tell him that I want to dump my rebuilt classic for a fast car."

Over the next month, I tried to work up my courage to tell Dad, but it never seemed to be the right moment. Then, one hot summer day, the door of opportunity burst wide open.

That Thursday, Dad left to attend the City of Seattle's car auction where, twice a year, the City sold off its oldest fleet of cars. When he returned to work, he ambled in with some exciting news.

"Today, the City had nearly a hundred pieces of equipment up for sale. I bid on thirty-five of their retired cars, and I got lucky," he told his parts manager Rod and me. Smiling, he handed me his bidder's report and said, "I bought eighteen of them."

Car purchases at Lincoln Auto Wrecking averaged two a day and never more than five or six. This was unbelievable! Dad tapped the paper in my hands. "As you can see, I ended up buying more than my share." By his smile, I could tell that he was pleased with his bidding success.

After lighting up his cigarette, he announced, "Tomorrow we'll all have extra work to do. The City gives buyers only twenty-four hours to pick up their vehicles. I could use both of you to help me for as long as it takes."

We both instantly agreed.

I hadn't yet read the list to see what kinds of cars he'd purchased, and that was the biggest surprise of all. Dad plucked the bid sheet out of my hand and proudly reviewed the results. "I bought three '54 Chevy pickup trucks from the parks department and fifteen retired police cruisers—they're all 1955 Chevrolets. Four are wrecked, but the rest are drivable."

Holy cow! Police cruisers! My jaw really hit the floor this time. I could already imagine myself behind the wheel of one of those babies.

Dad announced his plan. "If the three of us get an early start tomorrow morning, we should be able to get all the cars back here in six trips and, hopefully, finish before the afternoon traffic kicks in."

"Do you want me to ask Gerry to help?" I knew he would be all over this opportunity.

"That's a great idea," Dad said and then winked at me before heading back into his office.

I immediately called Gerry to ask him about it, and he exclaimed, "Count me in!"

The next morning the four of us crowded into Dad's old Ford tow truck and, as we drove, he laid out the game plan. "I'll tow the cars that don't run, and you guys can start driving the police cruisers back to our shop. We'll wait for each other there and then jump back into the tow truck and repeat the process until we're finished."

When we arrived at eight o'clock, I noticed that three of the cars were unmarked detectives' cars painted dark blue. What's more, they were two-door Chevys. Based on my previous experience in the back seat of a police car, I had assumed the police department had only four-door cars.

The first patrol car in the lineup wouldn't start. When I opened the hood to jumpstart the cruiser, I noticed the engine was an eight-cylinder. It was my lucky day. I'd never driven a car with a V8 engine.

"Gerry, look here," I hollered. "This one's an eight-cylinder." I knew he'd be as excited as I was.

With jumper cables and Dad's help, we got the first three cars started. Then Dad quickly hooked his tow truck to one of the four wrecked Chevys, and, in tandem, we all got underway. As soon as the first stoplight turned green, I tested the acceleration. It slid me straight back into the seat. The car was quick on the draw—and my pulse picked up its pace! At the next stoplight, Gerry and I looked over at each other with conspiratorial smiles. The moment the light changed, we hit the gas, squealing the tires on our police cruisers. The power test only lasted a few seconds; I knew Dad was in plain sight and may have heard us. My heart skipped a beat—this was not anything like my snail-paced Model A.

Back at my dad's shop, I parked my police car and then walked over to Gerry who was just closing the door of his high-powered machine. He couldn't wipe the smile off of his face. "This car is fast! Now I know how they catch the bad guys."

After holding back for most of day, we played a little cat-and-mouse as we made our final trip northbound on Aurora. We stayed far enough behind Dad to keep out of his vision. These last two patrol cars still had their police logo on the doors. Someone at the City's shop must have forgotten to remove the markings. So, now, we felt like real policemen. I puffed up my chest and pulled my hat down over my eyes to conceal my youth. I quickly passed Gerry, and then he poured on the power and passed me. Back and forth it went. I wonder what the other motorists thought as they witnessed our recklessness. We probably raised some eyebrows as we squealed our tires and weaved in and out of traffic in our police cruisers.

The nine-mile, one-way trips were sheer pleasure. We made five trips in just over three hours to help move those eighteen vehicles.

When our transportation group had finished its task, Dad came over and thanked both of us for our help. I jumped in my little four-cylinder Model A to give Gerry a ride home. As we chugged along, I recognized that my once-cherished classic car had officially lost its luster.

"I'd sure like to own one of those undercover cars," I sighed.

"You should go for it."

I grinned in anticipation, "I think I'll do a little detective work."

Later that afternoon, I did some homework on the three undercover cars. I discovered that the City of Seattle pulls and sells its vehicles as soon as the speedometers reach 100,000 miles. With proper maintenance, most cars last a lot longer than that. I didn't know for sure, but based on average mileage calculations, I guessed my Model A probably had close to 250,000 miles so the 100,000 miles didn't concern me one bit.

That night I asked Dad, "What plans do you have for the auction cars?"

"I plan on selling six or seven of the best ones and taking apart the others."

I left the conversation at that and headed to bed. As I lay there, I couldn't stop dreaming about owning one of those two-door Chevys. The thought kept circling in my head. It seemed like the perfect car for me. The acceleration was intoxicating, and two-door cars were the only ones popular with the kids at school.

I wasn't looking forward to discussing the subject with Dad, but my desire now outweighed my reluctance. I worked hard to prepare my line of reasoning.

While Dad read the paper on Sunday morning, I built up my nerve, took a deep breath and approached him. "Dad, I'm ready to move on and sell my Model A. I really want to buy one of those blue detective cars. What do you think?"

Dad sat back in his chair and frowned, then reached for his coffee. "Are you sure this is the right move for you? Maybe I shouldn't have let you drive those fast police cars."

"Dad, you know I can't keep my Model A forever."

"Let me caution you, Junior. Falling for a car is a little like falling in love: the excitement can blind you and cause you to move too quickly. You need to make big-purchase decisions with your head, not your heart. Take some time to cool off before you make up your mind. In a few weeks, if you still want to trade up, I won't hold you back."

Telling me to wait was not what I'd hoped for, but at least it wasn't a "no."

After finishing his breakfast, Dad asked, "By the way, what do you think you can get for your car?"

"I have a friend at school who offered me four hundred dollars just last month. I've seen some in the paper for three hundred or less, but I think my upgrades make mine worth more."

He nodded. "I think four hundred would be a fair price for your car."

I was eager to find Gerry and share my promising news.

He slapped me on the back and said, "You're one lucky guy."

Everything worked out better than I'd expected. A month later, I sold my car and purchased the '55 Chevy detective car from Dad for six hundred dollars, which was his cost.

I was definitely in love with my new powerful machine. But, as the weeks passed, the knowledge of the dormant power under my hood left me feeling restless again.

Ed's 1955 Chevy in front of his parents' office

I soon found the antidote to my dissatisfaction: street-racing. The need for speed dominated my next two summers. Adrenalin poured through my veins as I competed with other like-minded street racers. As teenagers, we never thought of racing as dangerous. Yes, it was illegal and risky, but our only worry was getting caught by the police.

During the summer, I raced three nights a week. I couldn't hold back. However, I didn't see it for the addiction that it was. My parents thought I was out cruising or chasing girls, but instead I was wholly focused on finding a worthy opponent for a quarter-mile race.

For safety purposes, we selected streets without any stoplights or heavy traffic. To ensure a fair start, a passenger from one car or the other volunteered to step outside and be the flagger. He'd raise his arm and wait a few seconds for the racers to prepare, and then he'd thrust it downward to signal the start of the race. My quick reaction time in popping the clutch gave me a huge advantage. The squeal of tires, the tire smoke, and the roar of the engines produced a new crop of goose bumps every time.

After each race, one car would circle around to pick up the flagger, and then both vehicles would vacate the area because we never knew if the cops were on their way. After we beat the same challenger two or three times during a summer, we didn't waste our time with that opponent any longer. If we were racing for gas money, the stakes were three dollars to help the winner cover gas and tire wear. But, really, the biggest reward was the bragging rights.

I won more than my share of the races, and, after a great finish, we usually headed back to the local drive-in burger spot to bask in our victory. On my way home, I always looked forward to the next night of racing. The double thrill of winning and staying one step ahead of the law kept me in the game. Perhaps, if I'd had a losing streak, I would've given up my sport sooner.

During those days, Gerry wasn't always available to race with me so my younger cousin, Ron, often stepped in as co-pilot. Ron added to the experience by keeping a written record of the make and model of all the cars we raced, which car and driver won and the date. The journal grew thicker with every passing month. Sometimes when we were not racing, Ron, Gerry and I spent time with friends reviewing "the book" and reliving our victories.

Eventually my luck turned, and so did my opinion of street racing. During my last year in high school, I managed to pick up three speeding tickets, and, consequently, I lost my license for ninety days. The last ticket required me to attend a driver's education course, which got me thinking about the safety of my thrilling hobby. That class made it crystal clear: all street racing was irresponsible and dangerous, not only for the drivers, but for the onlookers and any innocent bystanders. I'm sure we traveled at more than twice the speed limit during our short but intense street races. My epiphany had come too late to save my license, but at least I'd never hurt anyone. For the ninety days, I was back to riding my old three-speed Sears bike: a humbling experience for any eighteen-year-old.

On my long bike rides around town, I made up my mind to hang up my racing gloves. I would be off to college soon, and I knew I didn't want to jeopardize my future. By the time my license was reinstated, my racing days were officially over.

Chapter 7

Real Estate 101

For years, my grandmother had been living with one daughter and then moving to live with another—all very possible with five daughters in Washington state. I grew very close to her because of all the time she spent in our home. I loved my grandma with all of my heart. She was kind, funny, loved to laugh, gave good advice and, on top of that, she was a great cook. What more could a teenage boy want from a grandma?

When I was seventeen and a junior at Lincoln High School, Dad called me to the kitchen for a father-son chat.

"I've found a house for Grandma," he announced.

I was confused. "I didn't know she was looking for a house. Isn't Grandma happy living at Aunt Sophie's?" I asked.

"Your mother and I think she would enjoy having a small home all to herself," Dad explained. "I have a proposition for you. How would you like to be part owner of Grandma's house?"

"Me?"

"You've worked hard over the last few years, and I know you've put most of your money in the bank. What do you think about investing some of it in real estate where you can earn more than just bank interest?"

"I'm not sure," I answered hesitantly.

"Take a look at the house. It's only five minutes away," Dad said with a slight smile. "Mom and I have checked out a dozen houses over the past few months, and this is the best of the bunch."

"How much would it cost me?"

"Well, the price of the house is seventy-five hundred dollars, but thirteen hundred would cover your share of the down payment and closing costs," he explained. "The house payment will only be seventy dollars a month. With her Social Security check, Grandma can afford to pay fifty-five dollars, and I'll take care of the difference."

I liked the idea, but I was also protective of my savings. If I made this leap into becoming a homeowner, after my recent car purchase, I would only have about five hundred dollars left in the bank. I knew it would take quite awhile to build my savings back up again.

"I'm interested, but I'm not sure I want to spend that much of my money," I admitted.

He responded, "Son, everything in life is a tradeoff. But, with this choice, you have a chance to make a bigger return on your money than at the bank and, at the same time, help provide a home for your grandma. If you would like to see it, we can all meet the real estate lady at the house on Sunday."

"Sure, I'll take a look at it," I agreed, starting to see the bigger picture.

Dad, Mom, Barbara and I drove over to see the house on Sunday afternoon. It took only a few minutes to get there from our house. When we turned the last corner, Dad pointed to a little white house on the left side of the street. It looked like it had been painted recently, and the yard had been kept up.

As we pulled into the driveway, the first thing I noticed was the cute white picket fence that surrounded the front yard. The real estate lady got out of her car, walked up to the house and let us in the front door. The interior sparkled with a fresh paint job. The rugs and the wood floor were in great shape. I could picture Grandma standing in the kitchen looking out at the yard. I found myself quickly becoming emotionally attached to the house. My desire to be part of the purchase was growing.

I walked quickly from room to room and realized that this house was nicer than ours. It only had two bedrooms—one less than ours—but it was newer and had a bigger backyard. There were three fruit trees out back, as well as a smattering of other plants. I knew in my heart that Grandma would love it.

The first home Ed purchased

I was sold. "Count me in," I said with a grin just before we all got back into the car. Dad offered his hand, and we shook on it.

In the following weeks, I grew a few notches on the maturity scale or, at least, I felt like I did. Whenever I thought of Grandma's house, I tingled inside. I was now a novice investor and proud of it. About a month after purchasing the house, I decided to tell my friend Jeff about my investment. To my surprise, he didn't think it was a good idea.

"You're crazy!" he blurted out. "You could've bought a bigger engine for your car with that money or even a whole new car. Who wants to own a house?"

Despite the harsh words from my friend, I still felt good about my decision. I trusted Dad's wisdom about the investment, and I was happy to help my grandma.

During my weekly visits, she repeatedly expressed her gratitude in her heavily accented rendition of English.

She'd say, "I love dis garden with all dee plants. I love dis 'ouse. And, oh, dee kicheen! It so nice to 'av 'ouse all to me."

Ed's Grandma Anna

Many months after she moved in, she was still beaming with a smile so wide that it nearly reached her ears. To me, that smile was worth more than any financial gain.

Grandma was never lonely in her new home with five daughters and their families regularly dropping by. She was always ready to serve cookies, a piece of cake, or, better yet, hot homemade doughnuts. If I was there during lunchtime, I usually got a bowl of delicious homemade polish sausage soup made with vegetables from her garden. *Yum, yum!*

If I stopped by to introduce a girlfriend, Grandma was always very interested and friendly. Later, in private, she would let me know what she really thought of her and if she might be good for me. She always favored the ones who were the sweetest. I chuckled to myself about her matchmaking skills. I appreciated the help, but I wasn't ready to get serious. I was still in high school!

Life moved on and four years later, when I was a sophomore in college, Dad made me a surprise offer. "Would you like to buy out my share of the house partnership?"

I was stunned, and I couldn't figure out why he would ask that. I was pretty sure he didn't need the money. "Why do you want to sell off your half of the house?"

"I want to give you a chance to own a whole house rather than just a half. You're bound to feel more complete," he smiled. "It will only cost you another thirteen hundred dollars. I'm not marking it up. Plus, in just a few more years, the house will be paid off."

Right away, I knew that was a whale of a deal. After renting the house to Grandma for four years, it must have built up some additional value. Without hesitation, I found my checkbook and bought the other half.

Grandma passed away four years later, leaving an empty spot in my heart. At that time, I was newly married. After Grandma died, my bride and I sold our one-bedroom home and moved into Grandma's old house, where we lived for another two years.

Ten years after my original purchase, we sold the house for eighteen thousand dollars. Thanks to Grandma's need and Dad's willingness to share, I was able to get a head start in Real Estate 101.

The great financial return and priceless memories that went along with being a homeowner are something a savings account just can't compete with. Ever since my original teenage house purchase, I've had an affinity with "dirt investments." And, over the years, that kinship has served me well.

Chapter 8

Going Full Throttle

I purchased my first boat and trailer for two hundred dollars during the summer before my final year of high school. It was a second-hand, fourteen-foot, flat-bottom wood boat with a forty-horsepower Mercury engine. The boat was so light two people could pick it up.

In order to get it to the boat launch, I installed a trailer hitch on the bumper of my '55 Chevy. Thirty minutes after heading out for our maiden voyage, my friend, Tom, and I were ready to launch the boat at the public boat ramp under the Kenmore Bridge. It was located on the Sammamish Slough, a narrow waterway that runs between Lake Washington and Lake Sammamish, about twenty minutes north of Seattle.

I backed the trailer down the ramp and partway into the slough. Tom disconnected the front cable, and the boat slid smoothly into the water. There was no place to tie it up, so I tossed my shoes into the boat and waded to the side of the ramp to pull it out of the way.

While Tom took care of the car and trailer, I stood next to the boat in three feet of water and kept it in place by holding onto nearby cattails. Some ducks paddled nearby, all in a row.

With still no sign of Tom, I glanced back at the boat. The seat cushions, my shoes, the small cooler with our lunch and our lone oar were now floating *inside* the boat, gently rocking on top of four inches of water.

Just then, Tom returned, saw the predicament and immediately understood the problem. "Where's the drain plug?"

"I don't know!" I said, panicking and feeling stupid.

We quickly pulled the boat closer to shore. Tom hopped in, and we both searched frantically for the tiny hole and the plug. My precious boat was starting to sink. Tom found the incoming gusher and stopped most of the flow with his finger. After a few stressful minutes, I finally found the plug near the floating cooler. We tipped the now very heavy boat just enough so I could reach underneath and insert the plug by screwing it in from the outside.

Once we solved the sinking problem, the next order of business was to bail the water out of the boat. All we could find in the car was an empty two-pound coffee can so we took turns. After thirty minutes of hard work, we finally got most of the water out. The interior was sopping wet, and there was still about an inch of river water in the bottom, but we were as ready as we were going to be for our first day on the lake.

"Tom, let's push the boat around," I said. "That way, when it starts, we'll be heading in the right direction."

As Tom held onto the boat, I braced my left leg on the motor support and tugged on the starting rope. Nothing happened. Six more pulls and the same result. With this new predicament, my optimism about the day began to fade.

"I think the cattails might be getting tangled in the prop," Tom suggested.

"Okay, why don't you push us out a little further and jump aboard."

Unfortunately, I forgot there was a current in this slow-moving river. We drifted downstream as I continued to yank on the blasted rope.

Trying to help in every way he could, Tom advised, "Cut back a little on the choke."

Not wanting to add to the strain on my right arm, I switched to my left and pulled with vigor. The engine had started just fine in my driveway a few days ago. I knew it should work, and I had to get it started now. I had no choice.

Eight pulls later, the motor finally shuddered to life. It spit water and bellowed smoke as I pushed the throttle into gear. Relief washed over me as the boat jumped into motion.

A few high-fives to celebrate and we got underway with only a half mile to go before we would enter the north entrance to Lake Washington. We traveled slowly since the signs proclaimed a NO-WAKE ZONE and a FIVE MPH SPEED LIMIT. High dirt berms along both shorelines blocked the scenery, but we enjoyed the sun on our faces as we made our way downriver towards Lake Washington.

Tom announced, "Now the whole lake is our playfield!" Not surprisingly, we were anxious for the speed limit to end. "Look!" he pointed out. "We're almost there!"

"As soon as we get past the signs, I'm going to pour the power to this baby," I said.

When we came up beside the last sign, Tom raised his arm in the air and shouted from the back of the boat, "Hit it!"

As we raced into the lake's wide opening, the cattails faded from sight, the high dirt berms disappeared and the scenery changed. On the right, I could see a marina and boat storage business. Next door a sign advertised the Kenmore Air seaplane business. Straight ahead, as far as I could see, was nothing but open water.

We spent many days on the lake that summer. Although we loved the hot, cloudless days, we weren't deterred by less than perfect weather. When the water was smooth, the boat could reach thirty-five miles per hour at full throttle. Without a windshield, the wind brought tears to my eyes that ran down both cheeks. Even though I could hardly see, it was still pure excitement when I drove it flat out, full speed ahead.

One day while we were out, foreboding clouds moved in and a storm whipped Lake Washington into a frenzy. I decided that we'd better head back when we started taking small waves over our bow. With my nerves on high alert, I drove cautiously towards the end of the lake. We were making good headway when a big wave suddenly crashed into the boat. Without a windshield, twenty-five gallons of water poured in over the bow and flooded the interior.

Frightened, I immediately turned and headed for the closest shore. Tom attempted to bail water with his hands, but that quickly proved ineffective. The boat struggled with the extra weight as it rode very low in the water. Even at this slower speed, the smaller waves now easily rushed in over the bow and sides.

It took almost five minutes to reach a dock, and we got there just in the nick of time. With a borrowed bucket from a kind-hearted homeowner, we bailed water for over an hour before we were able to limp back to the boat ramp at the Kenmore Bridge.

On a calmer day, we undertook a trip to the far end of the lake. We had been planning to make the long run to the end and back for a few weeks. With beautiful blue skies overhead, we flew across the water, taking in the view. There were definitely sights worthy of slowing to see, especially when we got close to some of the beauties sunbathing on the boat docks.

Ten miles from our launch site, we buzzed two girls sitting out on their beachfront lawn. When the girls waved, it seemed as if my boat had a mind of its own, instantly circling back to visit their dock. Of course, Tom and I didn't object.

After introducing ourselves and speaking with them for awhile, Tom posed the question, "Would you like to go for a spin?"

I explained our end-of-the-lake mission. The girls looked us over and agreed to a short ride. Tom and I winked at each other. We felt proud to have our first female passengers.

Unfortunately, we quickly discovered that the boat performed best with only two people onboard. With all four of us, the little boat would only blow water, and the bow tipped up at a thirty-degree angle. Trying to remedy the problem, all of us crowded towards the front to try to drop it down. Once we got the boat's nose back in the water, we were good to go as long as we didn't slow down.

Although the closeness was a nice fringe benefit, it didn't compensate fully for the embarrassment I felt from my boat's lack of robustness. Before long, we returned the girls to their house. They smiled at us as they waved goodbye, but I was certain that they weren't overly impressed.

When it came time to waterski, the maximum load the boat could handle was a driver and one skier. (In those days, you weren't required to have an extra person to serve as a spotter.) Skiing got a lot easier when I discovered one of my high school friends lived on the western shore of Lake Washington. The backyard of John's parents' house was a water paradise with a thirty-five-foot dock.

Since it was a high dock, three feet above the waterline, we no longer had to start skiing from the middle of the lake. Whenever I had a friend or two who wanted to go skiing, I made a call, got permission and then gave them John's address. At the prescribed time, I showed up in my ski boat and met my friends at John's dock.

After giving my novice skiers some specific instructions, I'd pull away slowly to tighten the rope and then wait for the signal. Often, the first few starts were failed attempts. But, I was happy to swing around and try again. I never tired of teaching someone to ski. I'd keep pulling them until they either got up, or they tired and wanted to give up.

My instructions must have been effective because I taught dozens of my friends to waterski during the summer of '58. My students usually learned in less than half an hour. Afterwards, Tom commented, "You could have made a lot of money if you had charged a fee for your lessons."

"I feel the thrill of success right along with them," I replied. "I could never charge for something I enjoy so much."

As the summer rolled along, some of my friends wanted to try bolder things such as slalom waterskiing. None of us owned a slalom ski, so we just used one of the double skis. Unlike single skis, double skis had only a tiny, one-inch fin so it was awkward to control and nearly impossible to execute sharp turns. But with practice, by mid-summer, Tom and I became proficient at slalom skiing.

One day Tom proposed a challenge, "We should try to master a step-start off John's three-foot dock. I'm going to invest in a slalom ski, so we can do this right. They are three inches wider and come with a four-inch fin."

"Okay, you get the ski, and I'll give it a try."

During the first two weeks with the new ski, we crashed and burned. Every time we jumped off John's dock, we sank deep into the water, and the rope was jerked out of our grip. We immediately realized that we needed to time the jump perfectly so we wouldn't sink so far into the lake, but we quickly found out that getting the timing right was tricky. Armed with competitive spirits, we refused to give up; after each failure, we swam back to the dock, climbed up and did it again, sometimes until dusk. We made countless attempts during each outing, and we always paid the price with sore muscles the next day.

Finally, near the end of the second week of trying, we did it! By focusing on the speed of the boat, the rope and our balance, we were able to pinpoint the exact moment to make our leap. What a thrill to jump off of the dock and hit the water at the split second before the rope was taut. We sunk only inches, and then, like rockets, we flew forward, skimming fast across the water with a hoop and a holler. Each success brought cheers from curious onlookers. We felt like acrobats and conquerors.

In the spring of 1959, we heard about an annual event dubbed the "Slough Race." The race, which had its inaugural year in 1928, boasted over one hundred entries. The starting line was located near a barge a half mile from the end of the lake. From there, the race course continued for thirteen miles up the winding and very narrow Sammamish Slough. Obviously, the five-mile-per-hour limit was ignored for this occasion.

Some of the competing boats were like miniature hydroplanes from as far away as Idaho and Oregon. Others were local boats but twice as long as my boat and with three times the horsepower. Camera crews perched themselves in the most severe turns to catch the inevitable crashes. My friends and I, along with over forty thousand local fans, watched from the banks of the river.

Excitement was in the air even before the race began. As we sat on our blanket in the tall grass, we could hear the roar of each boat's engine long before it came around the nearest bend and into our view.

All boats got their start with a five-minute delay behind the previous racer. They flew through the twists and turns at breakneck speed. A number of ninety-degree turns posed serious problems for drivers. Boats often slid completely sideways in the turns and sent a wall of water up onto the embankment, drenching the excited fans.

There were numerous crashes as boats careened into floating logs, bridge supports and sometimes each other. When boats ran into trouble along the way, spectators would jump into action to help them get back to racing. It was clear that power and speed could be a dangerous combination on this narrow river, but that added to the thrill. Although I did envy the drivers, I knew that watching had to be much safer than racing.

The day after the race, the local newspaper announced a special event would be added to the Slough Race the following year. For the first time, a limited number of boats would be allowed to pull water-skiers in a five-mile competition. Each participating boat would compete according to its engine size.

I called Tom right away. "Did you hear about the new ski race classification for next year?"

"I heard about it on the radio. I was going to call you. Are you thinking what I'm thinking?"

I quickly made an offer. "If you'll be the skier next year, I'll pull you behind my boat."

"Let's do it!" Tom exclaimed.

The next year, we couldn't wait for the spring ski race. I filled out the application as soon as it was available, and we were lucky enough to secure a spot.

A few days before the race, Tom and I had a quick strategy meeting. I said, "The slough has lots of sharp turns we'll need to anticipate. It will be more difficult to maneuver with you skiing behind the boat, but I'll go as fast as I'm able. You just hold on."

"You do your part, and I'll do mine. Just remember to glance over your shoulder once in awhile, to make sure I'm still on the end of the rope. You can't win without me," he joked.

Finally, the race day arrived. We got into position and waited for our turn to go. When the flagman dropped his arm, I took off like a bullet, my forty-horsepower engine pushing for all it was worth. When I turned back to check on Tom, the sun reflected off of his white knuckles. The crowds cheered at every turn. It felt like we were in the Olympics! Tom had become a great skier, and I knew we had a chance to finish well.

Four miles up the crooked river, just when I was beginning to count on a good finish, I attempted to make a hard left turn. I misjudged that particular section, which turned left and then right in a tight S-curve. With my adrenalin pumping, I was going way too fast to make the turn. I backed off the throttle, but it was too late.

My little boat was out of control and careening towards the shore. I closed my eyes and braced for impact. The boat and I ended up in the bushes. Tom was okay, but not completely safe from other speeding boats until he swam to the shore. For us, the race was over, but the bragging was not.

"We almost won! I'm sure of it, even if we didn't quite finish," we told our friends.

I reentered the same event for the next two years, each time with a different buddy as my skier. Both years we narrowly missed the trophy, but the reckless fun and the cheers of the crowd made us feel like winners.

The Slough Race continued until 1976 when a high-powered boat completely missed a turn and flew up onto the embankment, badly injuring a spectator. After that, the sponsor could no longer buy insurance for the race.

When I think back to the races, I realize how crazy and dangerous they actually were. The cheering crowds, which included my friends and me, sat mere feet from the slough's edge and the out-of-control boats—something that would never be allowed today. It's actually surprising that nothing worse than that one serious injury transpired throughout all the years of slough racing.

Chapter 9

Cool Cars for College Guys

In the spring of 1960, I was nineteen years old and finishing up my first year of college at the University of Washington in Seattle. At the beginning of my freshman year, I had joined the Sigma Phi Epsilon fraternity but continued to live at home. I spent many afternoons with my buddies at the Sig Ep house, which was located near the middle of Greek Row, on the corner of Forty-sixth Street and Twenty-first Avenue Northeast, and only one block north of the University of Washington campus.

One sunny day, while I was eating lunch at the fraternity house, I heard the alluring roar of a high-performance car. Within seconds I was outside.

There, in the parking lot, surrounded by at least a dozen Sig Eps, was a sparkling white Corvette. We gazed longingly at the convertible sports car as our frat brother, Alan, got out from behind the wheel and soaked in all of the attention. When he raised the hood to show off the powerful fuel-injection engine, we all began to drool. The top of the engine was accented in chrome. I didn't know if I'd ever seen anything so beautiful. As groups of students walked by us down Forty-sixth Street, I noticed that the 1959 Polo White Corvette was turning heads faster than a mini-skirt.

I said, "This car is amazing and it looks brand new. How much horsepower does it have?"

"It's got two-ninety, and it's actually just over a year old," Al responded.

After a quick look, many of the guys were drawn back inside to finish their lunch, but I couldn't pull myself away. I was in awe of this beautiful machine.

"Anyone want to take a ride?" Alan offered.

There were a number of takers so I eagerly awaited my turn. The upperclassmen stood in line ahead of me. I was the sixth and final passenger.

Al said, "Get in and fasten your seat belt."

"Let's burn some rubber—make it worth my wait," I challenged.

"That will be easy," he responded with a glint in his eyes.

With the engine roaring and the tires smoking, the 'Vette shot down the street like a bullet. My body slid backwards and my head felt like it was glued to the seat. The power was invigorating. In just a few moments, we were already around the final turn and slowly coasting back to the fraternity house.

As I stumbled out of the car, my heart racing, I knew that one day I'd get a Corvette. I'd never been in a car that could go from zero to sixty in six seconds flat.

One of my fraternity brothers pointed up the street. "See those two black streaks? That was you and Alan striping the pavement." I marveled at the tire tracks; they started in front of the fraternity house and headed northbound as far as I could see. My '55 Chevy could never burn rubber like that.

"Man, your car is fast!" I said.

"That's because it's made of fiberglass. I've heard that Corvette bodies are so light, two men can lift one off the frame. I guess the light weight and powerful engine make it especially fast."

Alan was more concerned, however, about all the attention his car and driving had attracted. "I think it's time for me to take off before someone calls the police."

Sure enough, as Alan began to turn his Corvette around, a police car approached. The officer appeared to be on the hunt, and his gaze lingered on all of us. Despite the telltale black streaks on the pavement, the squad car passed by. Fortunately, he must not have had a description of the car causing the disturbance. Feeling lucky, Al casually drove away.

After that brief introduction to the world of Corvettes, I began to fantasize about owning one. Many afternoons, when I should've been studying, I found myself daydreaming about how it would feel to be in the driver's seat of my own Corvette convertible—preferably a red one.

A few weeks after the ride with Alan, driven by curiosity, I stopped by a car dealership to get a price on a new 1960 Corvette. The white one on the showroom floor was four thousand dollars. My goal was to find one for less than two grand. To stay within my budget, I learned that my dream car would have to be at least four or five years old. Even though I was tempted by the glamour of the showroom Corvette, I remembered the advice my dad had given me on more than one occasion: "Never buy a car you can't afford. Make sure you always have the cash on hand to pay in full."

I waited a couple of months in order to increase my car fund, saving as much of my part-time paychecks as I could. With twenty-five hundred dollars in my account, I got serious about finding the right car. I searched the newspapers every week for a Corvette but found few. Even the used ones were priced way over my budget.

Finally, after a month of intense searching, I caught a break. While getting a haircut at the local barbershop, I heard about a 1956 Corvette for sale. It sounded like it was within my budget and might be worth pursuing, so I called the car's owner as soon as I got home.

"A friend of mine at the Ninetieth Street Barber Shop gave me your number and said you had a Corvette for sale."

"Yes, my son does. He purchased the car new four years ago. He bought it with some racing options and took it to the race track every chance he got. He had lots of success there. It's a very fast car."

"Why is he selling it?"

"When he joined the Marines, I agreed to store it. That was two years ago. Now he's decided to re-enlist so he's asked me to sell it for him."

Trying to mask the excitement in my voice, I made an appointment to see the car in an hour. With my checkbook in hand, I headed out to find out if this car was as good as it sounded. I had high hopes, but I also realized that I might be setting myself up for a disappointment. After all of that racing, the car could be a worn-out dud, especially if it had chips and fiberglass cracks from the track.

Upon arriving, I was escorted to the garage to see the car. My first impression of the Corvette wasn't good. The car had been sitting, uncovered, for twenty-four months. It was completely caked with dust. This definitely wasn't a good way to sell a car. I did, however, notice one good thing: it was my dream color, Venetian Red.

The soldier's dad said, "My son applied a preservative to the chrome and completely waxed the rest of the car before he parked it. It should clean up nicely. Here, I'll show you." He walked toward his workbench and continued, "If you had come a few days from now, I would've had time to clean it."

He grabbed an old towel, wetted half of it and cleaned off the right front fender. I was shocked to see the improvement. The fender looked great, much better than I had expected.

The gentleman reached inside the driver's door and released the hood. He slowly raised the dusty bonnet until the hood latch clicked into place. Immediately, I took notice of the twin carbs and high-compression heads. Everything else under the hood looked "bone stock," that is, the parts looked the same as those in the dealership Corvettes.

"Can you start it up?" I asked.

"Sure thing," he agreed.

"How many miles are on this car?"

"Thirty-six thousand," he said over his shoulder as he reached in to turn on the ignition.

The Corvette started up quickly, with a distinct rumble coming out the exhaust pipes—just like Alan's Corvette. "What's the oil pressure gauge say?"

"Fifty pounds," he reported.

I knew that was a good indicator of a strong-running engine. I closed the engine compartment and asked, "Do you mind if I sit in the driver's seat?"

"Help yourself," he offered as he pulled the door open.

I slid inside and gripped the spoke steering wheel; it felt so good and natural. I noticed the deluxe push-button radio and turned the dial until soft music poured out of the dash speakers. I brushed my hands across the seat and found perfection. This car was beginning to feel like it belonged in my garage.

"If you're serious about buying it, you might as well look it over real good," he offered.

"Hey, that's a great idea. Would you happen to have a flashlight? I'd like to take a peek under the car."

"Yeah, I've got one right over here."

After I completed a thorough examination, I gave my report. "It looks pretty good."

"Would you like to take it for a short drive?" he offered. "I'll go with you, but we can't go far because it's not licensed for this year."

"Sounds good," I replied.

We took a short drive, and I was in heaven! My chest felt tight as my heart revved up just like the Corvette's engine. I struggled to contain my excitement.

Boy, did this car handle well! I was in love.

Dad had always taught me to be a cool customer in negotiations. Trying to follow his advice, I composed myself and casually asked, "How much does your son want for it?"

"He would like to get eighteen hundred," he said.

After walking around the car and kicking the tires a few more times, I boldly made my offer. "I can give you fifteen hundred cash today."

He hesitated for a few moments, and I held my breath. Then he said, "Son, you've got yourself a deal."

I was ecstatic! I got the car I wanted, and I got it at a great price. I would even end up with extra money in my bank account. My spirit soared all the way to the bank, and I returned in less than an hour to complete my purchase.

The car, as it turned out, had an additional option. Just before I drove away, the seller pointed out a fold-down convertible top stored under the attached hardtop cover. The bargain had just gotten a little sweeter. This car was definitely worth the wait.

I parked the Corvette in my folks' garage and, with help from Gerry, cleaned it up in two days. We washed it three times just to make sure we didn't miss a spot. Then we added a wax job and, boy, did it shine. We also gave the interior a deep cleaning, and, by the time we finished with a vinyl dressing, it looked almost new. Each hour I invested in working on it doubled its beauty. I was completely in love with my Corvette.

Ed's dream 1956 Corvette

Because I didn't want Dad or Mom to judge my car until after I'd detailed it, I'd asked them not to take a peek until I was ready. Now it was showtime!

I wanted Mom to be the first to see the finished product. I carefully backed the car out of the garage and walked into the kitchen to invite her outside. She knew what was up and brought along her camera. She took a couple of photos of me with the car and then gave me a big hug. "This car looks brand new. It's very nice. How about giving me a ride around the block?"

I opened the door for my mom and smiled to myself as I walked around to the driver's side. Despite the familiar-sounding request for a ride around the block, there would be no tire burning on this trip.

When Dad came home from work, I repeated the big reveal for him. I told him to turn around until I pulled the sparkling car out of the garage. From his "good job" comments, big smile and slap on the back, I knew he thought I did okay.

Now I was ready to show it off to my buddies. I took it down to Dick's Drive-In where a large group of my friends hung out. They all instantly loved my Corvette and wanted to take a ride in it with the top down. My frat brothers were particularly impressed that, in only three months, I had fulfilled my dream of buying a Corvette.

What began as a fantasy turned into an intense love affair. I jumped at any excuse to drive my sports car. When I put the car through its paces, the roar of the mufflers and the pull of the high-performance engine telescoped up through the seat cushions. At moments like that, I was in Corvette heaven!

In 1961, Tom and I took a spring break trip over to see some girls we knew at Eastern Washington College in Cheney, a small town close to the Idaho border. The trip was well worth taking; we enjoyed visiting our friends, but the best part was the drive there and back. The weather was great so we traveled with the top down the entire time. We peeled our shirts off to soak up the eastern Washington sun.

On our way back to Seattle, we first had to traverse the flat and sparsely populated eastern half of the state. As we were driving down a straight piece of highway on State Route 2, Tom said, "Let's see what this car can do."

Without hesitation, I pressed the pedal to the floor. The speedometer raced passed ninety miles per hour and, before I knew it, I was going a hundred.

"Do you want to go faster?" I yelled over the roar of the wind.

"Top it out!" he urged.

The brief pleasure carried some risks, but they were hard to measure against the offsetting reward. Tom and I wore enormous grins as I buried the throttle into the floor.

The Corvette surged ahead. We went faster and faster until the speed dial crept upward and tapped on the one-hundred-and-twenty-mile-per-hour mark. At this crazy speed, the telephone poles looked like picket fences. I decided to ease off the throttle.

Seconds later, I noticed a large road sign indicating a sharp left turn dead ahead. I applied the brakes and didn't get a lot of response from the car.

Suddenly concerned, I yelled, "Tom, you'd better hang on. We may not make this turn."

Still going about eighty miles an hour, I depressed the brake pedal with both feet and tightly gripped the steering wheel. The tires locked up, and we skidded straight ahead, completely missing the turn. Out of control and still going fast, we flew off the road, plowed down a steep embankment and bottomed out. Dust and dirt filled the car. I couldn't see a thing. It was like being in a dust bowl.

As we came to a stop, Tom started waving his hands to clear the air. "That was as close to rolling over as I've ever been!"

I was shocked, embarrassed and shaken by the danger I'd put us in.

Choking on dust, I sputtered, "That was definitely a very close call."

We got out of the car to survey the damage. My beautiful red Corvette looked like we had just driven it through a dirt farm but otherwise seemed okay.

As Tom watched, I climbed back in, started the Corvette and turned it around. Now we had to get it back up the hill and onto the road. I applied light pressure to the throttle to control the tire spin while Tom pushed for all he was worth. Thankfully, after a few attempts, the Corvette crawled up the steep embankment.

Once the car was back on the road, Tom jumped in and said, "We are two very lucky guys."

My sentiments exactly. I felt very thankful.

We drove at a more civilized speed back to Seattle, our conversation somewhat subdued.

I enjoyed tinkering around with the car and gave it several upgrades. Some additions proved to be more useful than others, like the car alarm system I installed.

A few months after our dirt farm adventure, Tom and I cruised to Golden Gardens Park in north Seattle on a Sunday afternoon to check out the girls. I parked the car in the upper parking lot with the top down, and we walked down to the beach.

About fifteen minutes later, I heard a horn honking continuously, as if it were stuck. I suddenly realized what I was hearing. "Tom, that might be my alarm. We have to go check it out!"

We raced up the hill to the parking lot, my heart pounding. I sprinted towards the spot where we had left the car. *Please don't be gone,* I repeated over and over to myself as I got closer. I reached the third row and saw my car, its horn still shrieking. I didn't see anyone nearby, but the hood was propped open and two electrical wires dangled carelessly over the fender.

Tom caught up and patted me on the shoulder. "Ed, it looks like your new alarm just paid for itself."

After my sophomore year, I decided to take a break from college. That July, I signed up for military duty in the U.S. Army. The reality that soon I would be heading off to boot camp was beginning to sink in. I knew that my Corvette would either need to be stored or sold. I thought of the car's first owner and wondered if, for the second time, the Corvette might be sacrificed for the military.

Ed in his army dress uniform

Plagued by indecision, I wondered if I should sell the car. I knew it made sense to sell it, but, every time I washed my car, I found myself admiring it as you would a fine work of art. I elected to hang on to my dream car at least a little longer.

One hot August day, Tom and I cruised to Carkeek Park. It was another beautiful top-down day. Knowing Tom would be very interested, I casually mentioned, "I think I'll sell my Corvette at the end of summer."

Tom looked shocked. "Are you serious? I've wanted to buy this car ever since you first took me for a ride. If you're really ready to part with it, you know I'd buy it in a second."

He bought my treasure a month later for two thousand dollars. From then on, he loved her as I had. The best thing about selling my Corvette to a friend was that I still got to ride in her. I now rode as co-pilot with Tom in the driver's seat.

Tom, the proud owner of Ed's Corvette

Two months later, I left for boot camp with Tom and another buddy, Bob. We had all signed up for the army together, and now we were heading to California's Fort Ord. Tom's mom had happily agreed to take care of the Corvette while we were away.

It didn't take me long to discover what every soldier knows: boot camp is no joke. It was tough for me, both physically and mentally. During all of the years I worked for my dad, I had been encouraged to think for myself. But, I quickly found out that my independent spirit didn't mesh well with the army. Although I figured I could handle my limited time commitment, I knew, within the first few weeks of training, that I wouldn't want to make it my career. Everything moved slowly in the army (much too slowly for my taste); certainly not at the Corvette-type speed to which I'd grown accustomed.

Ed's mom, Ed, Tom, Bob and Larry

Chapter 10

College Antics

Once boot camp finally ended, I continued to serve in the Army Reserves one weekend per month. In the summer of 1963, I decided to finish up the second half of my four-year degree. I transferred to Central Washington College in Ellensburg.

My new roommates and I were all former University of Washington transfer students and longtime friends. The three of us lived in a small, converted motel room, one mile out of town. Our rent was only one hundred and fifty dollars a month, split three ways. We didn't mind being squeezed a bit for space because we were getting such a great deal. Living off-campus gave us a lot of independence, but being totally responsible for all our expenses meant we had to be careful about money.

One day, my roommate John found an interesting article in the school newspaper. "Listen to this, guys," he said. "This article says, 'Some of the low-income families at Central Washington College may qualify for food rations from the federal government.'"

Food was an important concern for us, as was the money we spent on it. We had become very resourceful at making cheap meals. We took advantage of the neighborhood grocery store's sale items and bulk food discounts, and we bought the majority of our produce at a fruit stand a mile up the highway. We also benefitted from our twice-monthly trips back home to Seattle where we gladly accepted food donations from our concerned mothers. The pleasant aroma of homemade cookies, casseroles and soup filled our car as we made our trek back over the mountains.

When we heard about the offer of free food from the government, John had our attention. After he scanned the rest of the article, John explained, "To qualify for the Welfare Department Family Plan, we just need to show proof that we all live at the same address, and we need to be under the maximum income limit."

As college students with little or no income, we found it easy to qualify. We filled out the paperwork, and our first box of goodies was ready to be picked up just three weeks later.

I was the only one, out of the three of us, to have a car at college. Since it was a pretty nice car, I figured there was no reason to alarm the Welfare Department. On the two days a month we picked up our food supplies, I parked it several blocks away. At that time, I was driving a bright red 1963 Pontiac Lemans convertible, and it certainly didn't look like a welfare car.

From then on, once a month, we received a one-pound tub of butter, a generous bag of beans, a large sack of rice, a two-pound can of peanut butter and a bag of corn meal. Thanks to the government's generosity, our food costs were cut in half.

As college boys with too much time on our hands, we often played tricks on each other. The trick I remember most involved our welfare food.

Since we were poor college students, we didn't eat out much. Instead, the three of us took turns cooking in our small kitchen.

It was Monday night, which meant it was John's turn to cook, and he had pork chops and rice on the menu. We hadn't yet tried the welfare rice so we were about to find out if it was edible. While John was in the kitchen, Fred and I kicked back in the multipurpose bedroom and watched television. Fifteen minutes after hearing John bang pots and pans around in the kitchen, I decided to get up off the sofa to stretch my legs.

I walked into the kitchen to check on dinner. "How are you doing in here?"

"Would you mind stirring the rice while I go to the bathroom?" he asked.

"No problem, take your time," I agreed.

As I stirred the white rice around with a wooden spoon, a mischievous thought snuck into my head. *John's not that hard to fool; I should play a trick on him.* I opened the overhead cupboard and found a bag of small-kernel white popcorn. I quickly grabbed more than a dozen kernels and spread them around the edges of the pan. I stirred the rice around to hide my naughty deed. John was slow to return, and I started getting anxious so I turned down the burner.

A minute later John returned, looked over all the preparations, and announced, "Dinner will be ready in ten minutes." He took the spoon from my hand and started stirring the pot. "By the way, thanks for your help," he said.

I set the table quickly and returned to the TV room. I whispered to Fred, "I'm not sure exactly what will happen, but I'm playing a trick on John so just play along."

We turned off the TV and waited. There was no noise from the kitchen. I began thinking that maybe I had turned the temperature too low when, suddenly, a loud yell erupted from the kitchen.

"Hey, guys, come quick! Hurry!" John hollered.

The two of us raced into the small kitchen. With wide eyes, John gestured towards the stove as rice flew out of the pan and onto the floor. He reached down and scooped up eight or ten kernels of "popped rice" and exclaimed, "This stuff is amazing! Look at this special rice. It even tastes like popcorn."

He was so excited, his jaws just kept flapping. "I've never seen rice do this before; it must be a special brand. Hey, guys, if we could buy rice at welfare prices and market it as specialty 'popcorn,' we could make a fortune."

We ate dinner and laughed about John's money-making idea. For the next hour, he just couldn't stop talking about the special rice.

It turned out to be such a good joke that I didn't want it to end. I whispered to Fred, "Let's let it play out until morning." We laughed all the more as John continued his excited chatter; good ol' John didn't have a clue.

The next morning was a blur. We all had tests that day so, in the chaos of the morning, I forgot to confess to John. He had the whole day to figure it out, but he didn't. Unfortunately, the situation worsened because, by the end of the day, John had told dozens of students about his special "popping rice." I don't know if anyone believed him.

When I finally confessed that evening, John wanted to club me. Forty-seven years later, John and I still laugh about that prank.

———

Since eastern Washington winters are harsh, my dad loaned me a '55 Dodge station wagon to use at school. One Monday night, my roommates and I jumped in the Dodge and went to the local tavern a half mile up the road. Most Mondays we put studying on hold at seven o'clock and headed out to watch Monday Night Football.

That evening, during halftime, Fred excitedly told us that he'd heard there was a huge rat population at the county dump. Even though the county poisoned them once a year, hundreds of rats somehow survived. In between the yearly poisonings, the rat families multiplied like crazy.

"My friend told me rat hunting is a gas. There are supposed to be mounds of them, and they all come out at night after the dump is closed. He said it's easy to get around the locked gate."

Fred continued his pitch, "Come on guys, let's do the rat hunt next Monday. This is the time of year that the rats are supposed to be thrashing around like spawning salmon. I guarantee this hunt will be the most fun we've had in a long time."

John and I reluctantly agreed.

By the next day, Fred had convinced our friend and neighbor, Mike, to join the hunt. The four of us gathered at our house to discuss the plan. Fred took the lead, "We'll need ropes or wire to secure our pants to our boots because last year one of the guys had a rat run up his pant leg. He beat the rat out with his pistol, but his entire thigh ended up black and blue. Don't worry, it was probably a fluke! I'm sure we won't have any problems if we take precautions." Fred continued, "It'll be very dark and below freezing, so we should wear warm clothes and bring flashlights. Oh, and you'll need to get your guns from home this weekend."

"Don't you think we could go in a few months, when it's warmer?" I asked.

"No, we have to do it when it's really cold out. The rats are hungry, and my friend said they're more aggressive when they're starving. There'll be hundreds of them coming out of their holes, and we can just start blasting them."

We all agreed and began moving forward with our plans. That weekend two of us traveled back to Seattle to visit our families and do some laundry. At home, we gathered up our hunting rifles and a pistol. Except for Fred, a regular bird hunter, the rest of us felt like we were gearing up for a dangerous safari.

After arriving back in Ellensburg late Sunday afternoon, we decided to drive over to the local gravel pit to test our weapons. That was the easy part. It's not hard to hit stationary pop cans.

When Monday evening came, we set off on a mission only testosterone could inspire. To ensure our aim would be straight, we made a very brief stop at the tavern. Then we jumped in my old station wagon and headed out towards the cutoff road.

All four of us were suited up for battle and heavily armed. We had a total of four guns and two hundred bullets between us. What we lacked in experience we tried to make up for in firepower.

After we reached the turn off, we drove almost a mile down the long and bumpy dirt road. As we neared the dump, we saw several adult rats cross just in front of our tires. They looked surprisingly huge in the glare of my headlights. We continued for another quarter mile before I stopped the car at the edge of three acres of garbage. An old, crooked sign hung from the locked gate, and it read, KITTITAS COUNTY DUMP: KEEP OUT AFTER DARK. We all laughed at the sign and slowly drove around the gate.

With the glow of the crescent moon completely doused by cloud cover, the area was as dark as a jungle. The only visible patch was the narrow strip illuminated by my headlights. The car had fogged up from our breath so we each rolled down our window and tried to spot our targets. As we listened, we could hear some rat activity in the distance. When I cut the engine, I heard a strange rumbling noise nearby.

Fred barked orders like a military sergeant. "Everybody get out of the car and spread out in front of the headlights. Hurry! I'll turn the lights off for a couple of minutes to bring the rats out of hiding. Keep your shooters ready for action, but don't pull the trigger until I turn the lights back on."

We followed his instructions and quickly took our places in front of the car. Within seconds, Fred reached into the car and killed the lights. Instant blackness flooded the area. Fear and anxiety swirled around in my head, but I listened carefully, waiting for the enemy to approach.

At first, I heard only a faint noise, but it quickly grew in intensity. It sounded like a lot of tin cans being thrown into a dumpster. The noise grew louder and louder. The rats must have been attacking the new day's garbage. With our lights off, the rat community didn't seem to notice us; or maybe we just weren't interesting enough to distract them from their dinner. Like a swarm of frenzied bees, the rats were aggressive with the garbage, and I could feel them getting closer.

Suddenly I felt rats running around my feet. I took a deep breath and tried to remain calm. Even though I had my tall work boots on and my pants cinched with wire, my heart was thumping hard and fast.

I'd had enough. I yelled, "Fred, turn on the lights!"

He finally pulled out the headlight switch and yelled, "Shoot those nasty critters!"

The high beams illuminated the area and turned it into a battlefield. The rats were everywhere; they had come out of their bungalows in droves.

I took aim and pulled the trigger on a fat one just six feet away. It flew two feet into the air, landed on its back, then flipped over and continued to run. As I fired a second shot, it quickly disappeared into a hole in the ground. By now, all our guns were blazing and hundreds of panic-stricken rats were running in circles, trying to flee from the flying bullets and the blinding light of our headlights.

Staring at the sea of frantic rats made it hard to focus, aim and shoot. It looked to me like our little ambush was not working out as well as planned. With my heart still pounding, I jumped back into the car to reload. Within a minute, my roommates and Mike had joined me in the safety of the station wagon.

Mike wanted to call it quits. He said emphatically, "It's way too dangerous out there. I almost got shot! I've had enough of you, John. You're dangerous with a gun. You fired a bullet right between my legs!"

John apologized, "Oh my gosh. I'm really sorry. I got a little carried away when I tried to gun down one of those big fat ones."

We all agreed to end the hunt. I started up the Dodge and turned it around. As the headlights swept across the area, I was surprised we didn't spot any dead rats, only some live ones scampering away. It looked like they might be laughing at us.

To soften the blow to our egos I suggested, "The rats might have carried the dead and wounded ones into the tunnels for tomorrow's breakfast." Everyone mumbled their half-hearted agreement.

Although we talked about it, round two never did happen. Once was enough. While we never would have admitted it out loud, we all knew that the rats had won.

Chapter 11

I Met My True Love

For my senior year of college, I lived in a larger house on Ruby Street with Jeff and ol' "dodged-a-bullet" Mike. My former roommates, John and Fred, had graduated the previous summer.

It was the first week of January, 1965, and the weather in Ellensburg was cold enough to cause frostbite. Winter quarter was slated to start in just a few days. In less than six months, I would be graduating. I was planning to study hard to keep my grades up until I hit the finish line. Unfortunately, my remaining business and economics classes were going to be my toughest yet. I had enjoyed college, but I looked forward to having my diploma in hand. I was ready to get on with my life.

On Saturday, around eleven o'clock, my housemates and I drove to a restaurant located just across the street from campus. Because we had slept late, the breakfast crowd had thinned considerably by the time we arrived. As soon as we walked in, the waitress directed us to an available booth on the far side of the room.

While we waited for our food, my friends and I discussed the party we were hosting that night. Jeff and I divvied up the food and clean-up duties and assigned Mike to pick up the keg of beer. Two of our friends were driving over from Seattle, and they had asked us to set them up with blind dates. But, that task had proven to be more difficult than we'd expected. We had completely struck out. The party was set to start in eight hours, and we hadn't lined up any girls to go with them. It looked like our Seattle friends would be dateless.

John, Ed's dad, Ed and Jeff

As we discussed our dilemma, I heard female voices in the booth right next to ours. I looked over my shoulder and eyed three attractive girls sitting on the other side of the planter: one blonde, one redhead and one brunette. *Maybe we should invite them to the party*. It was a long shot, but it was worth a try.

I leaned over and said, "Hi, girls."

They answered, "Hello," in unison.

The six of us exchanged small talk for a few minutes. Then Jeff and Mike, unaware of my idea, finished their breakfast, said goodbye and headed off to the gym. Even though I'd have to do it by myself, I still planned to take the risk and invite the girls.

Because it was awkward for me to talk through the plant divider, I decided to ask the girls if I could join them.

"Now that my housemates have abandoned me, do you mind if I sit with you?" I asked.

"Not at all," the tall blonde offered.

"By the way, I'm Ed," I said as I slid into their booth.

The friendly blonde girl responded, "My name is Diane, and these are my roommates, Marsha and Connie."

Trying to make polite conversation, I asked, "How long have you been going to Central?"

"We're all freshmen," Diane said.

"Where are your hometowns?"

"Diane and I are from Bainbridge Island," Marsha, the redhead, explained.

"And I'm from Richland, one of the Tri-Cities," Connie, the brunette, added in a quiet voice.

Even though she appeared to be the shyest of the group, as the conversation went on, I felt my eyes continually drawn back toward the quiet brunette.

We talked for almost half an hour, exchanging bits of information. In the process, I learned that Marsha was in my typing class.

After the conversation began to die down, I awkwardly sputtered, "Would any of you be interested in going to a function at our house tonight? It's less than a mile off campus."

I tried to sweeten the deal by adding, "Some of my buddies from Seattle are driving over for it."

The girls looked at each other and slowly shook their heads. The answer was a unanimous, "No, thank you." The rejection would have been easier for me to take had my housemates stuck around.

After a few uncomfortably quiet moments, the conversation turned to next weekend's plans. Connie and Diane said they were both going to Seattle. Diane would take the ferry to Bainbridge Island, while Connie was planning to visit her two married brothers.

"My friends and I travel to Seattle every other weekend, and we're heading there next weekend as well," I told them. "If you ever need a ride, give me a call."

In the '60s it was common for students to catch rides with each other, especially for long trips across the state. Each passenger was expected to chip in a dollar or two to help pay for gas. Postings on the school bulletin board and word of mouth were helpful ways to hitch a ride.

Diane and Connie looked at each other. "Actually, we would love a ride! Thank you for offering," Diane said.

We exchanged information and decided on a time to leave that Friday. As our conversation wound down, I suddenly remembered the annual dinner-dance function I was going to next weekend in Seattle. My date, who attended Washington State University in Pullman, had called two nights before to tell me she had to bow out. I had already invited two of my best friends and their dates to the function. Now, it seemed I'd be going stag.

I looked across the table at Connie, the pretty brunette. "Would you consider going to a dinner-dance with me while you are in Seattle next weekend? It's a semi-formal event, and a few of my good friends and their dates will be coming as well."

After a few moments of hesitation, she surprised me by saying, "Yes, I'd like to go. It sounds like fun." She smiled shyly, "I'll be staying with one of my brothers, but I'm not sure which one yet. They both live in Lynnwood and not far from each other."

"All I need is an address and phone number, and I'll be able to find you. Lynnwood is not that far from my parents' home in north Seattle."

By Monday, I decided it would be a good idea to get to know Connie before the dance. I gave her a call and asked if she could meet me at the library the next evening. "We can study for awhile and then stop for a Coke," I suggested.

"I should be able to make it," she said.

I drove to the library on Tuesday and waited patiently. I was there for two hours, and she never showed up. On Wednesday morning, I called to see what had happened, and she said she had to help her roommate with a project. I decided to try again. This time I suggested a Coke date that afternoon.

"I'm sorry, I can't join you. I have a lot of homework," she said.

Now, I was getting concerned. Maybe this girl from Richland had a boyfriend, or maybe she just didn't like me.

I decided to try a third and final time. I asked, "Do you want to give the library another try on Thursday?"

She quietly said, "Okay."

After I hung up, I wondered why I couldn't get that girl out of my head. I'd only spoken to her three times, briefly, and she really hadn't done anything special except evade me.

I'd felt a connection when I talked to her the last time. I liked her soft and polite voice, especially combined with what I'd seen at the restaurant. However, I didn't have a clue what she was thinking. There was still a good chance she might stand me up for our date, like a deer that got spooked and ran.

Thursday evening started well; Connie showed up this time. We whispered our hellos across the library table. Hearing her voice and seeing her face made my heart skip a beat.

In a hushed tone I asked, "Do you and Diane still plan on riding to Seattle with us tomorrow afternoon?"

"Yes, we do. Would it be possible for you to pick us up in front of our dorm?"

After clarifying the details, we continued our whispered conversation for thirty minutes. The next hour was pure study, with no talking. After all, even romance has to occasionally take a backseat to bookwork. At nine o'clock, I walked Connie back to her dorm.

It was a cold night. While we walked, I built up my courage, took a chance and reached over to take her hand. I felt a pleasant tremor of electricity when our hands touched, and I was relieved that she didn't pull away.

I asked my most important question of the evening. "Are you still planning to be my date for the dance this Saturday?"

She smiled and nodded her head.

That Friday afternoon, Mike drove us all west on Interstate 90 towards Seattle. His station wagon was loaded with three guys and two girls. Jeff sat in the front seat next to Mike, and the girls and I squeezed into the rear seat with Connie wedged in between Diane and me. The poor girls had to endure the jokes and stories of us college boys. But, between the five of us, we talked the time away.

When we arrived, Connie directed Mike to her aunt and uncle's home on Lake Washington. It was a beautiful, large home and looked like a mansion from the outside. She and Diane were to be picked up there, in an hour, by one of Connie's brothers.

The next day, I called Connie to confirm our plans for the evening. I dialed the number she had given me for her brother. It turned out she had moved from that brother's house to the other. I wrote down the new number and finally got a hold of my date.

That night, as I drove to the new address, I was nervous—what if she wasn't there? What if she had changed her mind? It wasn't until she answered my knock that I finally relaxed. After Connie introduced me to her brother, Conrad, he discreetly slipped her some coins just in case she needed to call for a ride home.

When we pulled into the parking lot of the hotel that was hosting the dinner-dance, I saw my parents getting out of their car, two rows over. We waited for them to catch up to us, and I made a quick introduction. Mom and Dad were concerned about getting inside to check on the two tables reserved for their employees so we didn't talk much. I was anxious for my folks to get acquainted with Connie, but that would have to wait until everybody got settled.

As we walked into the lobby of the hotel, I explained the event to her. "This is the annual Western Washington Auto Wreckers Ball. It's a chance for the association members to treat their employees to a fancy dinner-dance."

After we climbed the stairs to the second-floor ballroom, I introduced Connie to our employees and their spouses and to the friends I had invited. We spent the first part of the evening eating dinner and chatting with the people around us.

As we finished our meal, the band cranked up the tunes, and Connie and I danced our way through the night. Luck was on my side; slow songs dominated the evening. I loved how well we were getting along. Dancing with her was wonderfully smooth and natural.

When I returned Connie to her brother's house around 11:30 p.m., I had a hard time saying goodnight. I had made up my mind earlier that I might try to give her a goodnight peck, but only on the cheek, so I wouldn't scare her away. As we said our final goodbyes next to the front porch, I reached over to plant a tender smooch on her right cheek. To my surprise, she turned and our lips met.

It was over in seconds, but it sent shockwaves through me.

"I had a nice evening. Thank you for inviting me," she said softly. Then she turned, walked up two steps and disappeared into the house.

I got back in my car and slid into the driver's seat. My mind replayed the kiss as I started my car and drove away. I was trying to understand if this unfamiliar feeling meant anything. I had enjoyed a splendid evening with an outstanding ending. Maybe that was all there was to it.

The next day, Connie and I were alone in the backseat as we drove back to Ellensburg. Diane was getting a ride with her mom, so I took the opportunity to get to know her better. When we got to the subject of past boyfriends, she hesitantly said, "There actually still is another guy in the picture. My boyfriend is attending Eastern Washington College in Cheney. We've been dating for five years with some breaks along the way."

I can't say I was happy to hear that, but I've never been one to run from competition.

"We both decided to date other people while attending separate colleges," she explained. "Dave thinks we should have some space from each other so we can be sure about our future relationship."

With my interest piqued, I viewed her response as at least a small opening. I decided not to ask any more questions; I was content just to be near her on the drive back to school.

As the weeks passed, Connie and I continued to see each other; by the end of two months, I was adjusting all my free time to be near her. She clearly had a hold of my heart.

After a while, she decided it was only right to let her former boyfriend know she was dating someone seriously. She felt she should go to Cheney and tell Dave in person. I didn't like that idea very much, so I convinced her to call him instead. I knew with their extended history, there was a chance that he could change her mind. I could tell it was going to be difficult for her. She didn't want to hurt him. She finally made the long-delayed call and afterwards felt better for doing so.

Throughout spring quarter, we continued dating and learning about each other's hopes and dreams. In May, I graduated from Central Washington College and started my real adult life back in Seattle. As summer arrived, I was certain Connie was the one for me. I didn't want to rush her or scare her off, so I held off on popping the question.

That summer Connie also moved to Seattle. She was sharing an apartment on Capitol Hill with a friend from her hometown and working downtown.

By July, just six months after first laying eyes on Connie, I decided the time was right. It was a beautiful summer evening. Connie and I went out to dinner and then drove to Green Lake. I found a quiet spot on the grassy slope by the lake. We sat down and talked. Excited energy coursed through me, but I was nervous about what I was about to do.

After a while, I asked Connie, "Would you like a piece of gum?"

"Yes, thank you," she replied.

With my trembling right hand, I reached into my pocket and took out a box of Chiclets gum. I opened the flap and tipped it into her hand. Out slid a diamond engagement ring.

"Will you marry me?" I said, tripping over those four little words.

She smiled and instantly said what I wanted to hear, "Yes!" Then, she reached over and gave me a big kiss.

I slipped the ring onto her finger; it was a perfect fit. I had just made the deal of a lifetime.

Connie and I were married four months later, on November 20, 1965.

Ed and Connie on their wedding day

Chapter 12

Dune Buggy Addiction

After I finished college and married Connie, I was back working at my parents' business, Lincoln Auto Wrecking. One day, Rod, the manager of the parts department, offered me an exciting opportunity.

"I'm planning to build a dune buggy, and I'm looking for a partner. If you're interested, we could work on the project on Mondays and Wednesdays after work. The finished product is going to be loads of fun."

I quickly responded, "I'm definitely interested. When do you think you'll start?"

"I am hoping to begin working on it next week. I asked your dad, and he gave me permission to work after hours in the repair shop. I think it will take about six weeks to build."

He went on to say, "My neighbor is willing to sell me his 1961 VW Bug with a forty-horsepower engine. It's not much to look at on the outside, but it runs great. I built a dune buggy out of a VW years ago in Montana. It stuck to the hillsides like glue. So, what do you think?"

"You've got yourself a partner!" I affirmed with a handshake.

Building a dune buggy from scratch was a real learning experience. I would have never taken on the task without Rod's expertise. During that week, Rod purchased the old, but functional, VW

Beetle for one hundred dollars. When the next Monday evening arrived, we were ready to start the project.

Our first job was to remove the entire body, fenders and all. That task only took one evening. After unbolting dozens of fasteners and unhooking the electrical system, we were ready to lift it off with Dad's boom truck. We discarded many items during our initial step: the dash assembly, windshield, doors and seats were all given the heave-ho. The VW-like appearance was now gone: all that was left were four wheels, a steering wheel and an engine sticking up in the rear. It was the stripped-down, ugly and naked beginnings of a dune buggy.

As I helped Rod put away the tools and equipment, I commented, "It feels like we accomplished a lot for one night."

"We did better than I expected."

Wednesday came quickly. According to Rod, we needed to shorten the floor pan by fourteen inches. He said that would allow the car to climb over large objects without getting high-centered. Sparks flew while I directed the open flame of the acetylene torch toward the frame of the car. I made two narrow cuts, fourteen inches apart, just behind the area where the seats had previously been. After an hour, the VW broke into two sections.

The front piece held the suspension and the steering wheel, but the most valuable part was the back section, which housed the engine and transmission assembly. At first I was pleased with my cut, but then I noticed a big problem; the brake line, clutch cable and gas line were torched in two.

I apologized, feeling embarrassed, "I'm really sorry. I didn't see those parts under the floor pan."

"It could have been worse. Good thing I removed the gas tank!" Rod patted my shoulder and said reassuringly, "It's no big deal. We had to cut them sometime in order to do a splice later."

We used large clamps to hold the parts together. He had me measure the pieces several times before he started the welding process. Rod finished reattaching the floor pan in just over an hour.

The next trick was to splice the brake lines, the throttle cable and the clutch cable. According to Rod, it was going to be a trial and error repair.

After we repaired the cut cables and jerry-rigged a new gas line, it was time to test start the engine. The buggy's key mechanism was converted to a toggle switch. We added some gas to the tank, then Rod said, "Here goes . . . let's hope it starts right up."

It smoked and sputtered but finally ran smooth. We tested the clutch rod and brakes, and they all worked properly.

Even though we were only halfway finished, Rod decided it was time to go for a spin. "Round up two old apple boxes from behind the office," he told me. "We need something to sit on."

I placed the two wooden boxes on the floor of our topless toy. I looked over at Rod and grinned as we both sat down on our makeshift seats. Wobbling precariously, I hung on for dear life as Rod drove throughout Dad's hilly five acres.

After fifteen minutes Rod said, "Now it's your turn."

On our final lap, I decided to test the buggy's limits with an eight-foot embankment. I circled around behind the hill and started down the incline.

Rod yelled, "You're going too fast!"

But it was too late. He groped for any possible handhold on the buggy's frame as we slid down the embankment. The front end dug into the dirt as we hit the ground. Without a steering wheel to steady him, he was tossed forward and nearly ejected. Dust and flying gravel engulfed us in the violent landing. As soon as he stood up and brushed himself off, he sternly pronounced, "I think it's time to call it a night."

The next week, we had numerous challenges to tackle. We built a set of roll bars and custom fit them inside the dune buggy. Then we formed a new windshield frame. Following Rod's precise markings, I drilled new holes in the floor pan and bolted in a sturdy set of Fiat car seats which Dad had donated to our project.

The third week, we mounted some mud tires that we found in Dad's tire shed. Those extra-wide tires and matching wheels greatly improved the look as well as the handling of the dune buggy. The next day, Rod approached Dad and offered to pay retail price for the tires we had taken.

Dad told us, "They're on the house."

I could tell Dad was getting excited about our project as well. I didn't expect free tires or seats. I think he was happy that I was learning new things.

"Next, we'll form the fenders," Rod said. "We're going to need some sheet metal; maybe we can cut the roof off of a junk car."

The fender project took two weeks to complete. We mounted headlights in the front grille and taillights in the rear fenders so the dune buggy would be street legal. The last task was to custom fit a flat glass windshield into the makeshift frame. Our dune buggy was coming together.

We painted on several coats of grey primer to make all the parts look more united. After that, we stood back to behold our creation.

We were itching to put it through its paces. Rod suggested a large gravel pit near Woodinville as a good place for our first practice run.

On a cold Sunday afternoon in April, we loaded our beauty onto Rod's car trailer. Twenty minutes later, as we approached the gravel pit just off of Highway 522, I saw three motorcycles racing up the two-hundred-foot gravel cliffs. When we pulled into the parking area, I was surprised to see there were two other dune buggies already there. They looped around the lot, chasing each other like dogs.

After we unloaded our rig from the trailer, they drove over to size up our buggy. I could see right away that both buggies appeared to be made out of VWs. The major difference between ours and theirs was the length of the vehicles; neither of them had bothered to shorten their floor pans.

Rod asked, "Which are the best routes up and down the hills?"

One of them said, "Follow us."

Our rig had no trouble keeping up as we bounced along after them. On our second run up the hill, we passed both buggies.

Ed's niece, Tracy, and nephews, Rick and Denny, sitting
in the dune buggy

When they turned back down, we kept going, throwing rocks, gravel and sand all the way to the top. Other than our rig, only the motorcycles were making it to the top. We were very excited with our homemade project.

One of the dune buggy drivers came over to us when we stopped for lunch and said, "Your machine is unreal." I felt my chest swell with pride.

Over the next few years, my interest in climbing steep hills and jumping dirt mounds grew. Dune buggies quickly became a raging fad and dozens started showing up in gravel pits around the county. Rod was constantly adding refinements to our buggy, and we were now charging up and down the two-hundred-foot cliffs with our brand-new double-wide balloon tires. It was rare for the competition to outperform our rig.

Ed and others with the dune buggy

In time, as with most things, the dune buggy thrill started to lose its pull. I decided to refocus my energy on my family and the business.

Chapter 13

Corvette Fever

In the early '70s, my passion for Corvettes still smoldered. This passion was ignited the day Dad challenged my brother-in-law Vuryl and me to find ways to help build our family-owned and -operated business.

By that time, Lincoln Auto Wrecking's inventory consisted of over four hundred American-made vehicles squeezed into our five-acre lot in north Seattle. After a week of intense brainstorming and research, Vuryl and I approached Dad with an idea we hoped he would support.

"Corvettes are the new rage. Several hot rod magazines claim that they're the only true American-made sports cars; they've even rated them on top of their list of collectable cars. We think that stocking parts for this high-end market could be very profitable."

Dad wrinkled up his forehead and said, "I'm not sure I like that idea. We've never bought a Corvette before. I'm sure those cars would be very expensive. It sounds like pouring money down a rat's hole to me. Can't you guys come up with a more practical idea?"

Armed with my research, I defended our position, "We've talked to some of our business connections in southern California, and they said there is a boatload of wrecked Corvette inventory down there. The prices have dropped two years in a row, and right now no one in Washington has a corner on that market. Many of the older, worn-out Corvettes are showing up in the *Little Nickel* newspaper ads. The asking prices are unbelievably low, averaging three hundred to five hundred dollars apiece. At that price, we could sell just a few parts, and we'd get our money back."

Still not overly excited about bankrolling our vision, Dad said, "I'll need a few days to think on it."

By the end of the week, he had softened up a bit. He starting asking questions about how we planned to find, buy and transport the cars.

"Vuryl and I have located people who, with our phone approval, will do our buying for a fee of one hundred dollars per car. Our purchases can be collected and stored until we have four to six Corvettes. Then they could be loaded on a car carrier and transported to Seattle."

"I'm impressed that you guys have everything worked out. But you can't tell me how long it'll be before you turn a profit." He turned to leave and then surprised us by saying, "Let's see how it goes. Don't go overboard."

We'd gotten the green light, and I was ready to peel out. Ordinary wrecked cars can be a little boring, but I was excited to expand into the uncharted territory of the classic Corvettes.

Vuryl was pleased as well. "I'm surprised your Dad went along with it. We'd better not let him down. You can bet he'll be watching the bottom line."

Within a month the first car carrier loaded with six wrecked Corvettes arrived. My hearted thudded in my chest as they were unloaded. We'd bought the cars with the help of an Oregon buyer who had traveled to four or five salvage auctions throughout Oregon and California. We also made a deal with a second buyer in the Los Angeles area to follow-up on the older Corvettes in the *Little Nickel* ads. By the end of twelve months, we had half an acre filled with wrecked Corvettes—nearly seventy crumpled sports cars were all lined up.

After Vuryl came back from his vacation, I updated him on our new division's progress. "Our customer base is growing and so are our sales, but we need to sell parts a little faster to keep Dad off our backs. I think now that the word is getting out we'll do even better."

Car carrier full of Corvettes

In spite of our successes, our buying frenzy was still making Dad irritable. He'd been watching our big dream slowly erode the company's bank account. After biting his tongue for almost a year, he couldn't hold himself back any longer.

"I saw another batch of those plastic cars being offloaded yesterday. I thought I told you not to sink the ship. You're spending the company's money like it's yours." He looked me in the eye, "Son, as of today, I'm cutting off your access to the bank account. Give me your checkbook. You've proved to me that you're more focused on buying than selling. In business, you need to keep those two in balance."

There was no smile, no jokes. What could I say? It was my parents' money, and I was spending it on Corvettes. I felt like a whipped puppy with no puppy chow in sight. I'd learned to never cross Dad, so I handed him the checkbook. As I did, I felt disappointment settle in the pit of my stomach.

Lincoln Corvettes' lot

I saw Vuryl several hours later and delivered the bad news. We discussed the dilemma for an hour. The profit margins on the Corvette parts were good; we just needed to pump up our sales. It appeared the solution was to find more Corvette customers for our existing inventory, and fast. The two of us met again after work to try and come up with a plan.

"Vuryl, whatever we do, we can't give up. We've come too far to throw it all away."

"Don't panic. I think the solution is to focus on some national advertising. We never tried that route because we knew it would cost a lot."

"I'll make some calls tomorrow, check costs and work up a short-term budget. We should also try to get a listing of all the current Corvette clubs and do a mailing," I added. "We should be able to present our game plan to Dad in a week or so."

We carefully narrowed our choice to one national Corvette magazine. Our ad would feature a picture of our "Sea of Corvettes," along with a brief summary of our inventory.

It took two weeks to put a sales plan together for Dad. As he listened, he rocked back and forth on one foot then the other. Dad finally gave us the go ahead, and I signed a contract for a quarter-page ad to run for three months.

Once our ad hit the paper, the news traveled far and fast. People hungry for Corvette parts started calling our new 800 number almost as soon as the ads ran. Our phone lines were overwhelmed with requests. It was like someone had lit a match; the phones were on fire! Some calls came from as far away as Hawaii, Alaska, England, New Zealand and Australia. Our out-of-town monthly sales tripled overnight.

Watching the miracle unfold for two straight months gave Dad renewed confidence in our business plan. "I never thought you guys could pull off this Corvette business idea, but you did!" With the checkbook in hand, Dad extended his arm towards me and restored my access to the bank account with a pat on the back.

Chapter 14

The Unbelievable Corvette

In the fall of 1974, four years after we launched our new venture, the Corvette division of Lincoln Auto Wrecking was booming. Fueled by our success, I began to get a little careless with spending and, of course, Dad noticed. I had begun buying some high-priced used Corvettes instead of just the wrecked ones; plus, even the wrecks were costing twice as much as when we first started.

Dad's frustration boiled over one day as another semi-truck load of wrecked Corvettes arrived. Before the big truck even came to a stop, my father stomped outside the backdoor of the company office to cool off. It was the first time two truckloads had arrived in the same week, bringing twelve more Corvettes. Out of the office window, I could see Dad standing on the back porch, shaking his head in disgust.

I had a sinking feeling as I watched him march back inside. Dad still controlled the money supply, and my bad timing was about to cost me.

He called me over the intercom, "Ed, I need to see you in my office."

The minute I entered, he barked, "I want you to stop buying those overpriced cars! The company account has been stripped to the bone again. I am tired of dipping into our personal savings to cover payroll. I need the checkbook back."

I didn't want to give it up because I couldn't function without it. I stalled a minute, and then he demanded, "Hand it over." I didn't attempt any negotiations as I took the checkbook from my left shirt pocket and placed it in Dad's outstretched hand. I silently watched as he locked the checkbook in the company safe.

When Vuryl arrived back at the shop, I informed him of our new predicament. "Dad's hot about the two loads of Corvettes that came in this week. We've been cut off again."

Vuryl was the calm one; he had probably expected this to happen.

"Let's offer a discount on all our parts," he suggested. "We'll see if that increases sales. We've got twelve used Corvettes for sale. Let's discount those too. Growing the bank account is the best way to earn the checkbook back. It worked three years ago."

I agreed with Vuryl's suggestions. But, the following morning, I developed a new sick feeling in my gut as I remembered something I had done. I went straight to Dad.

"I apologize for overbuying this month. I understand your concern with the checkbook, but there's a slight problem. I verbally committed to buy two additional cars that have not been shipped yet. They're both at the auction yard in Portland, but we'll lose our credibility if we back out."

"The wrecked Corvettes have taken over nearly half of our acreage. You need to stop buying for at least six months. There is nothing wrong with concentrating on selling regular Ford and Chevrolet parts. We'll go ahead with the Portland purchase because a Lincoln always keeps his word, but these are the last Corvettes you're getting for a long while."

As luck would have it, two weeks after Dad silenced my spending, I heard about the deal of a lifetime. Don, a friend and a state trooper, stopped by our office bubbling with excitement. He claimed he had just completed a state patrol inspection on an extremely unusual 1967 L88 Corvette with a 427-cubic-inch engine.

Vuryl and I were all ears. I asked, "Are you sure it was an L88 model?"

"Without a doubt," he confirmed. "The amazing thing about this car is the odometer only shows eleven miles. I was sent to do an inspection because this vehicle had never been licensed or titled in any state. The Department of Licensing was questioning the legality of the vehicle. The owner says when he first bought the car he began altering it to produce a winning combination at the drag racing track in Kent. He ran out of money so he parked the car in his dad's extra garage. Now he's lost his job and gotten a divorce, and he has to sell it. I feel bad for the guy."

"He claims there were only twenty-five street-ready race cars produced by Chevrolet's factory, which may or may not be true. Right now, it doesn't look very extraordinary because it's partially dismantled," Don chuckled. "It's kind of crazy, but, during the past seven years, he's removed nearly every mechanical part to look for ways to improve the car's performance. The motor, transmission and rear end are all scattered on the shop floor. In spite of the fact it's torn apart, this is a very rare car, and the guy is only asking thirty-three hundred, non-negotiable."

I was feeling more excited with every word coming out of Don's mouth.

"I've never heard of a car that old and rare with only eleven miles," I blurted out.

At that moment, all I could think about was what poor timing to have lost my check-writing privileges.

Don looked at his watch and reached for his jacket.

"What are the chances of getting this guy's phone number?" I asked.

"No problem. I'll give it to you. After my inspection today, the car is legal for anyone to buy."

I wrote down the owner's name and phone number in a flash. We walked Don to his patrol car and thanked him for the tip.

Vuryl and I looked at each other. We now faced an excruciating reality. We had just stumbled upon a gold mine but, without the checkbook, our hands were tied.

Vuryl said, "It doesn't cost anything to look." I agreed and dialed the owner Steve.

I asked, "Are you the one with 1967 Corvette for sale?"

"Yes," he said cautiously. "How did you get my phone number?"

I explained my connection to Don, the state patrolman, and he was suddenly more open to my inquiry. I asked about the car and told him Lincoln's Corvettes might be interested in purchasing it.

He sounded relieved to hear we were in the auto business. Then he added, "I don't want any tire kickers wasting my time."

My brother-in-law and I scheduled an appointment for seven o'clock the next evening. What we didn't tell him was, at this stage of the game, we were no better than any other tire kickers. Good deal or not, the asking price of this car was eight times more than we paid for an average wrecked Corvette. But we just had to see the car because we were fascinated by the low original miles and the extremely rare L88 engine. The prospect of seeing a seven-year-old car with only eleven miles on the odometer would long live in our minds. If it was true, someone might need to mop up my drool.

During the drive we chatted about what we expected to see, and Vuryl said excitedly, "We might be on our way to a real 'barn find.'"

When we arrived we were greeted and escorted through two sets of double-locked garage doors. Right away, Steve seemed more interested in showing us the boxes of new high-performance parts than the car. Vuryl and I pawed through the boxes, popping them open one by one. A lot of money was contained in those boxed parts. Vuryl and I glanced towards each other with matching greedy smiles.

As we stood up, Steve said, "Now, I'll show you my baby."

Together we walked to the back of the garage. A large white sheet was draped over what was obviously the silhouette of a Corvette. As Steve stepped over to the car, he gently slipped off the protective covering. Surprisingly, the Rally Red paint job looked to be in show shape. It was even sporting a fresh coat of wax—a little salesmanship, of course.

Vuryl and I tried to conceal our excitement as we examined the car. It was perfect in every way. Several minutes later, I asked for permission to sit in the car. I just wanted to see the odometer up close. Indeed, it recorded only eleven miles. Although we were not buyers this time around, we were certainly enjoying the moment. I asked one last question before we left.

"Steve, how could anyone verify the eleven miles shown on the odometer?"

He said, "It would be hard to do because anyone who could operate a drill in reverse for an hour could change the numbers. But, I can honestly tell you that this car has only been to the quarter-mile racetrack in Kent two times. I hauled it on a trailer on both occasions. After that, I tore it apart to add some performance improvements, but then I fell on some hard times. I was always thinking I would get back to my Corvette, so I kept it waiting in this garage."

Then Steve turned to me, as if remembering something, "Look here, there's one thing I forgot to show you." He opened the driver's door and started manually rolling up the window. "I never got around to removing the factory sticker."

As the window inched upward, the factory sticker appeared, only slightly shredded. It was still glued to the glass just as on any new car, showing all the options and the sales price. It was faded and difficult to read some of the information, but the important stuff was 100 percent readable.

"You can see what I paid for this car."

The car's list price of $6,250 was about one third more than the average '67 Corvette. The options Don had told us about were listed on the document.

Vuryl and I were bubbling with excitement as we returned to our own shop that evening. Vuryl said, "There must be some way to capitalize on this amazing find. I can't get that car out of my mind."

We started brainstorming but to no avail. Finally, I threw out a long shot. "Because Dad is out of town, the only way I can think of to buy this car is for us to find an actual buyer first. Then, we can justify heisting the company checkbook out of the safe. If we had the Corvette sold before we bought it, what could Dad say?"

Vuryl grinned, "I love the way you think!"

The next morning, I called two separate out-of-state Chevrolet dealers. Both had purchased several of our most vintage Corvettes in years past. The owner of the dealership in Detroit was not in, so I called the Chicago dealership. I asked for Bob, one of the owners, and I waited for the receptionist to locate him.

I whispered to Vuryl, who hovered over me, "This might be our only chance. I can feel this whole deal slipping through our fingers. I'm sure that in the next few days that Corvette will be gobbled up by someone in one of the local Corvette clubs."

Just then the phone came to life, "Hello, this is Bob."

I said, "I'm Ed from Lincoln Corvettes. I'm the guy from Seattle who sold you two '55 Corvettes a couple of years ago. Do you remember me?"

"I sure do! Both Corvettes were even better than you described. We did well with them. What do you have this time?"

I quickly transitioned into salesman mode, providing all of the details of this rare treasure. Bob asked a number of questions, seeming to sense the urgency of this opportunity. The last important fact I told him was the price. It very well could have been the deal breaker.

Masking my hesitancy, I stated bluntly, "The price is $4,500."

Without a moment's delay, he answered, "We'll take it."

I was both shocked and thrilled. I said, "Great, it's all yours. Thanks for doing business with Lincoln's Corvettes."

After I hung up the phone, I was speechless. Vuryl was shocked as well, "I can't believe you just sold, and made a huge profit off of, a rare car that you don't even own!"

I immediately called Steve to let him know we would buy the car. He was happy but told us we would have to pay in cash like any other buyer.

"No, problem," I answered.

Without hesitation, I went into the bookkeeping office where my sister was working. She looked over at me and said, "You know Dad's not going to be very happy with you and Vuryl."

"You're probably right, but this deal is too good to pass up." I opened the safe and seized the checkbook. I tucked it in my pocket, picked up my briefcase and headed to our bank. With pen in hand, I wrote a check and extracted $3,300 in cash. I was fairly confident Dad would forgive my insubordination; I had just put together the company's most profitable single-car transaction ever.

As soon as Dad and Mom came home from their vacation, I didn't waste any time confessing the checkbook violation. When I finished explaining, Dad sat back in his office chair, folded his arms and said gruffly, "I guess I can look the other way this time."

Then, not able to maintain his stern look any longer, he smiled proudly, his eyes crinkling. He looked me in the eye and said, "I'll let you have the checkbook again, as long as you promise to put your spending on a diet."

Amazingly, this story didn't end for almost thirty years. The Corvette was put together in Chicago by the new owner's son, but even he was not willing to drive the unbelievable car. So it sat in heated and locked garages. It was hauled with a trailer to some car shows during the next few decades.

Over the years, we saw the car advertised two different times. The first time it was priced at $75,000. Then, a few years later, the asking price was $125,000. Much of the value was due to the odometer reading, and the rest came from its race-car pedigree.

I lost track of the car for several decades. Then, one Saturday afternoon in the summer of 2003, I received a call from an old friend who worked at a Chevrolet dealership in Oak Harbor, Washington.

He asked me, "Do you remembered that rare Corvette you bought and sold all in the same day? It was about twenty-five years ago. I think it had only eleven miles on the odometer.

"I could never forget that car," I told him.

"I was just reading a recent issue of a national car magazine, and a high-performance Corvette, just like the one you sold, was featured at a major classic car auction in Bloomington, Illinois. I don't remember; what was the color of the car you sold?"

I said, "It was Rally Red. Did the article say how many miles were on the car?"

"At the time of the auction, the car was documented to have only thirteen miles. Without a doubt, this is the car you sold in 1974. Sit down for this surprise: The red L88 Corvette was sold to the highest bidder for $615,000!"

I sat down hard on my office chair and asked my friend to repeat the sale price.

"Here, let me read this part to you," he offered. "'Following the sale, several car experts claimed the transaction was the highest dollar amount for any Corvette, ever.'"

I asked my friend to send me a copy of the article, and he quickly sent me the entire magazine. I read the article about twenty times and then tucked it away in my personal collection of car memorabilia.

Our most unforgettable Corvette made a fair profit for Lincoln's Corvettes; however, the car's biggest reward wasn't realized until decades later when it sold for a record price. Even though our profit was comparatively small, we felt like winners too, in our own way.

I guess it's better to touch something for a small profit than to completely miss the opportunity and earn nothing. The fact that this car made history and grew to become so valuable is truly unbelievable; it's flabbergasting!

Chapter 15

One Legacy Ends,
Another Begins

B y the end of 1974, I began to wonder if there might be something better for me on the other side of the wrecking yard's fence. These fleeting thoughts turned into deep contemplation as I began to think seriously about independence.

It had always seemed disrespectful to even consider doing something else for a career. I recognized that working under the family umbrella offered a great deal of protection and would continue to provide security throughout my working years. However, restlessness was building up inside me. The safety of staying in the family business lacked the risk and adventure I craved. Armed with my business degree and management experience, I longed to accomplish something all on my own.

Week after week, I tossed in my sleep. Connie easily recognized my dissastifaction. With her encouragement, I finally got up the nerve to approach my dad. I had to do something. I was already thirty-three; my clock was ticking!

At the end of a long winter workday, I asked my dad if he had time to talk. He agreed and sat down with me in the privacy of my office.

Most dads look forward to their kids taking over their business, and I was aware that was true in my case. However, I took some solace in the knowledge that my sister and her husband were both heavily involved in the management of the business; I knew they were quite capable of taking care of it without me.

Still, the words did not come easily. "Dad, I'm struggling with what I want to do with my life. I really appreciate the opportunities you've given me. You've taught me so much over the years. But, I've lost my enthusiasm for the wrecking yard. Even the thrill of growing the Corvette business doesn't inspire me anymore. I'm so sorry. I don't want to hurt you and Mom."

"Don't feel guilty," he said lightly, "that happens to a lot of people."

At this point in the conversation, if Dad had looked upset or even uncomfortable, I would have been willing to put the brakes on my plans. For him, I would do almost anything. I studied his expression and waited expectantly to see what else he had to say.

After drawing a deep breath, he continued, "I'd never want to hold you back." Relief washed over me; his response was like sweet music to my ears. Then he added, "Do you remember all the jobs I had before I started this business in 1952? You're a lot like me, and I've always liked working for myself the best."

"Dad, I'm so relieved to hear that. Thank you." I could sense the love in his response. I knew it wasn't what he'd hoped for, but he didn't allow me to feel even an ounce of guilt. He really was one incredible dad.

Although I had Dad's blessing to leave the family business, I realized I couldn't break away until I knew where I was going. At that time, Connie and I had two little girls, so I knew it was not a good time to make a foolish choice. We had purchased a brand new home in Kirkland back in 1968 so we also had a substantial house payment to consider. Now that Dad had offered an open door to leave, my restlessness subsided. I knew, if I kept my eyes open, I'd find the perfect opportunity at the right time.

Twelve months later, tragedy struck. On March 16, 1975, in the dark of the night, Dad crossed Aurora Avenue near 145th Street. He was hit by a speeding car and thrown into and over the windshield. The driver of the car didn't even bother to stop as Dad lay bleeding and unconscious in the middle of the highway.

My dad died a week later of massive internal injuries. The pain and shock of Dad's death was difficult for the entire family to bear. My dad's personality was larger than life, and we loved him so deeply that his absence left a gaping hole in all of our hearts. Mom struggled with the loss of her adored companion until her death twenty-five years later.

With one eyewitness's account of the hit and run, plus evidence from a broken mirror near the scene, the police were able to trace the vehicle to a rental car company. The officers interviewed the driver who denied he was at the wheel. After a few days of being questioned, the suspect moved to the Midwest. With no solid proof of fault, no charges were ever filed.

Life moved on, as did my own desires to make a new start. Twelve months later, Vuryl and I were invited to join a group of other auto wrecking owners on a commercial fishing trip sponsored by a local metal-recycling business.

During lunch, the men on the boat began talking about Seattle's towing contract that was going to be up for grabs. For weeks, it had been a front page story in *The Seattle Times*. The current contractor had been caught red-handed, violating some of the contract conditions, and he was being prosecuted. The Seattle City Council decided to put the impound contract up for rebid.

Group of auto wreckers on fishing trip

Although I'd seen the story in the news, I hadn't given it a second thought. However, as I headed home, I couldn't stop thinking about the towing contract. I was anxious to talk to Connie about my idea. I excitedly told her about the conversation on the boat and the possible business opportunity.

"What do you think?" I asked, trying to suppress my enthusiasm.

She looked uncertain but still said, "Let's check it out."

On Monday, I met with Mom, Vuryl and Barb to let them know that I was thinking about starting my own towing company. I needed to see how they all felt about me leaving. Without hesitation, they gave me their blessing.

Vuryl and Ed's sister, Barb

I visited City Hall the very next day. I was happy to find out that the City gave all applicants ninety days to submit their bids and paperwork. I quickly procured a thick pre-bid packet from Seattle's Municipal Building. Then I began to read through pages of documents to find out what was involved in a towing bid. It was a little overwhelming to see that it was nearly fifty pages long.

Basic equipment was first on the list of required items. The bidder needed to have small, medium and large tow trucks – ones big enough to tow buses and semi-trucks. The real estate requirements were also larger than I had guessed. We would need to have a strategically located impound storage lot with a minimum amount of square footage.

Those first two requirements should have been game-ending for me. However, I was determined to find a way to become a legitimate bidder.

A week raced by, and the clock was ticking. Several realtors had already warned me that it would take some time to locate property meeting my specifications. Feeling a little disheartened, I decided to visit a trusted friend at his family's towing business in Lake City. They had been in the business for decades, and I wanted to pick his brain.

Ralph, the owner of Ralph's Towing, said, "I'm happy to help you because I'm not at all interested in getting tangled up with the City. I tried it once, and there was too much red tape for my taste. City work is a high-energy business. Now that I think about it, it would fit your personality perfectly."

Then he told me something that floored me. "Did you know that the oldest towing company in Seattle has been up for sale, off and on, for over two years?"

"No, which one is it?" I asked, surprised.

"It's Cordes Towing. Have you heard of it before? It was started way back in 1917. I actually had coffee with the owner, Ernie, last week."

"That's very interesting," I said. "I'd love to talk to him. Can you give me his number?"

Ralph and I talked about towing for an hour. That night, Connie and I put our heads together to discuss the exciting information.

We both agreed that contacting Cordes Towing was our best move. I made a call early the next morning and arranged lunch with the owner.

The meeting with Ernie went better than I dreamed. He said he was eager to sell and would make me a very attractive deal. The bargain included a dozen trucks, large and small; two of his biggest trucks were rated to tow buses. In addition, he had a collection of over two dozen contracts with local repair shops and also a handful of Northwest trucking companies who were weekly customers.

I asked if he knew of any real estate to lease and he said, "This is going to be the best part for you. I have three locations around town that fully qualify for police impounding. The rents are very reasonable, and I would be willing to sublease to you." I was speechless. I couldn't believe how quickly all the pieces seemed to be falling into place. He told me the addresses to drive by, which I quickly jotted down.

After hearing about this amazing deal, I asked the most important question. "What is your asking price?"

"I'm nearly eighty, and I've been wanting to retire for quite awhile so I'll give you my rock-bottom price. I'll sell you everything for eighty-five thousand dollars. My two big trucks alone cost me that much."

With my heart pumping, I realized that price was better than fair. For the first time in my life, I had no notions to dicker.

"Ernie, I'll buy your business under three conditions: my wife agrees, I can secure a loan from the bank and I'm successful in winning at least one zone of the City contract. What I need is a ninety-day option to buy your tow company."

Ernie's shoulders drooped slightly. "I would prefer to just sell it and be done with it. I'm not sure I want to wait around."

"If I win, I'll need your company. But, I don't want to be in the tow business without a City contract to support my purchase. I'm sure you can understand my position. If you won't sell on these terms, I'll need to make other plans."

After thinking for a moment, Ernie drawled, "Okay, you've got yourself a deal."

The five weeks flew by as I took care of talking to our banker, securing the loan and working on all the details in the bidder's packet. I was exhausted from the pressure. The paperwork was all finished. My old Corvette buddy-turned-attorney Alan reviewed it for us. With just over two weeks to go, we felt confident that everything was in place except for the final bid numbers.

Connie and I decided to take a week off in mid-August to visit some friends in northern California. I had been racing around for weeks and needed a break before the time came to submit the September bids. We were staying with good friends and enjoying their pool with our daughters, when I received a phone call from Vuryl.

Ed and Connie and their daughters Wendy and Trina on a family vacation

"A letter came in the mail today from the City. Do you want me to open it and tell you what it's about?"

"Yes, please, it might be important."

After scanning the letter, he said, "For some reason, the City of Seattle has just extended the bid opening by thirty days. Won't that date change mess up your deal with Ernie?"

I was surprised by the news but not terribly worried. "I'll just phone him from here and ask for a thirty-day extension."

When Ernie answered the phone, I explained the situation and made my request. To my shock and dismay, Ernie responded, "No extension. You have two weeks left to decide. You either buy it by then or forfeit your five-thousand-dollar deposit. "

Unable to relax, Connie and I decided to cut our trip short. We packed up the car and our family of four and headed north to Seattle. We thought it would be best for me to speak with Ernie, face-to-face, to see if he would change his mind.

As soon as we got home, I set up a meeting to try one last time. The meeting only lasted a few minutes. When I returned home, I told Connie, "He isn't going to budge. Maybe he has a better offer."

Connie and I talked about it and decided it was best to just go ahead and purchase the tow company. My low-risk option had just turned into a high-stakes deal.

I called Alan and made an appointment to draw up the necessary purchase agreement and lease documents.

The legal papers were signed on September 1, 1976, giving Cordes Towing a new name and owner. We decided to call our new venture Lincoln Towing. The City contract bids were due to be opened in thirty days, but at this point we were already committed, win or lose.

Chapter 16

The Day of Reckoning

The new City of Seattle contract bid date was fast approaching, and I felt the pressure bearing down on me. I knew a lot was riding on the results. On top of that, I now had the additional demands of running my own business.

The lowest bid per tow, combined with the lowest daily storage rate, would win the contract. But, if we bid too low, we could end up trapped in a contract and losing money for three years. We'd done our research and come up with our bid numbers, praying before writing them on the final document.

Connie and I were both up early on the day the bids were due. We sat down to breakfast together, but we hardly touched our food. The official deadline was October 1, 1976, with bids to be in the clerk's hands and time- and date-stamped by 10:00 a.m. sharp.

"I felt you tossing and turning all night," Connie said. "How do you feel about our chances?"

"I think we have a chance, but there's no way of knowing what it'll take to win it," I answered.

"I saw you rereading the contract last night," Connie commented. "Did you make any more adjustments?"

"No changes. If I were a betting man, I would say we have a 30 to 40 percent chance of winning at least one zone. I'd be extra happy if we won the high-visibility, high-volume zone downtown."

I dashed off to work to clear my desk, but I couldn't concentrate on anything. I decided to get a head start and not risk being late with our bid.

I drove downtown and backed my Chevy pickup into a parking stall right in front of the Municipal Building. With my bid packet tucked tightly under my right arm, I took a seat in the fourth floor lobby. I looked up at the wall clock; I was thirty minutes early. I watched several groups of people arrive, hand the clerk an envelope and sit in the chairs arranged around the room. I didn't know a soul. I concentrated on keeping my eye on the clock, which now read 9:40 a.m.

My strategy was to hold my envelope, keeping it secure until the last few minutes. The elevator door opened and more people got off. The waiting area was getting crowded. At that moment, I had a strange feeling. I didn't want to go, but I felt a sudden urge to use the restroom. One more look at the clock, and then I dashed out the door to find the men's room. Just as I began to panic, someone came out of an office and directed me down the hallway to the right. When I raced back through the glass door and reentered the lobby, I had less than five minutes to turn in my bid. With sweaty palms, I silently presented my packet to the clerk.

The lady stamped my large envelope and said, "You're sure cutting it close," as her machine printed 9:56 a.m., October 1, 1976, on the top of my envelope.

I returned to my seat with my heart still pounding.

Three minutes later, a large door opened and an official wearing a badge announced, "Those who submitted a towing contract bid, follow me."

Six members of the lobby group, including me, were ushered into a conference room.

A lady carrying an armload of bid packets followed us into the room. She set the packets on the table, cleared her throat and stated, "No contract decisions will be made until tomorrow afternoon. Winners will be notified by phone and posted in our lobby. A press release will also be issued at that time and all decisions will be final. Today, I will open and read the bids for each impound zone, including the daily storage rates. The other portions of each bid packet will be reviewed privately by committee. Please refrain from asking questions or making comments. Good luck."

As the public servant began to read aloud, I recorded each bid on my yellow notepad. I was surprised how similar some of the bids were to mine. A few were far higher and seemed like sure losers, but many were uncomfortably close. The stack was almost empty, and my bid had not been read.

Then the clerk announced, "This is the final bid, and it's from Lincoln Towing."

Slowly, she exposed my secret bids to everyone in the room. My bid amounts had been completely confidential. No one except my wife knew them.

When the bid process was over that morning, I couldn't say if we were winners or losers. It was going to be very close. In the prime zone, we were one dollar and fifty cents below the impound price of the next lowest bidder, and we had identical storage rates. Even though we appeared to be in the running, I knew that any mistake or unmet requirement in the thick bid packet was grounds for elimination. In addition, the contract contained dozens of pages of criteria other than price, any one of which could be the deciding factor.

I took my time getting back to the office. I knew, once I got there, I would face questions I couldn't answer even if I wanted to. When I arrived, I told everyone who asked, "Everybody, including me, will have to wait until tomorrow for the official outcome."

I left work early and headed home to see Connie. When she heard the front door open, she immediately gave me a long hug.

Then, with hope in her eyes, she asked, "How do you think we did?"

"There's a strong possibility that we might win one of the high-volume, downtown zones. For those two zones, I think it will be down to two bidders: the Canadians and us. Nobody else was in the running. I really hope they don't find any mistakes in our packet that would disqualify us."

"How many bid packets were turned in?"

"Six. Well, there were six separate companies with some bidding several zones each. "

"What happens next?" she asked.

"We were promised a quick review, with a final, official decision by tomorrow afternoon."

I wrapped Connie in a hug and said, "Let's not talk about the business or the contract tonight, my stomach is in a knot. I just want to relax and have some family time."

"That sounds good to me," she agreed, planting a kiss on my lips.

My work phone rang the next morning at eleven o'clock. The caller introduced herself as the director of consumer affairs for the City of Seattle.

"I have some good news for you, Mr. Lincoln," she said. "You have been selected as Seattle's new towing contractor for two zones. Can you come downtown today and sign the documents before two o'clock to make it official? We don't want to release the results to the news media until after we've both signed the contract."

"I'll be there before two."

I thanked the director, hung up the phone and took a deep breath. I could hardly wait to tell Connie and our employees the news.

I decided to call Connie first. The phone rang only once before she picked it up. "I've got great news," I exclaimed. "We won both of the high-volume tow zones—Capitol Hill *and* downtown."

The next day, *The Seattle Times* came out with an article announcing the winners of the towing contract. I held my breath as I scrolled down through that section of the paper. There it was—our name in print—and now it really felt official. Lincoln Towing was declared the winner of two of the six zones.

The article went on to report that the term of the contracts would be three years. Lincoln Towing's zones would cover the entire Capitol Hill area and all the streets in downtown Seattle. The article closed by announcing that the all-important start date for the new contractors would be November first.

Chapter 17

Off to a Bumpy Start

With the contract in hand, it was time to expand our tiny crew. When we purchased Cordes Towing, a few of Ernie's drivers and office workers had agreed to hire on with us. So far, we'd been running Lincoln Towing with just that small handful of people. Two of those former Cordes employees who were there from day one, John and Marvin, stayed on with us until we retired over twenty years later.

My first task was to hire a general manager. Through my business connections, I found out about an experienced and highly recommended candidate. I contacted Darwin and invited him out to lunch.

After we both arrived at the restaurant and introduced ourselves to one another, I explained my situation. "I just recently purchased Cordes Towing, and I am interested in talking with you about a management position. Ralph from Ralph's Towing recommended you. He said you would be able to help me get my business off to a good running start."

"That sounds like an interesting challenge," Darwin said. "Tell me more about the position."

After discussing the details with him, he said he would think about it and give me an answer the next day.

The following morning, Darwin called and agreed to come onboard. He was a valuable employee in more ways than I had expected. For several years prior, he had managed tow companies that had contracts with the City of Seattle so he was familiar with the City's procedures. He worked by my side, and together we tackled the challenges before us.

We began by focusing on finding qualified people to join our growing company. Luckily, Darwin knew a lot of people in the industry. He recommended employees he was confident would be great additions.

Darwin with wheel-lift truck

Pam was hired to be the player-coach of the office. She was put in charge of the dispatchers who communicated assignments to tow truck drivers, as well as the release clerks who dealt with the sometimes volatile public. Her job was a critical and highly stressful one that involved staffing the office twenty-four hours a day, managing incoming phone calls, serving customers, and handling all private-channel communication between the tow truck drivers and the office. It was always a wonder to me that Pam could manage all that at once and, on top of it, still love coming to work.

We were vigilant in our efforts to gather a pool of mature, qualified drivers because we understood that they were crucial to our long-term success and steady growth. We put policies and benefits into place to maintain a level of professionalism and to set ourselves apart from the competition. Uniforms for every driver, health insurance, vacation and sick pay were all new to the industry. Dad and Mom had offered those benefits to their employees, so Connie and I decided it was the right thing to do. We hoped these policies would increase employee morale and also help us retain workers. With the benefits we offered, we quickly found out that it wasn't difficult to attract seasoned drivers and dispatchers.

Because of the relationships Cordes Towing had established, from the very beginning, we had a steady stream of calls from repair and body shops. We also purchased Yellow Page ads so we had additional calls for a variety of services: jumpstarts, car unlocks, flat tires, and accident and breakdown-related towing.

The City contract kicked in at midnight on Monday, November 1, 1976. Minutes later, we received our first police call for a double-fatality, head-on crash at Valley and Fairview. Two trucks were dispatched from our Fifth and James location. After the police and emergency workers gave the go-ahead, our two trucks hooked the cars up. It turned out to be a real struggle to winch apart the smashed-together vehicles. After trying three separate cable positions, with our trucks pulling hard in opposite directions, the vehicles finally released their grip on each other.

The challenges continued at an alarming rate. The next morning, as a driver headed out to the first police call of the day, his tow truck's motor blew up in the middle of the Ship Canal Bridge. He had to call the office for a tow and leave the police waiting for a third truck to arrive at their scene. Unfortunately, from the very start, our mobile mechanic had to spend almost twenty-four hours a day keeping our ragtag fleet on the road.

After the first few weeks, it became obvious to Darwin that we had a tiger by the tail. "Twelve trucks just aren't enough," he insisted. "We need to add three or four more trucks and drivers to fill them. We are getting buried in police calls, and we can't keep up. If we don't do something fast, the police officers will start complaining to the City."

"Where is the best place to find some good used trucks?" I asked him.

"Well, it's pretty clear that the old stuff from Cordes Towing isn't going to hold up well with our new volume of tows. You might want to consider some dependable new trucks. Do you want me to make a call for you?"

"Sure," I said.

The next afternoon, a tow manufacturer representative came by driving a brand-new, white Ford one-ton tow truck. It was equipped with a hydraulic boom.

Because Seattle was known as the Emerald City, Connie and I had decided to paint our trucks green and white. When I saw the shiny white truck pull up, I immediately pictured it with our green accents and name painted on the side. I walked out to meet the salesman. The truck looked very professional and modern especially compared to all of Ernie's old trucks.

"I'm not sure Darwin knows what he's doing," I told the salesman. "Once I spoil a few drivers with new trucks, I'm liable to create a revolt from the guys stuck driving the old ones."

He smiled and said, "Actually, there's nothing like a new truck to pick up everyone's spirits."

I walked around the truck twice then opened the door and hopped in. "This truck is nice," I admitted.

"White works well with the color scheme of your other trucks. All you'd need to do is add a splash of green, and you'd be good to go," the salesman said enthusiastically.

I was impressed with his demonstration of the newest hydraulic equipment. Our small fleet was made up entirely of old-fashioned mechanical trucks with antiquated chain drives to power the winches.

"How many one-ton tow trucks do you have ready for sale?" I asked the representative.

"I have just two ready to go, but I could have more ready for you by next month."

"If the price is right, I might be interested in talking about more than one truck," I said, trying to work a volume discount into the deal.

He thought for a moment and said, "I'll have to get back to you after I discuss that with my boss. How many trucks would we be talking about?"

"Let's base the deal on four trucks," I said. "And I'd be willing to take delivery of two this month and two next month."

The salesman mentioned the advantages of leasing the trucks, which was tempting because I didn't want to visit my banker again so soon. By the next day, the deal was done. Within twenty-four hours, I had two newly leased trucks in the lot and twelve drivers on their best behavior, walking around and drooling over the new additions. Before putting them into service, we added a bit of green to the trucks, lettered the doors with our name and logo and installed a two-way radio.

Darwin was surprised with my speedy purchases and joked, "I guess I should have asked you for six."

Regrettably, I now had to face my banker again in order to secure funds before the arrival of next month's purchases. I had leased the first two, but I wanted to buy the second batch. I preferred owning to "renting" my trucks because that's the way I was used to operating. I decided that a line of credit would be a smart way to hold my future costs down.

The loan officer was a serious fellow, and he wanted to know how I was going to produce enough profit to make my payments. I showed him my contract with the City of Seattle. "This block of business should produce more than enough profit to make the payments." The banker didn't appear to be impressed. Fortunately for me, his boss interceded, and the outcome was tipped in my favor.

When we neared the halfway point of the second year of our contract, the banker and I had become friendly enough to be on a first-name basis. To his amazement, I never missed a payment. By then, Lincoln Towing's fleet had grown to twenty trucks, eight of which were brand new. I had a lot of pride in our fleet, but I still needed to replace a few more of Ernie's old, ailing trucks. I visited the banker again to discuss my replacement plans for the upcoming year.

I took my usual seat on the opposite side of his large desk. "I would like to talk about increasing my line of credit so I can replace some more of our older trucks."

I was surprised by his cool reception, "We have looked over your file, and we are unable to extend you additional credit at this time."

"But I have never missed a payment, and I have a large City of Seattle contract. Won't you reconsider?"

The banker seemed nervous as he pointed to his ledger. "The only collateral the bank holds is the titles to your tow trucks. Your City contract could get cancelled for failure to perform adequately or a dozen other reasons. In a worst-case scenario, our board of directors would be left with just those trucks, and they are not at all interested in getting into the towing business. Therefore, your current loan balance cannot be increased. I'm sorry."

I drove back to the office with my tail between my legs. As I considered the banker's rebuff, I knew I needed to find a way to do things differently. The next day, I called a staff meeting to brainstorm cost-saving ideas. My bright and creative staff had many suggestions: staffing adjustments, overtime controls, cutting back on Yellow Page ads, shutting down the truck's engine when waiting longer than five minutes, and asking managers, including me, to serve as extra tow truck drivers during the busy afternoon impound hours. We began to put these ideas into place, but, for now, my plans for more new trucks would have to wait.

———❦———

A few months later, I received an interesting call from Berg Construction, the owner of a lot we were leasing. Mr. Berg said, "I'm not usually a seller of real estate. I like to buy and hold for the long haul. But, I have my sights set on a large piece of property, and selling the Sixth Avenue North location would make my purchase possible. Since you are the lessee on that lot, I thought I'd give you the first option to buy."

We discussed the price and terms. Mr. Berg wanted cash in thirty days or no deal. Although I was very interested, the $120,000 price seemed as unreachable to me as the peak of Mt Everest. It just wasn't going to happen. But, I told him, "I'll sleep on it."

After I set the phone down, I wasn't sure how I felt. I had just been offered the first option to buy a choice piece of real estate, but I had no idea how I could come up with the cash in time. Although the price tag was big enough to choke on, I knew it was fair.

Sixth North had proven to be very valuable to our company. We currently had one hundred and fifty impounded cars parked on the lot. Every other Saturday, our public auctions were held there. Only a four-minute walk from the Space Needle, it really was a perfect downtown location with convenient access to the freeway. This could turn out to be a very wise investment. For the first time, I considered tapping into our personal savings account. It was fairly healthy but nowhere near the asking price.

I shared the news with Connie at dinner that night. "I think I've run across another deal of a lifetime."

Connie listened carefully and then pointed out a downside I hadn't thought of yet. "If Mr. Berg sells it to someone else, more than likely, we'd have to move out," she surmised. "Where would we put all of those cars? We'd also have to find someplace else to hold our auctions. Is there any way we can afford to buy it?"

With Connie agreeable to buying the lot, I couldn't stop thinking about how great it would be to own it. It was on a quiet dead-end street, bordering the Broad Street tunnel, and only a block west of Aurora Avenue. It was a great commercial lot, void of buildings, with easy and convenient tow truck access, and it was equal in size to half a city block. To top it off, our business was already using it and couldn't afford to lose it.

As a last resort, I talked to Connie's brother, Conrad, who was a banker. "What does a guy do when he's offered a once-in-a-lifetime deal but can't come up with the cash to make it happen?"

His answer turned out to be profound. "A piece of something is better than all of nothing," he said. "You might want to consider taking on a few partners to spread the burden and the risk. My customers do it frequently. Actually, I might be interested if you decide to take that route."

With his advice echoing in my head, I slept on it. The next day, I called a couple close friends: Bob, our accountant, and Jack, a college friend and fraternity brother. I hoped they might consider becoming partners. To my delight, after hearing about the opportunity, they both said yes, and with Conrad onboard, we formed a four-way partnership. We all quickly became the proud owners of a piece of prime real estate just a block from Seattle Center. Lincoln Towing leased the property from our partnership, which provided an immediate return on investment for the partners and allowed our company to keep its convenient and much-needed storage lot.

A few years later, Conrad decided he wanted to invest in another parcel and sold us his share. Now Connie and I owned 50 percent of the land. Lincoln Towing continued on as lessee for the next twenty years, after which time we all sold it for a healthy markup. Dad's advice about "dirt investments" had paid off once again.

Chapter 18

A Lesson Twice Learned

I learned another valuable lesson, this time from my young daughters, about being a good father.

After getting home from work each evening, worn out from my hectic day, I looked forward to having a chance to unwind. I was always happy to see Connie and the girls but, right after dinner, it was my habit to settle into my easy chair, put my feet up and cruise through the evening newspaper. The day's stories held my interest, and I relished the opportunity to digest them one by one. I just had to read them before they became yesterday's news.

I sometimes felt guilty for not interacting more with the girls. However, the two of them, ages two and four, always seemed to play well together.

On one particular evening, I had been reading the paper for thirty minutes when Wendy walked right over and stopped directly in front of me. I guess I didn't hear her soft little voice as she asked me something. With my nose behind the pages, I couldn't see her as she wound up her powerful little fist and smacked the newspaper right out of my hand. I sat there shocked. My hands were still outstretched but held no paper. The news lay crumpled on the rug beneath me.

Then, in her most serious big-girl voice, she asked, "How come the newspaper is more important than Trina and me?" Stunned and unable to come up with a reasonable explanation, I simply apologized. "You're right. You are definitely more important than the newspaper. From now on, I'll try to do better."

Wendy and Trina

I held out my hands and pulled her to me in an embrace. I said, "You and your sister are two of the most important girls in my life."

That night, I told Connie what had transpired. Guilt pricked my heart as I recounted the earlier incident.

"Honey, this is not a new problem. I understand that you are tired when you get home, but we get so little of you. It would be great if you could find a way to connect with us while you relax in your easy chair. I think that would be great for our whole family," she said gently.

Hesitantly, I nodded in agreement.

The next day, I knew what I had to do. I picked up the phone, dialed the *The Seattle Times* and canceled my much-loved newspaper.

It was obvious, almost immediately, that giving up the paper was one of my best fatherly decisions. Quality family time was on the rebound. Yes, I missed the news, but my daughters' smiles and laughter while we played games and joked around in the evenings erased any second thoughts about my choice.

Weeks later, as we played the board game Chutes and Ladders on the rug, I received an extra bonus when Wendy announced, "You're doing much better, Daddy."

Fast forward five years. By then, I had made the decision to restart the newspaper. I rationalized my change of heart by telling myself I could simply delay reading it until after the kids' bedtime. But slowly, as the months passed, the newspaper began to routinely sneak into my hands just after dinner.

One evening, as I was reading the paper, my youngest daughter Trina, now seven, asked me to play a game with her. I was tired so, for the third night in a row, I told her to go ask Wendy.

Trina and Wendy

About fifteen minutes later, something caught the corner of my eye. I looked up for a moment, but I didn't see anything. After an hour of reading, I got up from my chair and noticed a paper airplane lying on the floor. As I picked it up to throw it away, I noticed something carefully drawn on the wings. I flattened it out to reveal the entire picture. My daughter had drawn a portrait of a man reading a newspaper. With the newspaper held up in front of his face, only his eyes and hair were visible. But the headline on the front page was boldly displayed. It read: DAD READS PAPER AND IGNORES DAUGHTER.

My heart felt very heavy as I held the picture and walked down to Trina's room. I found her lying in bed, and I realized she must have been there for quite a while. She sat up when I took a seat on the edge of her bed. I felt a tug on my heart as I saw her tear-filled eyes. I took her in my arms and held her tight.

"You are precious to me, and I love spending time with you. I'm so sorry that I haven't been treating you that way."

I promised to be more available to both girls and to keep working on my dad skills. I knew the main ingredient was time.

Several decades passed, and I still have that paper airplane in my file as a reminder to keep my priorities straight and be true to my word. I even shared this story once at a men's retreat, years ago, and there were not many dry eyes in that roomful of dads. Some felt the sting of regret for off-kilter priorities that were too late to take back. Others, including me, recognized that we all have plenty of room to improve on this most significant job of fathering.

Fifteen years later, I received a love note from my daughter, Trina, who likes to write poetry.

Treasure

He shines with joy.
He overflows with compassion.
He's a beacon to me of unshakeable devotion.

He sparkles with smiles.
He generates much laughter.

He's a ready supplier of genuine embraces.

He stands with integrity.
He leans on his Savior.
He's a man full of life and love.

He's my father.

Chapter 19

A Cry in the Night

Like most couples, when our daughters were young, we would occasionally arrange a babysitter and schedule a date night. On one such evening, in the fall of 1979, Connie and I were returning home around ten o'clock from a Christian seminar in Seattle. We were running a little late to relieve our sitter, so we hurried a bit as we traveled through the severe rainstorm towards home.

At that time, most of the winding two-lane roads in our rural neighborhood had no streetlights. The last couple miles to our house were uphill, through a heavily wooded and twisting stretch of road without any guardrails for protection. On the left side, drivers faced a dangerous sixty-foot drop-off. On the right, there was a shallow drainage ditch three feet wide. No shoulder existed on either side of the road. On this very rainy night, the drainage ditch was overflowing with water runoff, sending a cascade of water down the hill.

During the day, this stretch of the road was beautifully canopied with evergreen tree branches from both sides intermingling overhead. But, in the dark of night, this beauty was concealed, and the surroundings took on a more sinister feel. On this particular evening, not even the moonlight penetrated the overhanging trees.

Our windshield wipers were maxed out as we reached the final two miles of our drive home. With the poor visibility, I was thankful that we were following behind the taillights of two other cars. When we stopped for the four-way stop at the bottom of the hill, our journey home was almost complete.

In turn, all three cars pulled away from the stop sign and headed straight ahead toward the darkened and windy road. After covering only a short distance, the brake lights of the two leading cars flashed, and they both stopped abruptly. I pulled up behind the unplanned caravan. I immediately spotted four red flashing hazard lights from two cars just beyond our trio: one in the shallow ditch and one beyond it in our lane.

Just seconds later, the cars in front of us moved forward, veering around the obstruction by briefly entering into the oncoming lane. Their taillights rapidly faded into the darkness of the stormy night. As we rolled forward, our headlights found a brawny man attempting to direct us around the vehicles. I could hear the disturbing sound of a blaring horn, muted by the downpour.

We didn't know it at the time, but the small car's flashing taillights and ceaseless horn were speaking volumes. The other car appeared to be a full-sized sedan; it was blocking the right lane, a car length ahead of the VW.

Before moving on, I said, "I don't think this is too serious, but I really can't tell what's happened. Can you? It's not a good place to have an accident, even if it's minor."

During that brief moment of hesitation, Connie turned to me and said, "I think I hear a voice coming from that car. Someone sounds upset."

Just then, the drenched man in the street walked over to the passenger side of our Buick. He was a large man in his thirties, dressed in a dark work jacket and jeans.

Connie lowered the window a little and the man calmly said, "The lady in the VW barely drove off the road. Her car isn't damaged, but she's still a bit hysterical. She seems to be over-reacting, but I'm sure she'll be fine in a few minutes. I'll wait for her to calm down and make sure she can get her car out of the ditch."

As he backed away and waved us forward, he said, "Thanks for stopping."

"No problem," I said, putting my car into gear. I turned to Connie. "That's nice that he stopped to help. We'd better get home for the sitter."

I slowly drove forward and passed by the VW and the man's Dodge. Though I had redirected my focus toward the road ahead, in an instant, my thoughts were yanked back to the cars in my rearview mirror. All of a sudden, I had a very unsettling feeling. I braked to a stop only two hundred feet up the road.

"Why are we stopping?" Connie questioned.

"I'm not sure. Something's bothering me. Maybe we should help out. That lady's car might be tough to get out of that mud. And, if she doesn't calm down, she'll need a ride home. In the dark and rain, it's dangerous for them both to be stopped there. I think that guy needs an extra hand; we should go back."

I put the car in reverse and carefully backed down the left lane. I thought it was safer than trying to turn around on the narrow road. I was thankful for my backup and hazard lights, even though they didn't illuminate much. I decided to back around the man's car and park in the space between the two vehicles. I wanted to reassess the situation and discuss a game plan with the Good Samaritan before stepping out into the rainstorm.

When we stopped the car, our headlights lit up the man's Dodge. Immediately, someone rushed past us.

"There's the man we spoke with," Connie said.

Without turning around, he moved briskly towards his car. Strangely, he didn't even bother to look at us. He opened the driver's door and jumped in.

"What's he doing?" I wondered aloud.

Then, suddenly, he started his car and took off. It seemed important at that moment, and I knew it couldn't hurt, so I quickly memorized his license plate number.

"Write this number down quick before I forget it." I grabbed a pen from my pocket, handed it to Connie and recited it.

"That's very weird! Why did he leave like that?" Connie questioned.

All of a sudden, the blaring horn ceased. We shifted our full attention to the VW behind us. The driver's door sprang open, and a woman stumbled out. She was screaming hysterically. We both jumped out of our car and met her in the downpour midway between our vehicles. We didn't know what to think.

"What's wrong? Are you hurt?" I asked.

The traumatized young lady shook her head and tried to answer, but she was crying so hard that she had begun to hyperventilate. Only a few words spilled out, frantic and jumbled. I had never seen anyone so panic-stricken.

Connie placed her hand gently on the woman's arm, and we tried to soothe her with our reassuring words. After a couple of minutes, she calmed down just enough to connect her thoughts. She was able to reveal bits of her terrifying story in the spaces between her labored breaths. "He was trying to kill me! He broke my window with his knife and was trying to open the door when you drove up!"

She started crying hard again and kept saying. "Thank you, thank you, thank you!"

"We better get out of here right now," I said.

There were just two routes off the hill, and, once the guy with the knife got to the top, he could mistakenly circle the hill and end up right back where we were standing.

"Where do you live," I asked.

Through her sobbing she said, "About a half mile up and just around the corner, the first house on the left. My husband is there waiting for me to come home."

If I was able to maneuver her car out of the shallow ditch, we decided it would be best for Connie to drive the young lady home in our car while I followed in the VW. When I got into the driver's seat, I saw tiny pieces of broken glass scattered everywhere. I touched as little of the crime scene as possible. I put the VW in reverse and let out the clutch. The wheels began to spin. I tried to rock the car, and, finally, after numerous attempts, the tires got some traction. As soon as I backed out into the street, Connie and the young woman began to pull away. Since the headlights on the VW were broken, I sped up and stayed as close as possible behind our Buick.

When we arrived at the young lady's home, she shot out of our car and headed for the front door, screaming for her husband. He frantically rushed out of the house, followed by two aggressive-looking Husky dogs. She was so hysterical that her husband could not understand her. He looked from her to us, confused and suspicious, especially given the fact that I was driving her car. We quickly explained that we were there to help and that he needed to call the police. I decided I should stay and also speak with the officer while Connie drove home to relieve the babysitter.

By the time the police arrived, she had calmed enough to give a full account of what had transpired. "A car was tailgating me on the freeway," she explained. "When I took the exit, I got scared because the car was still following me, and it was almost on my rear bumper. I could tell the driver was a man. He started flashing his high beams at me. I got scared. I tried to drive as fast as I could to get away from him. I even ran the stop sign at the bottom the hill, but so did he. I was so close to home, only a mile or so away, and I started to believe that I might make it. But, as I drove up the winding road, he sped past me and cut me off. I swerved and my car skidded into the ditch. I tried to drive it out but my tires just spun. Then I looked up and saw him stop his car in the street in front of mine."

Then, with her eyes revealing the depth of her fears, she continued. "The guy stepped out of his car and walked towards mine. I was still trying to get my car to move, but the tires just kept spinning. He jerked on my door handle, but I had already locked it. Then he pulled out a long knife and demanded that I unlock my door."

She continued, "When I refused, he didn't say anything else. Instead, he slowly walked to the front of my car. I had no idea what he was going to do next. I was frantic. He just stood there looking at me through my windshield. I tried not to make eye contact.

Suddenly, he began stabbing his knife into my headlights. I could hear the sound of breaking glass: first on the left and then on the right. After that, I was alone with him in the darkness."

Tiffany broke down sobbing. When she was able to speak again, she said, "Rape and death flashed through my mind. I couldn't think of any way to escape. Then, I saw headlights in my rearview mirror, and I realized there was hope. I knew I had to find a way to stop the car. The man quickly stepped back to my driver's side and put his knee against the door. He held the knife behind his back.

"When the car slowed, I laid on the horn and screamed at the top of my lungs. But the car just passed by. Then he turned and aimed his knife at my wing window. He pounded away until it broke into tiny pieces, then he pushed his arm through. He tried to reach the door lock, but I kept smashing his hand with my foot. I knew I couldn't hold him off much longer!"

She stopped to gain her composure and wipe away her tears. After a moment she continued, "As I stomped on his hand, some more cars approached. He moved a few feet away and calmly began directing traffic into the left lane. I screamed and laid on the horn, but they just followed his hand signals and kept going."

She turned and looked at me. "Your car was the only one that stopped. I thought I might be able to get your attention so I kept honking and screaming. But, then you pulled away too."

She shuddered. "I thought I was as good as dead. He walked back toward my car, pulled out his knife and stared at me through my window. Then, suddenly, he looked up the road and saw you backing up. That's when he took off." She started crying hysterically, and her husband squeezed her to his side.

The policeman ran a trace on the suspect's car from the license number I had provided and then gave me a ride home. The offender's physical description, along with the license plate number and the vehicle make and color, was a perfect match to a guy with a long criminal record. Later that night, the police staked out the man's house. At three o'clock in the morning, the suspect returned home.

The sheriff questioned and arrested him. It turned out that he was a convicted rapist who had recently been released from prison.

The following week, Tiffany, Gary, Connie, and I all went downtown to the King County Police headquarters to identify the suspect in a police lineup. Months later, he was convicted of attempted murder and sent back to prison for eight more years. The young couple lived in their home for a few years longer, but, after they had a son, they sold it and moved away.

This ordeal taught me two valuable lessons. First, I need to look for opportunities to help others and not just pass them by. And, second, God has given us our intuition for a reason; I need to listen carefully for mine and be willing to respond to it. I'm no hero. I'm just a regular guy who stopped to help someone in need, and it turned out to be a more important detour than I ever imagined.

Chapter 20

Tow Each His Own

Near the middle of our first City contract, another chunk of choice real estate became available for lease. The City of Seattle owned a highly visible corner location. As soon as I found out that the old tenant's lease was not going to be renewed, I formally expressed my interest to Seattle's property management office. The property in question was located at the foot of the freeway exit ramp on the corner of Fairview Avenue and Mercer Street.

The lot was well-suited for vehicle storage. I estimated it would store about seventy cars—not as big as I would call ideal, but we could make it work. It was vacant except for a small portable building that had been occupied by a prior tow contractor as their release facility.

This particular lot had superb access for tow trucks; it could be approached from two main arterials, as well as from two I-5 freeway exit ramps. After unloading, the tow trucks could quickly and easily head off to their next tow. Since the lot wasn't very big, the less busy graveyard shift could easily transfer any vehicles not claimed within twenty-four hours to our much larger lot ten minutes away. Moving stale cars out created space for the next day's impounds. When I thought about the saying, "Location, location, location," I knew this lot was a great one to snag.

Signing that multi-year lease with the City turned out to be one of my smartest moves yet. The business exposure was better than we had ever dreamed. The daytime work traffic coming off the freeway was jam-packed all day long. On top of that, the nighttime traffic to and from the Seattle Center could be heavy as well. A lot of people would go this route to attend concerts, plays and sporting events, and also to access the ferries. Several times a year, traffic monitors were set up by the City to count the cars at numerous intersections. Our corner at Fairview and Mercer consistently ranked first or second in the state for the highest daily volume of cars. Exposure like that was hard to beat.

We were easily able to cover most of the cost of the new Mercer lease by simply giving up our lease at the corner of Fifth Avenue and James Street. We happily made that trade. The Fifth Avenue lot only stored only about thirty-five vehicles, had a steep driveway and, due to space limitations, required drivers to back every car into the lot from the street. These extra complications ate up valuable time. After leasing the Mercer lot, our average number of impounds per day increased by thirty percent. This improvement added quickly to our bottomline and made the police happy.

The four-to-sixes, as we called them, kept us on our toes. Each weekday afternoon, parking lanes on a handful of downtown streets converted to bus lanes. Although parking was legal up until four o'clock, if a motorist didn't clear out by then, their vehicle was ticketed and marked for tow. During peak afternoon drive times, one illegally parked car could back up traffic for blocks. Under our contract, we were required to quickly clear them. The faster we impounded cars, the faster the bus lanes were cleared and the faster the traffic flowed. This was the busiest and most stressful time for our company each day.

About fifty percent of the ticketed cars were driven away before the tow truck arrived. Many times, a frantic car owner would yell and sprint to their car just as our driver was about to hook up or just as he was pulling away. We were required to unhook the vehicle for the parking violator on the spot if we had not yet moved the car twenty feet. It was a race against the clock each day to clear the streets for the buses.

One blustery fall afternoon, I headed downtown in my ten-year-old pickup. I wasn't proud of "Old Blue" and, being the boss, I thought I would look much better in a brand-new, four-wheel drive Ford pickup. But for frugality's sake, I had decided to keep my Chevy half-ton truck and simply add a magnetic Lincoln Towing sign to each side.

I had a three-thirty appointment with Alan. When I arrived, I searched the street for a metered parking spot. After circling the block several times, I was running late. I definitely didn't want to be paying for wasted minutes at an attorney's rate. At last, I found one near the corner on Fourth Avenue. I jumped out of my truck, dropped my coins in the meter and dashed to the appointment.

About forty-five minutes into our meeting, Alan's secretary, Beverly, interrupted us to say that I had a phone call. Perplexed, I picked up the phone and heard my dispatch manager's voice on the other end of the line.

"Hi, Ed. Sorry to bother you," Pam said apologetically.

"That's all right, is everything okay?" I asked, a little concerned.

Just as she began to explain, she burst into a fit of laughter.

"Pam, why are you laughing, and what's so important that you called me here?"

"You won't believe what just came in through the gate," she said with a smile in her voice.

Completely baffled by this exchange, I asked, "What?"

"It's your blue truck! You got a ticket, and we just impounded it."

"Are you serious?" I couldn't believe it. I turned to Alan and said, "My towing company just towed away my pickup."

Laughing hard, he asked, "Did the tow driver know it was your truck before he hooked up?"

"I'm sure he did. It says Lincoln Towing right on my door."

When I finished my appointment, I made a call to my office to hitch a ride back to the tow lot. The driver was chuckling when he picked me up. I asked him to drive past the corner where I had parked. There was still plenty of time left on the meter, but, in my frantic search for a metered spot, I had parked in a bus lane. I glanced at my watch; sure enough, it was nearly four-thirty. I'd made the mistake handfuls of our customers made every day, and now I was paying for it; maybe not in cash (except for the ticket) but in pride.

When I arrived at the tow lot, it seemed every one of my employees was having a hard time keeping a straight face.

One employee asked, "Are you going to fire the driver who towed you in?"

I smiled and said, "Of course not, he did the right thing."

I saw the humor in the situation, but my ego had suffered a slight bruise. When I left work that evening, I looked forward to moving ahead with a new day. *By morning this should all be forgotten.*

At eight o'clock the next morning, I received a call from Alan. He was laughing when I picked up. He said, "Wait 'til you see the morning paper! Take a look at Walt Evans' column in the *Post-Intelligencer* [*P.I.*]. The newspaper got wind of your story."

Twenty minutes later, I stopped by the corner store and purchased the morning paper. I didn't completely believe Alan. *How and why would this mistake make it into the newspaper?* But, when I opened up the paper, there it was. The column was titled: TOW EACH HIS OWN. And there, in print, was my humbling story for all to see.

At the end of the article, Walt Evan's parting comment was, "Maybe there is justice in this world after all." For posterity, I decided to purchase six copies of the *P.I.*

That week, my phone rang off the hook with friends calling in to razz me. Connie took a copy of the article and, unbeknownst to me, had it framed with the ticket. She hung it in the Mercer dispatch office for all to see. Numerous times over the years, it served as a good way to lighten the mood of irritated impound customers.

I guess, in the end, it wasn't all bad. After all, for the small price of my pride, I got a load of free advertising.

Chapter 21

A Roller Coaster Ride

B y the time we had reached the third and final year of our first City contract, my confidence was in full bloom. We had expanded and improved our business in many ways. Our fleet had grown to thirty trucks, most of which were paid for, and we now had thirty-five employees on the payroll. To improve our efficiency, we leased a new phone system and purchased a state-of-the-art dispatch communication system. Lincoln Towing was operating like a well-oiled machine.

On a cold morning in February of 1979, I received a phone call from Al, an acquaintance and the owner of a small towing company in Lynnwood, just north of Seattle. He invited me to meet with him to discuss a potential businesss opportunity.

When I arrived, Al said, "Let me show you around."

I saw six tow trucks, small to large, four industrial forklifts ready to rent and a large truck-repair shop. I was impressed to see that he was running all three businesses from this two-acre facility.

After sitting down in his office with a cup of coffee in my hand, I asked, "So what is this business proposition you wanted to talk to me about?"

Al explained, "Marge and I would like to sell our business and retire. We think highly of you, and we believe that our thirty-year-old company would be a good expansion to your business."

I was flattered by their confidence in me, but I was surprised by their offer. I hadn't even considered expanding this far north. After answering several questions, he handed over a packet of financial information.

As I was driving home, my gut told me that I should pass on this purchase. But, I was also not one to let an opportunity slip by without at least giving it some serious consideration. So, the next day, I consulted with my brother-in-law Vuryl about the potential purchase.

He said, "If I were you, I would only consider the deal if the real estate was included." I fully agreed with his conclusion—no property, no deal.

Two weeks later, Al phoned me and asked, "So, what do you think of our operation?"

I told him, "It's impressive, but I'm not the right buyer for you. For me to be interested, I'd need to have the property thrown into the deal. And, to be honest, I just don't have the cash available to make it happen. I'm sorry."

Al called again a month later, saying, "Marge and I really want to sell to you. We've decided to include the property at its appraised value, and we are willing to carry the contract on the entire sale price."

I was shocked by the fact that he was bending to my terms and even offering to finance the purchase. The door to this deal had just flown wide open. I told him I'd get back to him. When I got home that night, I discussed the new developments with Connie and asked her opinion.

"Do what you think is best. But, if it was up to me, I wouldn't want to take on that much extra responsibility. It's a lot to handle, and you're already working six days a week."

After sleeping on it, the risk-taker in me decided to go for it.

I had Alan review the agreement, and, within a week, I signed on the dotted line. I had thirty days to hire a manager, take possession of the premises and make my first payment. I'd just added a couple more balls to the ones I was already juggling, but I felt up to the challenge.

By the end of three months, regret had settled in my stomach like a boulder. Shortly after my purchase was final, the new Lynnwood business suffered an unexpected drop in revenue. Several local tow competitors became aggressive in their marketing efforts and wooed away some of our larger accounts. To add to that, a number of the Lynnwood drivers had bad attitudes and customer complaints abounded.

I was frustrated and overwelmed; I had spread myself too thin. There was just no way that I could spend the required time up north to remedy all of the problems. I knew I had only myself to blame for the fact that I was trapped in the middle of this gigantic mess.

When my banker got wind of my Lynnwood business purchase and the added debt, he called me and asked me to come into his office. I sat in front of his big desk feeling very small. I braced myself for a browbeating, but, instead, he surprised me by kindly saying, "We offer free quarterly financial seminars for our bank customers. We have one in downtown Seattle in two weeks. I think you would find the information very helpful when you're making business decisions, and I strongly encourage you to attend."

He handed me a seminar flyer and then said, "You will need to gather up the last two years of your financial statements and a balance sheet listing all assets and liabilities. You'll also want to bring along the information about your equipment and property leases, both personal and business, as well as any other contracts that legally bind you." Seeing my hesitance, he reassured me, "Don't worry. This can only help you."

In the next two weeks, with Connie's help, I was able to locate everything required. As I looked over the documents I had collected, I felt uneasy because I knew I didn't have a very good grasp on this crucial information.

The hotel where the seminar was held was impressive. To my surprise, there must have been close to fifty people in attendance. The speaker introduced two certified public accountants who were his helpers. After just thirty minutes of instructions and graphs, my head was already drowning in details.

At the end of an hour, the instructor shifted gears and said, "If you only take home one thing from this seminar, remember the debt-to-equity ratio. This is the formula bankers use when deciding whether or not to make a loan. It can quickly make or break the transaction. The ratio can be found by taking all of the borrower's debt and dividing it by the sum of his cash and equity in equipment, inventory, and real estate. Bankers expect most loan applicants to have a debt-to-equity ratio of 2:1 or less. If a longstanding customer is requesting the loan, that ratio can be stretched to 6:1. Once the debt numbers get beyond 8:1 or 10:1, the risk is too great and the bank won't touch it."

During the last forty-five minutes of the seminar, the instructor asked everybody to calculate their overall debt-to-equity ratio. All documents were confidential and nothing was to be shared with the class. The three experts were available to help anyone who raised his or her hand.

After filling out the worksheet, I came up with a ratio. I knew it couldn't be right so I repeated all the steps and came up with the same answer. I raised my hand and held my breath.

One of the assistants walked over to my desk, and I asked, "Will you check my work?"

He studied my documents and my calculations and then said, "Do you mind if I get a second opinion? I'll be right back."

"I'm not going anywhere," I mumbled.

I saw him talking to the instructor, and then he returned and went through my paperwork with a grim look on his face. After a few minutes, he pronounced, "These numbers are correct. Your debt to equity ratio is 39:1. You're stretched tighter than a piano wire. If just one thing goes wrong, you could lose everything."

I was speechless. His words made the hair on my arms stand at attention. My body began to tremble. The seminar ended, and I headed home, chilled to the bone.

When I arrived, Connie asked, "Did you learn anything new?"

Immediately, I poured out the truth about our dicey situation. I could tell I was causing her worry, but I had to be honest with her. When I saw the concern in her eyes, I admitted, "For the first time in my life, I'm really scared."

As I lay in bed that night, my mind kept circling around the words, "lose everything." *How can I find a way out of the huge hole I've dug for myself?* My panicked thoughts were met only with silence; I couldn't think of any answers.

Faced with the reality of our tenuous financial situation, I put my efforts into trying to get the Lynnwood businesses into the black. I had the whole problem on my shoulders since I hadn't been able to find a seasoned manager for the job.

To add to the troubles up north, our forklift rental and delivery service was involved in a serious accident that destroyed one of our forklifts. Our driver Bob was towing a forklift southbound on the Alaskan Way Viaduct. Not realizing the bridge supports were ten inches lower on the right side, he slid from the center lane into the slow lane. The tall forklift mast immediately smashed into the cement and steel support. The Viaduct suffered fifty thousand dollars in damage, and there was an additional twenty thousand dollars in damage to the forklift. Fortunately nobody was hurt, but our insurance company was not at all pleased.

With all of the new problems I'd acquired through my purchase of Al's company, I was very thankful that the Seattle division of Lincoln Towing was going strong and growing every quarter. We had recently picked up a huge contract to tow hundreds of City-owned vehicles: everything from road graders to fire trucks fell under that valuable contract.

Overall, our Seattle operation was in great shape, but we knew the time was running out on our first City impound contract. That contract accounted for the vast majority of our business. I didn't like to think about it, but I realized that, if we lost it this next time around, the train could come off the track.

The largest truck in Lincoln Towing's fleet

In the last week of July, I received a letter from the City's Department of Consumer Affairs. The City Council was buried in their budget process so they asked if we would be willing to extend the existing contract at the current prices for six months.

I was floored by this great news. I'd heard of a thirty-day extension but never six months. This delay couldn't have come at a better time.

The great news traveled quickly through the company. It was like getting an unexpected bonus. However, I still knew that we needed to be proactive. "Let's use this extra time to win over some more commercial accounts. The larger our customer base, the more protection we will have in the future."

With the girls now in second and fourth grade, Connie started working part-time at Lincoln Towing. We had always made the major business decisions as a team, but it was fun actually running the day-to-day operations side by side.

The months passed by too quickly. As the bid submission date approached, I could sense the stress both at work and home.

"I sure wish this wasn't a bid process," Connie said. "It's too bad we can't just earn the business by giving good service. Instead, we're left with this guessing game."

"And I'd sure hate to guess wrong," I said darkly.

———

To calculate the winning bidder, the City had a precise formula. They took the amount bid per tow, multiplied it by the annual number of expected impounds and then multiplied that product by the number of years in the contract. For example, if the bid packet listed an estimate of twelve thousand tows per year over three years, then a twenty-six-dollar-per-tow bid would be recorded as a $936,000 bid. If another bidder's number was a nickel less per tow, that bid would be $1,800 under the first bid. I knew that this next contract could be lost by just a penny.

On February 28, 1980, with our moment of truth less than twenty-four hours away, Connie and I sat in our attorney's office in downtown Seattle. Together we carefully reviewed every detail of the fifty-page bid packet.

Alan turned to the final page. "It looks like everything is in order: the leases are signed, the trucks are listed, the insurance amounts are correct, the lot square footage is calculated, you have the financial review and the bank letter of credit has been signed. All you need to do is write down your final bids and sign the last page. I'll notarize your signature and make copies for your records."

After tossing and turning all week, I had zeroed in on a tight range for our bid numbers. Connie and I discussed it and had come to a final decision. I took a deep breath and watched her as she now put them in ink.

She remained very quiet as we returned to work. I respected her mood and joined her in the silent, retrospective atmosphere.

I was awake at sunrise for the important bid day, just as I had been three and a half years earlier. My confidence was waning as Connie and I each drove to work. I tried to get a few things done at the office, but, once again, I was too anxious to accomplish much of anything.

This time, we drove downtown together and we followed my ritual of arriving early. Despite Connie's prompting, I held onto our bid packet until the last moment. I dropped it into the official bid box at five minutes to ten.

We followed the clerk into the room along with more than a dozen tow company owners. When the bids were read for the zones, Connie recorded each one. As I looked over her shoulder, I quickly did the math and realized we were not in the winning position for any of them. In the most important downtown zone, we were in second place; not just by cents but *dollars* above the lowest bid.

The city official announced, "The winning bid packets will be checked for accuracy. We'll be calling the winners tomorrow afternoon and posting the results in our office."

When we got to work Pam approached me and asked, "How'd it go?"

"Not good! It wasn't even close. Our only chance of winning a zone is if the lowest bidder is disqualified."

Twenty-four hours passed. I made a slow trip downtown to the Department of Consumer Affairs, riding up the same elevator and walking down the same hallway as the day before. I took a left turn and pushed open the glass door. The bulletin board was straight ahead. I studied the official results and slowly dropped my head, wounded.

Chapter 22

Facing The Storm

We now had thirty days to put together a new game plan. We had to face the terrifying reality that 50 percent of our tow business was set to vaporize in April. Making exciting plans to grow during the past three and a half years felt a lot different than thinking about the painful cutbacks. We knew there was no way that we would be able to retain all of our employees.

This staff reduction was going to be hard on us. We had both made solid personal connections with nearly all of our thirty-five employees and their families.

As we discussed the challenges ahead, Connie brought up the other hurdles we still faced with the Lynnwood businesses.

"With our revenues in Seattle about to be cut in half, Lincoln Towing won't be able to support the Lynnwood operation," she stated candidly.

I knew that the towing expansion, the forklift business and the truck repair shop were all barely staying afloat. The huge monthly purchase payments were killing us, and we just couldn't catch a break with these businesses. Recently, a long-haul trucker had given our office clerk a bad check for twenty-two hundred dollars after we rebuilt his transmission. We were never able to collect a dime of that loss.

"Don't worry. I'll find a way to make it all work out," I said reassuringly, although, in truth, my confidence was fading.

As I sat alone in my truck that afternoon, I had a flashback from the banking seminar: "If just one thing goes wrong, you could lose everything." I knew I already had more than one big problem. Sure enough, there was a storm brewing, and I sensed we would soon be taking on water. If I couldn't come up with some quick solutions, the troubles we faced just might sink the whole ship.

Over the next few weeks, I came up with a plan. I contacted Bud, a friend and competitor in Lynnwood, and invited him to lunch. I told him I was putting Al's prior businesses up for sale. As soon as he told me he wasn't interested, I made him an offer he couldn't refuse.

He said he would sleep on it and get back to me in a few days. When he called, he said, "I'm not interested in the repair shop or the real estate. But I will buy the forklifts, the five tow trucks and the towing business."

After we finished the call, I hung up the phone and whispered, "Thank you, Lord."

Without further hesitation, we terminated the mechanics, closed the repair shop and put the property up for sale. Amazingly, we were able to find a buyer within forty-five days. The profits from the land and business sale were barely enough to compensate us for our year of losses, but the relief I felt after getting out of that mess made the deal seem sweet to me.

Soon afterwards, one of my Seattle drivers who lived in Auburn gave me a tip. He said, "The owner of Hinshaw Honda in Auburn wants to talk to you about starting a branch there."

Although I was gun-shy after my first failed expansion, I made an appointment and headed south the next day. The owner introduced himself and then told me he wasn't happy with the local tow company.

He said, "If you are interested in expanding, our Honda store has an extra, fenced storage lot you can use at no cost to help get you started."

The terms were just too good to pass up: a free facility and a large customer already in place. I decided to go for it since there didn't seem to be much to lose. We made a deal that did not require signing a lease agreement and included free rent for the first six months.

For the cost of a City of Auburn business license, a telephone number and one of our surplus trucks, we were in business. We transferred the truck and the driver who gave us the tip to Auburn. We promoted him to manager of that location. He was charged with the task of growing the business by building relationships with local repair and body shops.

This small but successful expansion lifted the spirits of our managers. I doubt anyone could do a startup any cheaper.

Despite some signs of growth and opportunity, we just had too much lost ground to make up. Without the City contracts, our towing volume had plummeted. We could no longer ignore our oversized payroll. Our company bank account was sinking below the critical point. Putting off a major layoff was no longer an option if we wanted to stay afloat.

Chapter 23

The Birth of the Pink Toe Truck

On a Saturday afternoon in May of 1980, just one month after losing the City contracts, I sat alone in our accounting office. I was sifting through paperwork and mulling over our company's new challenges when I heard a firm knock on the office door. Outside was a tall man holding a fat briefcase.

"Can I help you?"

"My name is Bill, and I have some pictures I would like to show you. It will only take a few minutes of your time."

My first instinct was to send him away; I didn't have time for this. But, I hesitated, studied the tired man and then said, "You can show me what you've got, but I am just about to lock up for the day."

Out came a handful of scenic pictures. Paintings of rivers and mountains were piled up on my desk. All were neatly framed, but, as I expected, none captured my interest.

"I'm sorry, Bill. Your pictures are very nice, but I'm just not interested. If you had pictures of tow trucks, it might be a different story."

Bill graciously thanked me for my time and began putting his merchandise away. As he closed up his briefcase, he said, "You know, I used to do some janitorial work at a police station in a small town in Arizona. On the bulletin board there, someone tacked up a picture of a funny-looking tow truck. It had actual toes extending from the rear of the truck."

"Now that's interesting. Before you go, would you mind sketching me a picture of it?" I asked.

In no time at all, he handed me a picture scribbled on a half-sheet of notebook paper. Immediately, a smile formed on my lips.

As Bill exited the building, I thanked him for the drawing. After I sat back down to finish up my work, I couldn't stop thinking about how much I liked that funny little truck. The idea definitely had potential.

The more I looked at the sketch, the stronger my feelings grew. I started to think that maybe I could actually build this "toe truck." I wondered how difficult that would be. What kind of a vehicle would I use? A truck like that would be great in parades. If it made people smile, maybe it could soften the image of towing in Seattle.

By the time I closed up the office thirty minutes later, I had decided to take a sneak peak at the automobiles lined up for our next abandoned-vehicle auction. Maybe one of them would inspire me.

I unlocked the gate, turned and walked up the first row. In the third row, I spotted a vehicle that seemed perfect: a wrecked Volkswagen van. My mind began to race. From the looks of the crushed left side and roof, it appeared to have been a rollover, but the damaged body didn't matter to me because it would need to be cut off anyway. My heart sped up a bit as I began to imagine this vehicle transformed. I glanced at my watch; it was time to head home.

While I drove, I couldn't think of anything else. I began working out all of the details in my head. By the time I turned into the driveway, I could hardly wait to share the creative concept with Connie and the girls.

As soon as I saw Connie, my excited words tumbled out. I eagerly showed her the sketch and rushed to explain the specifics of my novel idea. Before I could completely finish, she stunned me with her reaction. She didn't like it at all.

The VW van that was transformed into the Toe Truck

"That sounds like a crazy idea. People will think you've lost your mind," she said.

I walked away totally deflated.

For the next week, any conversation about the toe truck put a strain on our marriage. Finally, to keep the peace, I made a deal with Connie.

The agreement hinged on my ability to get the still hypothetical toe truck accepted into Seattle's Torchlight Parade. If I could do that, I had her permission to build it.

However, even I realized that it would be very tough to get accepted into Seattle's grandest parade. Out of several hundred applicants each year, less than a hundred commercial entries were selected. This special parade was the culminating event of the city's Seafair season. It was the only parade in the state that was televised locally. The year before, over two hundred thousand people had lined the streets, not to mention the several hundred thousand at-home viewers.

In spite of the obstacles that lay ahead of me, I decided to bid on the VW van at Saturday's auction. When the auctioneer dropped his gavel on the final bid, I was the winning bidder at one hundred and twenty-five dollars.

On Monday morning, I made a call to the Seafair office to find out how to apply for a spot in the parade. After identifying myself, I gave the receptionist a verbal "toenail sketch" of my plans.

Then I asked the most important question, "What are my chances of getting my truck into the Torchlight Parade?"

"At this point, almost all of the allotted space is committed. You'll have a much easier time applying to be in one of the smaller community parades. There are nine local parades to choose from."

Those other parades wouldn't get me anywhere with Connie. Plus, I recognized that, in order to get a decent return on my investment, I would need the large-scale exposure of the Torchlight Parade. I could see my dream project quickly swirling down the drain.

"I still want to pick up an application for the Torchlight," I said. "Is that okay?"

By the next day, I had completed the application and made an appointment for an interview the following week. I immediately decided to do a little extra prep work.

I hired Jim, a friend and commercial artist, to do a few concept sketches of what the finished product would look like. It took several tries before I was satisfied with the overall design. When Jim handed me the final drawings, they looked like what I had pictured but even better. The toes were no longer hanging off the back of the truck as they had been in the salesman's original sketch. Instead, they were positioned at the front, on top of the truck's cab. With an artist's rendition of the toe truck in hand, I felt confident that I could make a convincing presentation to the Seafair Committee.

During the interview, I informed the four board members that I had already purchased the VW van for my project. They smiled at my sketches, and I took that as a good sign.

I waited four very long days before the postman delivered the letter to my office. I carefully opened the envelope and saw the word ACCEPTED stamped on top of the first page!

For a moment, I was in shock. I couldn't believe I had just been granted one of the final spots in the Torchlight Parade. I could hardly wait to see Connie's reaction to this news. I walked over to her desk, coughed a bit to get her attention, handed her the letter and then remained silent.

Following a quick read, Connie looked up at me and graciously said, "You win."

After days of anxious anticipation, I could hardly wait to get started. And I knew I'd better move fast; the parade was just over two months away.

In preparation for my long shot, I had already contacted Ed Ellison, a former body shop owner and old friend. I knew he was a magician with metal and fiberglass. He had some extra time because he was semi-retired and did only small repairs out of his home garage in rural Snohomish County. After explaining my idea and what the project would entail, he said he would like to tackle it.

Ed Ellison, builder of the original Toe Truck

I called him with the good news and then towed the wrecked van to his house on Friday. We talked about our time constraints, and I gave him some basic instructions. I also handed over the artist's drawings.

Ed said, "This project is going to be even more fun than I imagined. You know I love a challenge. I can handle building your truck, but we will need help with the design of the actual toes. You'll need to find a sculptor."

"Maybe I can get some references from the Seafair Committee," I proposed.

After the truck transformation was well underway, I spoke with an official at the Seafair office, and she gave me a couple of names. When I spoke to Joan, the second artist on the list, she seemed like a perfect fit for the project. When I explained the design work, she responded with a good-humored laugh and set up an appointment to see the truck for herself.

By that point, Ed had been working on the truck for three weeks. He had used a torch to cut the VW down to its floorboard. Then he formed the new body with tube steel and added chicken wire. Once that project was complete, he spent six days applying fiberglass pieces to the chicken wire to create the outer shell. He went to great lengths to make sure the truck resembled the artist's drawing. It was now ready for the addition of its most important feature.

The Toe Truck's transformation is under way

On the day of her appointment, Joan arrived right on time and, within minutes of looking the unique truck over, she agreed to sculpt the toes. She handed me a list of supplies she would need and agreed to return the next day. The following morning, Joan set to work carving the large toes out of the enormous Styrofoam blocks I had purchased.

When she finished three days later, Ed went to work duct-taping the toes to allow the fiberglass to stick to, rather than burn through, the Styrofoam. As always, duct tape did the trick, and, in a week, the master craftsman's fiberglass work was finished. After mounting the big toe and its four pinkies, the Toe Truck stood tall at ten feet, six inches.

Joan's job is done

Suddenly, I had a "bright" idea. "Can the inside of the toes be hollowed out so we could mount light bulbs inside for night parades like the Torchlight? I think a 'twinkle toe' effect would add a nice touch."

Ed grumbled, "It would've been helpful if you'd thought of that before they were all mounted. But you're the boss."

The toes were unbolted from the roof of the truck, and, with a carving knife and large spoon, Ed spent several additional hours carefully removing a major portion of the Styrofoam, leaving a much lighter eggshell covering. He warmed up to my idea after he finished the job.

"That was like carving out a pumpkin—much easier than I expected."

The next morning, I showed up to Ed's house driving one of our regular tow trucks. I carefully hooked up my prized possession. It was finally time to move the nearly finished project to our mechanic's shop in Seattle.

After giving Ed a bear hug, I headed for Seattle in a tow truck towing the Toe Truck. As I drove, it seemed every person I passed was staring or pointing at my unique cargo.

When I turned into the driveway at Lincoln Towing, I felt like a proud father. The first person out of the shop was Mike, our mechanic and fleet manager. Prior to this Toe Truck debut, he had had numerous sneak previews of Ed's creation, and he had made many helpful suggestions during the process. Mike stood in the driveway, grinning, and immediately hollered, "You guys sure hit a home run on this one!"

The paint appointment was just five days away. Mike needed to start in on his own to-do list, which included a tune-up, a brake job, major rewiring of the headlights, taillights and roof lights, as well as contracting with a glass and upholstery shop to do the finishing touches.

When I towed the Toe Truck to the paint shop at the end of the week, I again received a warm and jovial reception. Everyone who saw the truck seemed to love it, and it wasn't even finished yet.

The manager of the paint store, Bob, pulled out the color chart and verified, "You said you want the truck to be pink, right?"

"I want it painted bright pink," I said, pointing to a very bold shade on his chart. "And, please, put on an extra coat so it won't fade for a long time."

"You got it," he confirmed. "I can tell this is a paint job we'll remember."

A few days later, I showed up at the paint shop to pick up the finished product. I had a camera in hand as I got out of my truck. As soon as I saw it, I thought it looked pretty in pink. My cheeks were bulging with a wide smile.

"Bob, thanks for the terrific job. It looks just like I pictured!" I said as I shook his hand.

"You're very welcome; it was a fun project for us."

By now, Connie had warmed up to the idea and even gotten excited about the advertising possibilities. And, of course, our girls were thrilled. They had visited at various times during the building process and were eager to ride in the back for all the upcoming parades.

Because the "Pink Toe Truck," as we now called it, was completed earlier than expected, we had an opportunity to enter it into several small community parades ahead of the Torchlight. The truck's debut event was the Queen Anne Parade on a hot July day in 1980. As I chugged up the highest hill in Seattle, I could hardly wait to see the public's reaction to our new mascot.

Connie and I were up front in the cab while both our daughters were dressed up as clowns and sitting in the back of the truck. We were all excited to be a part of this exciting debut. The parade official assigned us a number and signaled me to move forward to the middle of the group. Just as I put the Toe Truck in gear, J.P. Patches and the Wheedle, the Seattle SuperSonics mascot, jogged up alongside our truck.

"Can you give us a lift? We need to get to the beginning of the parade route and our feet are getting tired."

I looked down and spied a pair of size twenty clown shoes. "Sure, climb in. We have plenty of room."

J.P., a local children's TV icon, asked, "What is this rig? I've never seen anything like it."

"It's Lincoln Towing's Pink Toe Truck."

JP Patches, Trina, Wendy and the Wheedle

"I get it! What a fabulous idea. It's certainly an original," he commented heartily.

As we moved forward to the street where the parade officially started, our two guests jumped out and began working the crowd. We all waved to the spectators, and I tooted the "ooga" horn and activated the siren in short bursts. Nearly every spectator, from the young to the old, responded to the Pink Toe with a laugh or smile. I loved every minute of it!

Finally the big night of the Torchlight arrived, and the atmosphere in downtown Seattle felt electric. The granddaddy of parades was set to start at eight o'clock, and just thirty minutes later our

Toe was released to follow the caravan. The route began at Seattle Center's east parking lot, traveled down Fourth Avenue for two miles and ended at the Kingdome parking lot.

We were off! Our whole family was onboard, waving to the huge crowd. Spectators filled the sidewalk while others sat at the curb or in lawn chairs. At every block the response was repeated: huge smiles, claps and excited waves. Some took a little longer to figure it out, but, when they did, their expressions of confusion quickly transformed to knowing smiles. A few of the most enthusiastic folks even took off a shoe and waved their foot. I loved seeing all of the varied reactions to our special truck.

The reviewing stand near the Bon Marché department store was packed with radio and TV reporters. I stopped at the Master of Ceremonies platform for thirty seconds of pictures. The announcer was generous in his comments about our unique tow truck.

Getting featured on TV was bound to provide a much-needed boost for our business and, at the same time, put a more positive spin on towing. At that moment, I realized this crazy Pink Toe Truck idea might be my best one yet.

Chapter 24

The MGM Fire

On Wednesday, November 20, 1980, Connie and I flew to Las Vegas where we had planned to attend a national towing convention; we hoped to gather some sales and marketing ideas from other towers around the country. The convention coincided with our fifteenth wedding anniversary so we seized the opportunity and made it a combined business and pleasure trip.

After a short taxi ride, we arrived at the MGM Grand Hotel and Casino. This impressive hotel boasted twenty-five hundred rooms and all of the amenities associated with a high-end property.

Just after seven o'clock the next morning, a siren outside roused me. I was curious so I got up to look out the window. Other than a fantastic view, I couldn't see anything but the shadow of the hotel's main entrance off in the distance.

The siren silenced, I slipped back into bed. About ten minutes later, I was disturbed again by someone yelling in the hallway just outside of our room. I quietly got up, trying not to wake Connie. When I peeked out the doorway into the dimly lit corridor, I saw a man rushing down the hall, carrying a suitcase and yelling in a foreign language. I didn't know what was going on, but I decided I didn't want to get involved.

Connie, now fully awake, asked, "What's going on?"

"I don't know. There's a man out in the hall yelling something, but I couldn't understand him. He's speaking Spanish, I think."

"Do you think he's okay?" Connie asked.

I poked my head out our door once again. It was quiet, and the man was gone. But, what I saw instead prompted me to blink my eyes to be sure they weren't playing tricks on me. No, they didn't lie: there was definitely a haze of smoke in the hallway.

I immediately closed the door and turned to Connie. "I think we'd better get dressed and get out of here. There's some smoke in the hallway."

I quickly pulled on a pair of pants and added a shirt, shoes and jacket.

Connie asked, "How bad do you think it is?"

"I'm not sure, but I bet it's getting worse by the minute. Just grab your jacket and purse, and let's go!"

This time, when I opened the door, the hallway was filled with smoke. My heart raced as I considered our room assignment. We were on the nineteenth floor.

I said to Connie, "Just stay close and bend down to get some better air."

I started to go left, but Connie grabbed my arm.

"No! That's the wrong way. That leads to the elevators; the stairs are this way," she urged, starting to cough.

With me now in tow, she reversed our direction. We held our breath and jogged for the exit door that, by now, appeared as only a hazy green light. I pushed the security door open, and we stepped into the emergency stairwell. The stairs were already filled with many other people descending. Except for the coughing, it was eerily quiet as everyone made their way down the stairs as calmly and swiftly as they were able. I kept track of the floor numbers in my head as we descended. As we reached each new floor, the air quality improved but more and more people continued to flow into the stairwell.

Initially, everyone seemed to be under control with only anxious whispers filling the air. However, by the time we had descended ten flights of stairs and finally reached the ninth floor, the crowded stairway was jam-packed with hundreds of fleeing guests.

The stairwell was only wide enough to accommodate two people side by side. As the heavy traffic slowed our downward progress to a crawl, the noise level around us increased dramatically. The calm atmosphere was replaced by a surge of panic as fleeing guests began to feel trapped. I could see fear in the faces around us as voices became louder and more demanding.

Near the seventh floor, we came up behind a hotel guest who was impeding the traffic flow. A small elderly woman, dragging a suitcase, was clinging to the handrail and shuffling, one step at a time, down the stairs.

As I moved alongside her, I offered, "If you'll hand me your suitcase and put your arms around my neck, I'll carry you down on my back."

She never really answered me, but, waving her arms, she declined. Connie and I carefully slipped past her and slowly continued down another flight of stairs.

After ten long minutes of inching down the remaining steps, our feet finally touched the pavement outside. Fresh air had never felt so good. We coughed for a few minutes, clearing our lungs. Safe on the other side of the street and standing in a large crowd of shell-shocked people, we looked back.

The luxurious hotel had suddenly been transformed into a deadly inferno. Smoke poured out of all sides of the colossal building. As I stared at the destruction taking place, I began to realize the gravity of the situation. I was so thankful we'd woken up and gotten out safely.

Looking up at the MGM Grand, I noticed that most of the hotel rooms had no balconies, and the windows were made out of a single sheet of glass, not constructed to open. I realized that scores of people were probably still trapped in their rooms. As we watched, some of the guests smashed open their windows with hotel furniture to find a momentary breath of fresh air. Broken glass rained down. The smoke immediately billowed out of every broken window. Those trapped in the upper floors were screaming hysterically for someone to help them.

Firefighters raced around, pulling hoses and shouting to each other. Their ladder truck looked completely inadequate for this massive rescue effort; stretched to its limit, the ladder only reached the sixth floor of the twenty-six-story hotel. The scene before us was overwhelming.

The situation quickly went from bad to worse. In their panic and desperation, some hotel guests knotted their bed sheets into a rope in hopes of escaping the deadly smoke. When I noticed the first sheet rope swinging outside a room on the twenty-first floor, I couldn't believe what I was seeing. I nudged Connie, pointed in the air, and said, "Look at that."

Just then, a male figure put his leg over the window ledge and began sliding down the makeshift rope. There was really no way for him to get to safety. His rope appeared to be only four sheets long, and there were no broken windows directly below him.

After a few minutes, he attempted to climb back up without much success. He clung onto the sheet for nearly ten terrifying minutes before his strength gave out and he fell. We watched in horror, not quite believing what we were witnessing. I reached for Connie, pulled her close, and together we prayed for all of the people still inside.

Our thoughts turned to our two young daughters back home. Connie suddenly said, "We have to call the girls right away. What are they going to think when they hear about the fire?"

By the time we found a phone, there was a long line of people waiting to call home. After more than thirty minutes, it was finally our turn. Connie called Trina's best friend, Julianne, because our daughter was staying with her family. We both spoke to Trina very briefly to let her know that we were just fine and asked her to let Wendy know right away.

After we hung up, Connie and I walked around the hotel block, trying to find a place to sit down and figure out what to do next. When we saw the hotel pool, we sat down on the lounge chairs to rest. The chairs were filled with dozens of other guests watching the events unfold. As we looked up, we saw two helicopters plucking frantic guests off the roof.

After more than an hour, a security guard came to the pool area and said buses would be coming shortly to take us all to a gathering spot to be processed. Along with the other survivors, we loaded into buses and were transported to the Las Vegas Convention Center where the Red Cross was setting up a makeshift shelter.

At the convention center, we met up with some other tow company owners and were relieved to hear everyone was accounted for among our group. We were told to register with the Red Cross, and they would try to find us lodging for the night. Several hours later, we were given small boxes that contained personal items.

We went outside to wait in a long line for a bus with our friends, Ken and Marilyn, who owned a tow company in the Bellevue-Redmond area. After a few stops Ken, Marilyn, Connie and I were finally able to get off the bus. We quickly went inside the hotel and received a room assignment on a lower floor in response to Connie's request.

The first order of business was to get a cab and find a department store to buy underwear, pajamas and other necessary items. After our shopping trip, we grabbed some dinner and headed back to our new hotel. Other than the shopping bag and the clothes on our back, the room felt very empty. Connie turned on the television. Every channel had MGM fire pictures flashing across the screen.

While she was preoccupied, I decided to unpack my complimentary Red Cross box. I fumbled with the cardboard lid until it popped open. At the same time that I saw a toothbrush and toothpaste, I also spotted a movement in the box. My heart skipped a beat as I found myself eye to eye with the largest bug I had ever seen. Not knowing how fast this creature could run or how high it could jump, I quickly closed the lid. It was obvious Connie was fully stressed and didn't need to know about my most recent discovery.

In a very casual way, I said to Connie, "I'm going outside for a few minutes."

"Okay," she replied, hardly looking up from the television.

I walked out to the hotel parking lot and opened the boxes. Nothing happened with the first box as I dumped the contents out on the driveway. I opened the second box up slightly, set it down and then kicked it over. Out tumbled the giant bug. I don't know anything about cockroaches, but I'm sure this one could have won a trophy. After a few seconds the critter got his bearings and headed south, bolting towards a dark corner of the building.

I picked up our new cellophane-wrapped toothbrushes, put them in the boxes and carried them back to the hotel room. It was months before I shared my cockroach story with Connie.

Later that evening, the telephone rang in our hotel room. Expecting it to be someone from our convention group, we answered. Instead, it was a reporter for *The Seattle Times*. He said, "Are you the Lincolns from Lincoln Towing in Seattle? I have information stating that you were in the MGM fire. If you'll give me a few moments of your time, I would like to interview you."

I spoke with him as briefly as I could, but he kept asking for more details. When I hung up the phone, I felt drained. Reliving what we had witnessed earlier that day was very traumatic.

On Friday morning, our goal was to find a way to retrieve our belongings and catch a plane back to Seattle. We took a cab to the MGM to meet with security personnel and get our name on their list. We checked in at a table that had been set up outside the hotel for former guests, and we received a 10:00 a.m. appointment. At our assigned time, we began the long journey up the nineteen floors of stairs that we had retreated down the day before. A hotel security officer led us and another gentleman, who had the room next to ours, upward. By the time we reached our floor and pushed open the emergency door, our legs ached.

As we headed down the hallway, the security officer said, "I'm sorry, but you only have ten minutes. Please move quickly. We have hundreds of folks to bring upstairs today."

My room key was in my pocket, but it was obvious that I didn't need a key. The door lock mechanism and door jamb were completely smashed. I looked across the hallway; someone had rough-housed that security lock too.

The guard said, "The fire department had to break into every room to search for hotel guests, and they weren't going to wait for the pass keys."

Connie and I took a deep breath and entered our room. It looked the same except for a thick layer of ash and soot covering everything. The ceiling, the walls, the bedding and even our clothes hanging in the closet were filthy.

We grabbed our clothes from the closet, emptied the bathroom of our personal items, and stuffed everything into our suitcases. We joined up with the impatient security man in the hallway to negotiate the long stairwell for the third time in two days.

Once outside, we looked around for a taxi to take us to the airport. After waiting on standby for a few hours, Connie and I finally slid into our seats on a United Airlines flight headed to Seattle.

I turned to Connie and asked, "How are you holding up?"

She answered, "I only got two or three hours of sleep last night at the hotel. I could hear those sirens in my head all night long."

I said, "I did a little better than that, but I'm still wiped out. I can't wait to see the girls."

Connie, now drifting to sleep, mumbled, "Me too."

After the plane landed and we walked up the exit ramp, we were shocked to see several television crews. Each one had a large camera with special lighting attached. As soon as we entered the waiting area, a gentleman in a suit stepped in our path and asked if we might be the Lincolns. All of a sudden we realized that Seattle news teams were there to interview us about the MGM fire. We were questioned, along with Ken and Marilyn, who were also on the flight with us. The four of us were the first fire victims to arrive back in Seattle. We answered a few questions, the cameras shot some footage and then we rushed out, making a beeline for our cars.

It felt so good to be back on familiar ground. We savored our first night home with our girls, knowing that this event could have ended very differently.

The newspapers continued to carry news periodically about the MGM fire for months afterward. We learned that the fire broke out in one of the hotel's restaurants. It started when the uninsulated electrical wires of a refrigeration unit rubbed together as it vibrated. It burned for hours undetected until it flashed over at approximately 7:00 a.m. It traveled rapidly through the ceiling and then the air circulation system. Though the fire was contained in the attached casino and restaurants, the majority of the fire-related deaths occurred on the upper floors of the hotel where toxic fumes and smoke collected after rising up the elevator shafts and stairwells. The fire was estimated to have spread at the alarming rate of nineteen feet per minute.

After a thorough investigation, the fire deaths were blamed on a shocking number of installation and building-design defects. The wiring was faulty, the fire alarm never sounded and the heating, air-conditioning and ventilation system designs were all flawed, allowing for the rapid spread of deadly smoke. To add to all that, during its 1972 construction, the casino refused to spend the $192,000 required to install a sprinkler system. Sadly, that system would have prevented the whole disaster.

There were approximately five thousand people in the hotel and casino on that fateful morning. The fire was responsible for eighty-four deaths: seventy-nine people died from smoke inhalation, many while they slept, four people died from burns and the man who fell from the sheet rope died of massive brain trauma.

We learned months later that eight people had perished in the fire escape on the twentieth floor, just one floor above the flight of stairs where we began our descent. In addition, more than six hundred and fifty people were injured. The MGM inferno was deemed the second-worst hotel fire, in terms of loss of life, in U.S. history.

A week after the fire, we were contacted by the Seattle fire marshal's office and asked to testify about the need for improved fire safety codes in Seattle. Fully understanding the importance of more stringent codes, we agreed.

Soon afterwards, dozens of code changes were approved by the City of Seattle. The most important one made smoke detectors mandatory in all structures and required sprinklers in all new or remodeled commercial buildings. That day, construction safety in Seattle took a giant leap forward.

Though the fire experience had been traumatic, we were thrilled that, as a result of living through it, we were able to play a small part in improving the future safety of our city; that's a legacy we're happy to leave behind.

Chapter 25

Back to My Roots

Shortly after Connie and I returned from Las Vegas, I decided to explore the City of Woodinville for a possible satellite towing office. I wanted to find other ways to make up for our lost contract business. I stumbled upon a one-acre lot owned by our friends, Terry and Cherry. The lot was located right next door to their business, Vintage Auto Parts.

I gave Terry a call. "Any chance that lot next door to Vintage is still available?"

"Yes, it is," he eagerly answered. "I'd love to have you as a renter. I'll even lower the price especially for you. The property is already zoned light industrial so it's perfect for towing or auto wrecking."

As soon as Terry said those two magic words—auto wrecking—my mind kicked into gear, and I couldn't stop thinking about all the exciting possibilities. A towing-and-auto-wrecking combination business would work beautifully. I could hardly wait to tell Connie about my new idea.

At dinnertime, I shared my news. "I found the ideal lot to rent for our Woodinville expansion, and it's already zoned correctly. It's Terry and Cherry's lot and they've offered it to us at a good rate. I'm thinking we can do more than just towing. How would you feel about opening a classic car auto-wrecking business right alongside the towing operation?"

I felt my excitement growing as I explained my vision in more detail. "We could pick one classic car brand and market the parts nationally. It would be just like in the old days with Lincoln's Corvettes."

I excitedly continued, "Mustangs might be the perfect choice. They sold over a million of them in '65 and '66. I've seen a lot of old, worn-out ones sitting in driveways and carports. We could probably buy them up for next to nothing."

I could see Connie might need a bit more time to get used to the idea so I backed off. By the next morning, she was asking all the right questions. I knew she would come around. And, by the next week, she did.

I hadn't been this excited about something since I started the towing company. I called Terry and told him we would like to rent the lot starting January 1, 1981. That way we could get a head start on getting the fence built and the lot graveled.

A few nights later we sat around the dinner table with our two daughters. We had a great time discussing what catchy name we might give to our new business. We laughed a lot about some of the crazier combinations. Then I passed around several Mustang magazines so we could check on which names had already been taken.

We finally settled on Wild West Mustang Ranch. We all liked the idea of a Mustang ranch since it fit well in the rural horse town of Woodinville, and we thought the wild west part added a bit humor. I loved the advertising possibilities (little did I know).

The next morning, I wrote our new name on the business license application. A few weeks after the name was official, a friend laughingly said he thought our name was clever. When he winked at me, I was confused. "What did you mean by that?" I asked.

"You mean you really don't know about THE Mustang Ranch. It's a well-known 'house of ill repute' down in Reno."

When I broke the news to Connie, she was mortified, but I looked at the bright side: this naive mistake might actually make our business name more memorable on a national level.

With Connie and our managers at the helm keeping an eye on the towing business, I was freed up to work on the start-up details for the Mustang business a couple days each week. Once the ball was rolling for our auto wrecking company, I couldn't wait to make it happen.

I decided the first thing I needed to do was talk to Connie about accumulating some inventory.

"I think it would be smart for me to start buying some Mustangs while we are waiting for our license, that way we will be ready to open our doors when it does arrive."

"What's the rush?"

"We can't start selling until we have inventory to bring in customers."

"Where will you park them? The new fence isn't even finished yet."

"I can park them in the gravel area in front of our house," I suggested.

"You can't do that. The property here is not zoned for business, and I'm sure the neighbors won't be happy about it."

"I'll go over and ask them right now. If Don and Jeannie don't like the idea, I'll drop it."

When I returned, Connie asked anxiously, "What did they say?"

"Don said, 'I love old Mustangs, it's okay with me!' and Jeannie said, 'I don't give a hoot what you do, especially if it's only for a few weeks.'"

I was having a good time; it felt great to be out buying cars again. By the end of that week, four dirty, beat-up Mustangs—which I saw as gold mines—stood at attention in the gravel alongside our private road. I pushed my luck and extended my buying into a second week. Soon seven cars were lined up against our neighbor's fence. On the other side, two horses grazed in the tall grass, paying no attention to my mechanical ponies.

Connie was more than a little concerned. "You need to stop buying cars until we can move them onto the business property. It's starting to look like a junkyard."

"Okay, I'll wait. I know we're running out of space."

I kept busy interviewing parts pullers and office help. Connie ordered invoices and picked up office supplies. We bought a small copy machine and cash register and worked through the myriad of details so we could put up our sign and open our doors. Of course, wherever I drove, I was constantly keeping my eye out for any prospective Mustangs for sale.

Finally, on the morning of January 31st, when I stopped by the post office box to pick up our mail, I noticed there was a Washington State Department of Licensing envelope inside. I tore open the back flap and pulled out my long-awaited auto wrecking license.

Finally, we could call for our inspection and start towing the cars to the lot. Two weeks later, our final inspection was over, and we were now legal to open. I alerted the tow company to transfer my collection of Mustangs to our new business location just five miles away on Highway 9 in Woodinville.

There were so many details to take care of that I don't think I slept much for several weeks. I was thrilled to be back in the business of my youth.

A few weeks later, while I was having coffee with Don, a long-time friend from Seattle, he surprised me. His family owned a very successful auto-dismantling business that spanned four generations. They had recently moved their operation from Seattle to Woodinville.

Don said, "I've been meaning to stop by and tell you I'm so happy to see you back in the auto-dismantling business. My dad and I decided that since you're specializing in classic Mustangs, we'll step back. We currently have around fifty cars. We'd like to sell them all to you and give you the opportunity to have a corner on the market. We'll use the space for other inventory. When people call us for Mustang parts, we'll refer them to you. Plus, we'll give you a friendly packaged price."

"Wow, that's very generous of you both. That will definitely help us get started. Are you free this morning?" I asked. "I would love to see what you have in stock."

"Sure, I'll meet you there in half an hour."

I was still stunned when I got to my car. Did Don really just offer me their Mustang inventory and all their referrals? It was almost too good to be true: fifty more cars right away. We could possibly get hundreds of Mustang phone calls handed to us. Unbelievable!

After arriving at Don's business, he showed me their stock. I had a ballpark number in my head, and, when he told me the package price, it hit my number on the nose. We settled the deal quickly and shook on it. Don had just dealt me a fine poker hand.

I arranged to have our tow company pick up the cars. Now Wild West Mustang Ranch was definitely off to a blazing start.

By February of 1982, the Mustang business had accumulated over one hundred cars. They were all lined up, twenty-five to a row. Word was out! We sold several drivable used Mustangs a month, but, mostly, we concentrated on selling parts. We had become the place to find new and used Mustang parts. Mustang club members were delighted with our inventory. Out-of-state enthusiasts began calling in droves. Big-selling items included doors, fenders, bumpers, hoods, hubcaps, seats, engines, transmissions and sometimes whole bodies. We squeezed every ounce of profit out of the cars, right down to the radio knobs and gas caps.

The Mustang lot filled with parts cars

Soon after our first anniversary, we had enough cushion in our bank account for me to start thinking about purchasing even more cars.

I filled out an application to become an official bidder at the Insurance Auto Auction in Auburn, Washington. They sold over three hundred vehicles each week. Every brand from Audi to Volkswagen was represented. These "clean" Mustangs sold for up to twice the price I had been paying to private owners, but I stepped up and bought a few to measure the return on my investment.

The quality of the parts from these well-maintained Mustangs was unmatched. Even though the cars were often crashed on one side, the rest of the car was usually in great shape and their parts were in high demand. Within weeks of purchase, these cars paid for themselves and then some. I should not have waited so long to step up and buy the more expensive salvage.

The manager and the employees of Wild West Mustang Ranch turned nothing into something. In just over a year, our sideline Mustang business was turning a very healthy profit. I had a good crew so the business only required a day or two of my time each week. I spent the majority of my week working at Lincoln Towing.

The Mustang business had an amazing start, but Lincoln Towing was still the "mother ship." If it wasn't for its seed money, there wouldn't have been a Mustang business.

With the proper balance of marketing and advertising, the towing business had righted itself. Profits were once again strong, volume was growing, and we were even able to hire back some of our original employees.

Lincoln Towing was fast approaching a mile marker. A third try for Seattle's impound contract was just around the corner. Winning back what we had lost two years earlier was always in the forefront of my mind. I knew that the competition would be tougher than ever before. Over the last five and a half years, since our original winning bid in 1976, the number of tow companies in Seattle had grown by about 50 percent.

We had a great opportunity right before us. Even though we realized the end result was out of our hands, with a hope and a prayer, we were ready for our next shot. What a crazy way to run a business, always on the edge.

Chapter 26

Making A Comeback

In March of 1982, Connie and I completed the bid packet and submitted our bids. As we sat in the familiar room and the bids were read, I was hopeful. But, with the new and more complicated bid rules, the zone winners were not obvious this time. After striking out last time, I didn't take anything for granted.

The next day, when I picked up the phone, I heard the words I'd been waiting more than two years to hear, "Mr. Lincoln, I'm pleased to tell you that Lincoln Towing has been awarded a City contract."

Ed leaving the office

The administrator went on to explain that we were the successful bidder in three zones: the Northeast district, which included the University area out past Lake City, the Northwest district, which included the Ballard area all the way out to the Seattle city limits, and the coveted West Central zone, which included the greater parts of Seattle's business district. I thanked the caller and sat down, stunned. I couldn't believe this turn of events.

When official contract-signing took place, I was still in a blissful fog. If we had been victorious in only one of the zones, we would have celebrated. But, amazingly, out of the five zones we bid, we won the three we wanted most.

Connie said, "Now we really need to get busy and hire some more people. Even though losing the contract was difficult, I think it was good for us. We learned a lot from that whole experience, and I think we are stronger today because of it."

"Definitely," I agreed, "with all of our new commercial accounts we aren't completely dependent on the contract any longer. But it sure will be great to have the added volume again."

We couldn't wait to share the news with our managers and entire team. Our employees knew it was a big deal and congratulated both of us. After the experience of not winning a single zone, this victory was even sweeter. It took two full days to calm down from the adrenaline rush.

During the next three weeks, we interviewed and hired additional office staff and drivers. We purchased a few more tow trucks, opting for a mixture of new and used.

On the April first start date, our ramped-up operation immediately jumped into high gear. Not counting regular breakdown tows, accidents and service calls, the police calls added approximately twelve hundred tows per month to our workload. Our volume approached a 25 percent increase. The bank account healed up and produced a healthy reserve.

Our drivers were thrilled to be busy; the pace made their shifts fly by. No idle time was spent clock-watching. Most of our drivers were assigned a private tow or police impound the minute their shift started, and the dispatch office had tow calls lined up for them all day long. It wasn't unusual for twenty trucks on a nine-hour day shift to average ten tows each. The all-time, single-shift record was fifteen.

Most tows were your average breakdown or police impound, but once in a while we were called to assist in unusual situations. Most drivers hoped for a challenging assignment in order to earn some temporary bragging rights.

During one graveyard shift, our driver, Marvin, responded to a call at the Lake Union Marina. The car he was dispatched to tow was completely submerged. Retrieving a vehicle out of the lake proved to be awkward and extremely difficult. Marvin had to deal with a twenty-foot cement bulkhead and a car twenty-five feet underwater. Fortunately, the police scuba diver was available and ready to help.

Getting the submerged car up and over the bulkhead without getting hung up presented a huge challenge. Dealing with the steep wall ended up requiring two of our trucks. Naturally, the night crew took pictures to prove to the day shift that they could expertly complete a difficult task.

The *Post Intelligencer* published a picture and story of the episode in the morning paper. The newspaper ended its investigative report by saying, "The retrieval was professionally completed by Lincoln Towing." Next to the column, there was a picture of one of our tow trucks vertically suspending the accident vehicle above the water while the other tow truck winched it to shore. We happily pocketed another free advertising handout.

As we charged towards Lincoln Towing's sixth anniversary, we felt like we had some serious momentum. We had survived a rough patch but emerged victorious. I was proud of our highly trained drivers and staff; their dedication and professionalism fed our success and reflected well on our company's image. With our new balanced-business mix of 60 percent private and commercial and 40 percent police work, we were positioned well for the future, come what may.

Chapter 27

Lake Chelan or Bust!

Once again, our family was headed out for our annual vacation to Lake Chelan in eastern Washington. With the daily demands and stresses of business ownership, we didn't get away as much as we should. But this trip was the most-anticipated family event each year; a much-needed break from the six-day-a-week grind. I loved spending quality time with all my girls in Chelan: swimming, waterskiing and soaking in the sun. I couldn't wait to recharge my batteries.

We always stayed at Campbell's Resort on the east end of the lake, and every year we went there with our good friends, Arni and Elaine, and their kids, Kaylee and Nick, who were the same ages as our girls.

The trip to the lake was an easy three-hour drive over Stevens Pass on Highway 2. But, in the summer of 1984, there was a large construction project on the highway and one lane was closed for ten days. After a powwow with Elaine and Arni about potential traffic backups, we decided to take the longer, northern route over the North Cascades Highway. This alternate route is a beautiful drive. We thought the potential construction delay was a good excuse to take the scenic route, even though it would take an extra hour to get there.

Naturally, the girls were buzzing with excitement as we readied ourselves to leave early Saturday morning. We packed up my '69 Chevrolet pickup and also loaded the boat with extra luggage and lake toys.

Kaylee, Wendy and Trina taken at Campbell's Lodge
several years earlier

At eight o'clock, Arni and his family swung by our house in their aged Audi sedan. They decided to move a few of their larger items into our boat to free up some space.

We headed off in a caravan, going north on Interstate 5 towards the town of Burlington. About an hour into the drive, we both took a right turn onto Highway 20. Soon, the little Audi was passing me on my left side, and Elaine was waving at me to follow behind them.

In less than a mile, they made a left turn into a Texaco gas station, and I followed with my trailer. I watched Arni pull behind the station near a hose. He jumped out, ran around to the front of his car and opened his hood.

As I stepped out of my truck, he hollered towards me, "I have a small water leak. But I've had it for awhile; I'm not worried about it."

I said, chuckling, "Arni, you're one of the most optimistic people I know. Most people wouldn't go two miles down the road with a water leak, let alone two hundred."

"It's really no big deal. I think I just need to stop and add water every thirty miles or so as we go over the pass. I'll grab a few spare water jugs now and keep them in the trunk," he said, unfazed.

As soon as Arni filled his radiator, we resumed our caravan. We were off and ready to make our fifty-five-hundred-foot ascent over the North Cascades Mountain Range. This pass was much higher and steeper than our normal route up Stevens Pass, which tops out at forty-one hundred feet.

When we approached the curves at the base of the first mountain, we were making good time. I thought about what I had to look forward to on this vacation. Getting back in the boat and water-skiing sounded good. I also couldn't wait to have some alone time with Connie, relax by the pool with a good book and hang out with our friends.

We continued up the mountain, stopping occasionally for Arni's radiator refill. Even with the stops, Connie and I were enjoying the beautiful drive. It had been several years since the two of us had traveled on this road. I reached over and took her hand in mine.

Finally, we completed the steepest part of the climb and reached the very top of the pass. Suddenly, I felt the truck lose power and then quickly regain it. After it occurred a second time, I signaled and pulled over to the right shoulder of the highway for the fourth time in four hours.

I shook my head; I couldn't believe our luck. *Didn't we have enough car trouble issues in this caravan already?*

I checked my gauges and everything appeared normal, but, when I got out of the truck and looked under the engine, I spotted red transmission fluid leaking on the ground.

While Arnie was parking his car behind my boat, I walked to Connie's open window and said, "It doesn't look good. The transmission is leaking oil."

"What are we going to do?" she asked.

"I'm not sure yet," I admitted.

Arni trotted over to my car. "What's wrong?"

"My transmission is failing; it's slipping and jerking. It's been leaking enough oil to coat the underside of the truck. Take a look."

I pulled the release latch and raised the hood. When I withdrew the transmission's dipstick, the empty reading on the long metal rod confirmed we had big troubles.

I thought aloud, "The way I see it, we only have two choices. We could park right here and wait up to three hours for a tow truck. Or, maybe, if I drive with a gentle throttle, we can make it to a gas station in Winthrop, especially if I coast in neutral on the downhill stretches. It helps that we're over the top of the mountain. But if the transmission pump gets completely dry, we'll all be out of luck."

Arni, a fellow risk-taker and optimist, urged, "Let's go for it!"

I immediately put the truck in neutral, released the emergency brake and headed down the steep slope towards the town of Winthrop, ten miles away. I zoomed past breathtaking mountain landscapes and meandering creeks at breakneck speed. But, I couldn't appreciate the beauty we'd come all this way to see as I maximized my coasting speed.

Finally, Connie said, "Honey, you're scaring all of us, can't you slow down?"

"I can't, because if I do, we'll never make it. We have to go as fast as possible on the steep parts so we can make it over the flat and uphill sections ahead."

I returned my attention to my driving. There, just ahead of us, was a dreaded sharp turn in the road where, for safety, I had to slow my wounded truck. After rounding the turn at a greatly reduced speed, the next hurdle looked to be a flat one-mile section of road which slowed our coasting to a crawl. I had no choice; I reached around the steering wheel and carefully slid the shifter into drive. The truck lurched ahead, and we gained speed until we were going thirty miles per hour.

By now, I could tell the brake lining was getting hot, but I just had to ignore the smell. A sign on the right appeared like a beacon of hope, WINTHROP - ONE MILE. The tense crowd inside my truck watched my every move.

I announced, "I think we're going to make it. This last mile should all be downhill."

Our truck limped into town, on borrowed time, and then came to a halt at a four-way stop in the middle of the cowboy town. On our left was a gas station with a sign saying REPAIR SERVICE. This was too perfect. We made a left turn, and the Chevy hauled the boat trailer the last few yards to the service garage.

The shop owner came over, introduced himself and asked how he could help us. I told him about the transmission. He asked, "Can you pull the rig ahead about ten more feet to make more room at the gas pump?"

"I'd be happy to," I said.

I got into the truck, fired it up and put it into drive, but nothing happened. It would not move a single inch.

The owner said, "Don't worry. We can hook it up to the tow truck and get it out of the way."

Arni and his family parked in the far side of the lot. He calmly walked over to my truck, and said, "I've got a new name for you: Lucky Lincoln."

When the gentleman asked my name for his paperwork, I told him and he laughed. "My brother purchased a used tow truck from your business a couple of years ago. It's been a great workhorse."

After looking under my truck, he continued, "I think you pushed your transmission too hard. More than likely, your seals are ruptured. I've seen it happen many times from pulling a heavy load over this pass. If you want, I can order a repair kit from Bellingham. I should have your rig ready in three or four days."

"That would be great. We're headed to Lake Chelan for a week. I'll check in with you in a few days, and, when it's done, we can run back up here to pick it up."

I looked at Arni, and he nodded, yes, he would bring me back.

By now, Connie, Wendy and Trina were standing at the Audi discussing our next move. I told Connie the good news about the repairs taking only three to four days. "Luckily, the shop has a spot to park our boat," I added.

"But if we leave the boat here, the kids are going to miss out on waterskiing for half our time at the lake," Connie said sadly.

We quickly decided that the two of us would stay back and try to hitch a ride while everyone else continued on to Chelan. It would be a tight squeeze with all four kids in the back of their car, but it was only an hour drive.

We gave Arni a duffel bag to strap on his roof, and we told them all goodbye. The Audi, now weighted down with six passengers and as much stuff as we could cram in it, grunted its way toward Campbell's Lodge on the shore of picturesque Lake Chelan.

Determined to save our vacation, Connie proposed what seemed like a crazy idea to me. "Maybe we can find a ride for ourselves *and* the boat. We could check around and see if there's anyone with a trailer hitch that we can hire."

Connie was now the optimist, and I was the cynic. Hitchhiking a ride was one thing, but our odds of finding complete strangers to haul us and our boat and trailer to Chelan were miniscule.

"Let's go into the shops and ask if they know of anybody in town who would be willing to tow our boat to Chelan."

"It's worth a try, I guess," I conceded, warming ever so slightly to the challenge.

We went in and out of seven shops, and they all had the same answer. "This weekend is the annual four-wheel-drive hill climb event. Most of the truck owners in town aren't expected back from the mountain until Sunday night."

With the ninety-degree sun beating down on us, we walked the long block back to our truck. We had tasted victory as we coasted into this town, but now we faced a likely defeat. As we retrieved a snack from the cab of our Chevy, a four-door Dodge pickup, with a camper on the back, pulled up to the gas pump.

"Let's check it out," Connie said, laying down her snack and hopping into action.

We walked around behind the vehicle as the man began pumping fuel. Our eyes opened wide as we both stared at a rather large trailer hitch. Connie turned to the man, introduced us and filled him in on our plight.

He said, "I'm sorry to hear that. I'd like to help you, but I'd better first check with my wife. We would need to have our two kids ride in the camper. I'll see if she is okay with that."

When he returned, he said, "We'll tow it for you if our hitch rating is correct for the weight of your boat."

Together we confirmed it was doable. After a quick hookup, we were on our way to Lake Chelan. I assured the man and his wife we would be happy to pay for his gas plus some extra for helping us out of our jam. In just over an hour, we all arrived in the parking lot at Campbell's Lodge where we told the man he could put the boat in any empty space.

He shook his head and, with a twinkle in his eye, he said, "The job isn't done until I put your boat in the water. Remember, tomorrow, you still won't have your truck."

He backed our trailer down the boat ramp and launched our boat into the cool lake water. With my wallet in hand, I approached him and attempted to square things up.

The man said, "My wife and I talked about it, and we've decided not to accept any money. We are just returning the favor from someone who helped us when we had a flat tire several years ago. We knew there would be a right time to pay back that good deed."

We thanked them both and said our goodbyes. We got into the boat and pulled it over to Campbell's dock and then went to check in. On the way to the lodge's office, we stopped at Elaine and Arni's room and knocked on the door. All six of them were shocked to see us so soon.

Campbell's Lodge

Elaine said, "We just arrived ten minutes ago, and we only stopped twice to refill the Audi. How did you almost beat us here?"

"About thirty minutes after you left, we hitched a ride. And you'll never guess what followed us all the way here: our boat—and it's already launched and tied up at the dock."

We told them all about our adventure and the very nice couple who helped us out. They couldn't believe how well everything had gone. The "Lucky Lincoln" nickname has stuck ever since.

I guess my luck still hasn't run out.

Chapter 28

Mustang Madness

As we neared our fourth anniversary of Mustang mania, our business was firing on all cylinders. Our inventory was continuing to grow, and, in some rows, we even had to begin double-stacking the cars.

In January of 1985, I was surprised to receive a call from *HOT ROD*, a national car magazine. They inquired about the possibility of doing a story on our Mustang business.

I had no idea why they chose us, but I was quick to say, "Yes, of course!"

The magazine's representative said, "One of our editors will contact you for an appointment. If all goes as planned, we will be looking at a publication date in June."

A few weeks later, a man named Bruce called and said, "I'll be doing the story featuring your business for *HOT ROD Magazine's* Mustang Edition. Your wrecking yard has been mentioned by our readers as one of the best Mustang parts sources around. I would like to come out on March eighth to interview you and photograph your business."

On the day before the big photo shoot, the office was swept, the windows were washed, the eight used cars for sale were cleaned and the parts bins were straightened up.

It wasn't until Bruce walked into my office carrying a very large camera that the reality of this amazing marketing windfall really began to hit me. I could hardly contain myself because I knew what articles in magazines could do for a business. I had experienced their impact firsthand in the Corvette business.

He interviewed me about how the business got started and our future plans. I was questioned about where I found our cars, what sources I used and our overall success.

Then he went to work with his camera, snapping pictures inside the office and outside, too. He shot hundreds of pictures, including dozens among the rows of Mustangs. To get a broader shot, he often stood on top of the parts cars or used a stepladder. He even climbed inside a few cars, taking photos of dash gauges, steering wheels and seats.

When it was all over, Bruce said, "It was sure hard to shoot two hundred and fifty cars crowded together and get them in one picture frame. I'm going to have to do a lot of editing before I submit this story to my boss. But if it gets approved, I think I can still get it done in time for the summer edition."

When I got home from work, I couldn't wait to tell Connie and the girls about the experience.

"The guy from the magazine seemed really impressed with our business. He shot a wheelbarrow load of film. I'm trying not to get too excited about it yet because there is still a real possibility that it will never be published. His boss could change his mind. But can you imagine the amount of exposure we could get from this?"

"Yes, that would be wonderful. But don't get your hopes up too much," Connie cautioned.

May 1, 1985, is a date I'll always remember as the day an advance copy of *HOT ROD Magazine* landed in our post office box. With my heart pounding, I retrieved the treasure, immediately opened it and scanned the table of contents. Halfway down the list of articles, I saw a heading called USED—NOT ABUSED, referencing page 126.

Could this be it? I turned the pages anxiously and quickly spotted our two-page article which included a large picture of the Wild West Mustang Ranch. It featured a group of parts cars along with the story of how we got started collecting old Mustangs.

The article also clearly listed our phone number and address for ordering parts. I was over the moon!

Just before I put the magazine away, I flipped to the next page. I was shocked as I kept turning and turning the pages. The Wild West Mustang Ranch was featured on the next twelve pages. I counted a grand total of fifty-two photos of our little Woodinville business.

I felt like I was floating on air. *Unbelievable!* I went out to my truck and climbed into the front seat. Stunned, I sat in the parking lot of the post office and scanned the pages a second time. I considered pinching myself to make sure I wasn't dreaming again. I couldn't wipe the smile off my face even though there was no one there to see it. As I considered this unexpected and highly unlikely blessing, I prayed a prayer of thanks.

When I arrived at the Mustang Ranch ten minutes later, I waved the magazine in my hand and hollered to my manager, Brian, "Come and look. You've got to see this!"

After showing off the article and pictures to everyone at the Mustang business, I headed downtown to Lincoln Towing's accounting office. I walked in with the *HOT ROD Magazine* under my arm, on a mission to find Connie.

I strolled into her office with the magazine and a smile. When I told her they only gave us fourteen pages of coverage, she said lightheartedly, "Be serious for once, Ed."

Silently, I opened the page to our article and handed her the magazine. She smiled as she slowly read through it. Then, out of curiosity, she turned to the next page. As soon as she saw the page filled with Mustang Ranch pictures, our eyes met, and she gave me a questioning look. She turned page after page after page through all fourteen pages. A shocked look doesn't do justice to describing her reaction. She was so stunned she couldn't speak for nearly a minute. When she finally did, her eyes glistened as she said, "I can't believe this!"

By the summer of 1985, the Wild West Mustang Ranch was nearly busting its seams. We had grown so much that we could no longer find space in the lot for our new inventory of wrecked

Mustangs. For every car we bought, we had to send a stripped-down Mustang carcass to the scrap yard.

I spoke to Connie about our dilemma. "We can't continue to grow our Mustang business unless we expand. The storage lot is filled to capacity. We're now buying close to two hundred Mustangs a year, and we can still barely keep up with the demand. The parts are flying off the shelves. If we want to take full advantage of this surge of business, we need to consider looking for a larger location."

She paused and then asked, "How much property do you think we need?"

"I'd like to get five acres, but I checked on some land prices. If we have to settle for two or three acres, that would at least be twice the size of what we're leasing now. But it could easily take a year to find the right location. I'd love to stay on the main highway for visibility."

Connie, always the voice of reason, responded, "I know things are going well now, but are you sure this boom in business won't be short-lived?"

"Nothing is certain, but I feel like this classic Mustang craze is still building. If we're able to meet the increased demand, I think we could ride this wave for quite a few years. And, by next year, we should have enough cash to purchase the land ourselves. Then we could lease the property back to the business to cover our payments."

"Okay," she agreed. "Let's keep our eyes open for a new location."

By the end of the business quarter, our sales had doubled; in two more months, they doubled again.

After leaving the Mustang Ranch one day, I drove about a mile up the highway. A FOR SALE BY OWNER sign appeared on what looked like a small horse ranch. I stopped to inquire about the size of the property. It had originally included five acres, but the prior owners had sold a portion of it; two-and-one-half acres were all that remained.

The lot had two homes and two barns. One house was sixty years old; the other was fifteen. The Clines, an older couple, had lived there most of their married life. I was excited about this location. However, as soon as I saw the price, I knew the property was out of our comfort zone. We liked the Highway 9 frontage and the layout so much that we decided to make an offer anyway. But, just as we assumed, it was quickly rejected.

We looked at several other properties over the next five months but made no offers. I was really getting the itch to move to our own plot of land. Years back, when my dad offered advice about owning my own business one day, he'd always emphasized the importance of personally buying the land you're operating on. He said that the land will appreciate in value over time, and it will give you something tangible even if the business doesn't survive. His words lingered in my thoughts.

In January of 1986, I received a call from Mrs. Cline, who, with her husband, had rejected our prior offer. She said, "My husband passed away a few months ago, and I have reconsidered your offer. If you are still interested, I'd like to sell the land and houses to you, and I'm willing to accept your original offer."

After discussing the unexpected call with Connie, we both decided to take the leap. Ten days later, we personally purchased two-and-one-half acres of the former horse ranch. It seemed fitting that we would be converting it into our own Wild West Mustang Ranch.

I called Terry and let him know we were buying our own place, and we would like to move out a year earlier than we had originally discussed. Being the good friend he was, he said he was happy for us and that ending the lease early wouldn't be a problem.

Now that we were getting ready to move, Connie and I discussed what to do about the Woodinville branch of Lincoln Towing. We had been struggling over the last few years since there were already several towing companies in the area that were providing good service. We decided to simplify our business dealings by concentrating our attention exclusively on towing in Seattle and on Mustangs in Woodinville.

In April of 1986, after four months of prep work at the new property, the Wild West Mustang Ranch was officially ready to open its doors at our new location.

The new Wild West Mustang Ranch office

Our customer base and inventory continued to swell. One year later, the move was a proven success. I found out that we could squeeze four hundred Mustangs into our back lot, a dozen used cars in the front lot and I kept buying at a rate of about two hundred Mustangs per year. Brian continued to do a fantastic job of managing the crew and selling parts.

Inside the new parts office

Thanks to *HOT ROD Magazine* we continued to receive parts orders from Iceland, Europe, Australia and many other places around the globe. We could not believe how far the news spread. New orders arrived daily. It was amazing to me that our small business was known in the far corners of the world.

Mustang parts cars

Chapter 29

Ten Most Wanted List

It was a gorgeous summer day in August, 1988—the kind that shows off Seattle's amazing views without the colors being muted by a wall of gray skies. I was planning to head downtown in a couple of hours to volunteer myself at the office, as I often did on Monday and Friday afternoons. On those two weekdays, I regularly offered my services to my manager, whether that meant answering phones or hopping in a tow truck to do my part.

On this particular Friday, our now eighteen-year-old daughter Wendy was working as a dispatcher and release clerk at our small downtown office. It was an extremely busy day because, in the late afternoon hours, a number of extra streets needed to be cleared in preparation for the Seafair Torchlight Parade that evening.

At about ten-thirty in the morning, Wendy answered the police hotline and was asked to go out into the lot and visually double-check the vehicle identification number on one of the recently impounded cars. When she approached the car, she noticed it had Texas plates. She looked on the dash and carefully copied the entire number. Back in the office she verified that the number matched the one in the computer. Then she picked up the phone and confirmed that the information the police had received about that vehicle was correct.

"I don't want to alarm you," the police dispatcher said, "but the registered owner of that vehicle is on the national *Ten Most*

Wanted list. We will be sending officers over right away. If the suspect comes in to get his car, I need you to handle the transaction just as you normally would. Our officers will wait to apprehend him until he is clear of your building to ensure everyone's safety. All I need from you, or any other employee at your office, is a quick and discreet call after he arrives."

At that moment, I'm sure Wendy was somewhat concerned but probably not panicked since she's not the worrying kind. Besides, it definitely wasn't her first time dealing with a high-intensity situation at Lincoln Towing.

She had worked the night shift a number of times and encountered her fair share of angry drunks. In addition, she regularly faced the rowdy post-Seahawk-game crowds. After yet another loss by the team, they were often frustrated, even before realizing their vehicle had been towed. When that happened, they had to catch a cab to our office. By the time they arrived, tired and angry, our release clerks had the joyous job of asking them to pay some more of their hard-earned money to retrieve their vehicle. And, as an extra bonus, the clerks were also obliged to inform customers that they would need to remit payment to the city for the parking ticket they were given. This was not a combination that lent itself to polite customers. But, regardless of the intense situations she faced, Wendy was always cool and courteous under fire.

Around noon that day, I exited the freeway and took the Mercer off-ramp towards our downtown location. I called in my code on the two-way radio. Wendy responded by activating the arm on the electric gate and, just as I drove up, it began to rise. She saw me through the office window and waved as I drove through the security gate and parked my truck.

After entering through the rear door, I asked my employees, "Do you want me to make a lunch run?"

Wendy and several others gave me their orders for burgers. The restaurant was just a few doors north of our office. I headed out on foot, completely unaware of the potential drama ahead.

(Wendy later admitted, "I kept the information from you, so you wouldn't make me leave. I didn't want to miss any of the excitement!")

Within minutes of my departure, the phone call she had been waiting for came in.

The caller said, "I can't find my car, and I saw a sign with your company's name on it. Do you happen to have it?"

After verifying the make, model and the fact that it had Texas plates, Wendy confirmed that it had been towed for a parking violation and was in our Fairview lot. It was *him!*

"Okay, I'll come and get it," he said.

Wendy immediately telephoned the police dispatcher to let her know that the suspect would be in the office shortly.

"Don't be worried," the dispatcher said reassuringly. "Although you can't see our officers, the tow lot is currently surrounded. Just try to relax and follow your normal routine. We'll make sure the suspect is unaware of our presence until he is out in the open. But, please, do your best to keep your lot clear of all other customers and employees when you send him out to his vehicle."

Soon, a police helicopter could be heard off in the distance. Within ten minutes, a taxi dropped off a customer. Wendy and the other staff members wondered, could it be him? The man entered the office and walked directly towards John, the other dispatcher on duty. When the customer gave his license number and asked to pick up his vehicle, both Wendy and John knew this was the guy they'd been expecting. Between the *Ten Most Wanted* list suspect and my daughter, there was only a half-inch-thick protective glass window.

Picking up some paperwork, Wendy calmly strolled to the private back office and quietly phoned the police. When she told them he was in the office, the dispatcher asked, "Is he the man with the light brown jacket?"

Wendy confirmed and then walked back out to her post.

Following standard protocol, John asked for the customer's registration. The suspect said he had it in his car's glove box. John politely asked him to go and retrieve it.

All eyes were on the suspect as he exited out of the office's side door and walked briskly towards his car, parked only a stone's throw away.

Still completely in the dark about the entire scenario playing out at my lot, I headed back from the nearby restaurant, carrying multiple bags filled of food. As I neared the office, I noticed a policewoman crouched low behind the cement ramp next to our driveway. I was perplexed but still processing the scene as I came up behind her, a french fry dangling from my lips.

With a firm wave of her hand, she stopped me and, without turning her head, said in a low-toned voice, "Don't go any farther."

I was very concerned when I realized she was looking in the direction of our office. All I could think of at that moment was my daughter is in there. Looking up the sidewalk, I spied three other officers ducked down, hiding alongside the Pink Toe Truck, just twenty-five yards beyond us. My heart raced as I realize something very serious must be going on.

When I looked down, I saw that the officer already had her gun in her right hand. Just then, I heard a signal over her radio and, suddenly, the lead officer ran towards our entrance gate with the two others following close behind. One officer stumbled and fell to the ground; his gun wildly firing off a bullet. The others sprinted toward the corner and past the gate. Five additional officers rushed in from the far corners of the lot. They zeroed in on the suspect, who was in the middle of the lot walking in the opposite direction.

I heard an officer shout, "Freeze! This is the police. Put your hands in the air!"

The man looked over his shoulder and hesitated for a moment.

Before his hands reached for the sky, the lead officer tackled him, sending both of their bodies skidding across the gravel. The other officers jumped into action: one pinned him facedown on the ground, while another put a rifle firmly against his back. All of the officers circled around and had their guns drawn and pointed at the suspect, who was ordered into the spread-eagle position. The surprised man did not resist as his arms were pulled behind him and handcuffs were firmly snapped around his wrists. Then, he was forcefully brought to his feet and shoved into the back of the police car.

Man being taken in for questioning

Two hours later, a reporter from one of the local TV stations showed up at the office and asked to interview me about the high-profile arrest. After I answered his questions, the cameraman photographed the lot and the suspect's vehicle. By the time they were finished, I was exhausted from the afternoon's hype.

As I got ready to get back to work, Wendy spoke up. "I don't think it was fair that they interviewed you, since you weren't even involved. John and I were the ones who talked to him and met him face to face, and nobody even asked to interview us."

I hadn't deliberately stolen the spotlight, but I knew she was right. After all, I really was just a spectator holding bags full of burgers and fries while this all went down. I apologized and thanked her for handling the situation so safely and professionally.

It was Torchlight Parade day, so we needed to quickly change our focus to handling the myriad of calls and logging in the numerous vehicles impounded for the police department. The freeway exit ramps were jammed beyond capacity as citizens poured into town early to secure a spot for the parade.

I joined the other tow drivers, driving a spare truck, and helped to clear the last few streets of the parade route. All the while, I kept wondering about the whole story behind the *Ten Most Wanted* list suspect.

Later that afternoon, the police department called our office with an update. "The man we arrested and brought in for questioning was, unfortunately, not the man wanted by the police. The vehicle was registered to the criminal who is on the *Ten Most Wanted* list, but your customer today bought the car just last week in Texas. His description of the man he purchased the car from matches the description of the true suspect."

Hours later, after getting out of jail, the man came to our office for the second time. The poor guy had just completed a two-day drive from Texas. It was his first time visiting Seattle and only his second day in the city.

After the way he was welcomed to our area, I wondered if this gentleman would ever come back. I guess, if he's a glass-half-full-type of person, he might at least find some solace in the fact that he left town with an interesting story to tell his family and friends about his adventure in the Pacific Northwest.

Chapter 30

The Fun Meter

My Mustang manager Brian and I traveled to San Francisco to attend a trade show in the fall of 1989. We visited many automotive booths throughout the morning. As lunchtime approached, we ran across a booth selling a humorous item that seemed somewhat out of place.

Being a sucker for silly gadgets, I said, "Hey, Brian, look at those."

The vendor, a guy named Gene, was selling Fun Meter buttons. They were simple round buttons with a pin on the back and an adjustable arrow designed to measure the amount of fun a person was having. Brian and I chatted with Gene for a few minutes about his interesting product.

He grinned as he showed us his collection. "Everybody in business needs to have a little more fun, don't you think? This Fun Meter provides a special kind of light humor. The adjustable dial makes it unique because it can be set on minimum or maximum fun or anywhere in between. So far, my customers have mainly been convention groups who purchase them to give away in their welcome bags."

Before we continued on our way, he gave both of us a couple of complimentary buttons and a business card. We each pinned one of them on our shirt and continued to walk around. Within minutes, one participant approached us and wanted to know where we got the "cool buttons." We happily pointed him in the direction of the Fun Meter booth.

"Let's go to the mall across the street for lunch and see what kind of reactions we get from these buttons," Brian suggested.

"I bet I can get more comments than you," I countered, always looking for a challenge.

As we walked around the neighboring mall, it didn't take long for two different store clerks to notice our meters and ask, "Where did you get those?"

At the restaurant, our waitresses laughed and said, "How clever."

That evening, we were still wearing our buttons as we boarded our flight back to Seattle. Before the plane took off, one of the flight attendants stopped by our seat and asked us to buckle up.

"What's that you're wearing on your shirt?" she questioned.

I explained, "It's a Fun Meter that's adjustable and can be set to your current mood based on how your day is going. If it's been a hard day, you're probably going to turn the dial back to minimum fun. But, as you can see, I've set my Fun Meter dial on maximum, which is where I plan on leaving it."

After the plane was in the air, the announcements were made and the seat belt lights were turned off, the flight attendant stopped by again. As she batted her eyes, she said, "Do you have any extra buttons? My coworker and I think they would be fun to wear while we work."

Brian looked at me as he reached in his jacket pocket for his spare Fun Meter. I hesitated, but Brian assured me, "We can get more, later on."

This friendly and attractive young lady was just too hard for us to resist. We both reached into our pockets and handed over our spares.

Back in Seattle, Brian and I continued to wear our Fun Meters whenever we remembered. The comments we received were too numerous to count. I never moved my dial off maximum fun. Sometimes friends would mess with me and slyly switch my pointer to minimum fun, but, as soon as I noticed, I'd readjust it back to where I wanted it to stay. I was having a blast!

After two weeks of showing off my Fun Meter, I decided to call the meter salesman and get a price. I knew we wouldn't make very much money off of them, but that wasn't the point. It was just something that tickled me, and I had already seen it do the same for others.

Gene answered, and I said, "I stopped by your booth last month and I've had a lot of fun with your Fun Meter. How much would it cost me to buy a batch of them?"

"I remember you," he said. "I thought you might call. My minimum order is fifty at $1.49 each. I'll pay the freight. There is a 20 percent price break, however, at two hundred and fifty units."

"I think fifty meters will be plenty." I knew I could easily give away or sell a couple dozen, but fifty? I figured a few months from now the leftovers would probably still be in the box, forgotten. *Oh, well. It will be a fun experiment, regardless.*

A week later, a small box arrived at my Wild West Mustang office. I opened it with anticipation. I wasn't sure what I was going to do with all fifty of these conversation pieces. When Brian walked by, I called him over to show off the box of meters. "How many do you want?"

He said, "Five or six."

I was disappointed with his answer. Maybe he wasn't as excited about them as I'd thought. I probably should have asked him before I ordered the whole box. Suddenly, I questioned whether there was really seventy-five dollars worth of fun inside that box. But quickly my thoughts moved on to the more important items of my day.

On the weekend, Connie and I attended a party. I wore my Fun Meter on my shirt, though Connie would've preferred that I'd brought it in my pocket. When she expressed her preference, I responded with a smile, "But I already have six in there." (Catching people's attention to elicit a response was something I lived for, but my whimsical notions sometimes embarrassed my wife.)

By the time we came home, my pockets were empty. I gave away two to my friends and sold the other four for three dollars apiece.

On Monday, I told Brian about the party and how many people stopped me to ask about the button. He replied, "What if I make up a twelve-inch cardboard sign, saying ARE WE HAVING ANY FUN YET? I could pin a dozen meters around the sign and put it on the sales counter. I think it would be a good impulse-buy item."

Fun Meter buttons

At the end of a thirty-day test period, Brian had sold three dozen Fun Meters. He said a few customers even returned to buy an extra one for a friend. By the end of the month, we were out of stock. I decided to order a second batch of fifty. When we were running low at the end of the second month, I placed a call to the meter man to try to get a discounted price.

He said, "If you will order one hundred at a time, I can give you 15 percent off the price."

I placed the order, got off the phone and said to Brian, "We're going to get a 15 percent discount, but I think this time we should try to increase our profit margin. Do you think we could raise the price of the meter by a dollar and not lose too many sales?"

"I'm not sure that will fly, but I'll try it out," Brian agreed.

Fly it did; the sales continued to be brisk. Every day, I made sure I had three or four in my pocket just in case.

The Fun Meters generated smiles and levity in the midst of everyday life; that was what really interested me. After all, they had nothing to do with towing or Mustang parts, and I certainly wasn't making a living off of the petite profits.

I ordered one more batch of five hundred and received a 30 percent discount. We eventually managed to sell all those, but it took quite a while.

By 1991, I was on to other things. Even though the Fun Meter had been entertaining, after two years of selling, my interest was waning.

In the fall of 1994, Connie and I attended a Western Washington Towing Association fundraiser auction. About halfway through the auction, I was surprised to discover a Fun Meter in the inside pocket of my sport coat. I hadn't seen one of those for a long while. As far as I knew, this was my last Fun Meter out of the seven hundred I had ordered. I told the auctioneer I had a personal item to auction off for charity and showed him my Fun Meter.

He said, "It's always good to have something personal. I want this Fun Meter to be the last item auctioned. You can tell the story of its journey, including finding it unexpectedly in your pocket tonight. Then I'll sell it."

And sell it, he did. Bidding for the plastic pin-on, dollar-fifty button started at five dollars. Then I added some history and stories about all the smiles it had generated. As the clincher, I explained how I had just discovered the last remaining button in my pocket. When the gavel dropped, the successful bidder stepped forward.

This one little Fun Meter button had just sold for the record price of one hundred and twenty-five dollars. The Fun Meter had worked its magic one last time. Smiling, I returned to my seat.

Chapter 31

Laughter at My Expense

When our daughters were in junior and senior high school, the unfinished basement was a big draw for their friends on weekends. Both boys and girls would come over and enjoy playing games on the foosball and ping-pong tables. In the summer months, kids filled our backyard, playing shuffleboard, volleyball and badminton.

Usually the Friday night group migrated upstairs to the family room to eat pizza, share stories and maybe play some cards or board games. Lots of laughter spilled out of this room during those nighttime get-togethers.

Many times, if the gathering was small, Connie and I would find ourselves in the middle of the kids' fun. Our girls didn't push us away; just the opposite. Sometimes we would play games with the group, and other times, Wendy or Trina would ask me to tell one of my stories. Often they were told at my expense. If the story brought laughter, it was common for me to be asked to tell another.

One of my repeat requests was for a true story that happened in 1986, when the girls were in their teens. Connie, Wendy and Trina, along with Marcia, our Brazilian exchange student, were eating snacks in the family room and watching the movie *St. Elmo's Fire*.

I walked into the darkened kitchen to get a snack. Without turning on the light, I opened the refrigerator and slid a Coke off the bottom shelf. Just as I closed the door, I felt something on my stockinged foot. I let out a small yelp. In the relative darkness, I looked down just in time to see a large insect, dark in color, dash across the floor. It scurried up to the pantry door, then turned on a dime and came twelve inches back in my direction before momentarily hesitating.

There was just enough light from the TV screen to get a fix on what I was up against. I quickly realized I was staring at the largest spider I had ever seen. I didn't have the luxury of time to look for a fly swatter. I figured if I didn't smash it on my first try, this spider would disappear within moments into the pantry, among the soup cans and the boxes of cereal. If that happened, I might never find it and, worse yet, one of my girls might. For all I knew, it could be a female spider about to lay hundreds of eggs.

I was only one giant step away from a possible kill. I just needed to make a swift and precise jump. At the moment just before I made my move, I really wished I was wearing shoes. I slyly raised my right foot, taking on the *Karate Kid* stance, and prepared to launch my attack. With a measured leap, I lurched towards my prey. My foot came down hard on the spider. I cringed as I sensed a crunch and then felt a disgusting amount of spider juice wet my sock. When I lifted my foot in victory, even the floor had a gooey spot.

Immediately, my heart began to slow to its normal rhythm. I was thankful I had killed the spider on my first try. I decided not to alert the family; I didn't want to give them any nightmares. I snatched two paper towels off the roll, folded them in half and bent down to scoop up the repulsive mess.

Since I was living with four females, I thought it best to discard the remains well out of sight, so I carried the smashed spider out the backdoor to the garbage can. I turned on the overhead porch light and opened the lid.

At the last moment, my curiosity about this enormous arachnid got the better of me, and I decided to take a final peek. I slowly opened the paper towel, and I was shocked by what I saw. The paper towel was very wet with smashed innards and some dark-colored skin, but it wasn't a spider at all. It was a large—and now obliterated—purple grape. I laughed out loud at my foolishness.

I surmised that, when I took the Coke from the refrigerator, the grape must have rolled out onto the floor. Then, when I took a step, I must have kicked it and sent it rolling towards the pantry where it hit the door and "ran" back towards me. I can only imagine how ridiculous I would've looked to any spectator who had seen me covertly lift my leg in order to catch the grape off-guard before bravely leaping through the air to destroy it.

Moments later, I went back into the house. The girls paused the movie for a second to ask me what the yelp and loud thump were about a few minutes earlier. Feeling a little sheepish, I simply walked past and said, "I don't know what you're talking about."

On another day, once my pride was restored, I knew I would tell them of the heroic actions I took to save them all from the enormous and terrifying purple grape.

Another story, regularly requested by friends and family, happened years earlier, back when my girls were eight and eleven.

After running errands on a beautiful summer day with my two daughters, we were headed home. I was driving my fully loaded used 1979 Cadillac that day; it had every automatic button and feature known to man. My young girls were seated in the front seat right beside me; all three of us in a row. We were cruising with the sunroof open and enjoying the sunshine as it filtered in.

When I reached our mailbox and grabbed the mail, I saw that our neighbors' newspaper was still in their box. On a whim, I decided to do a good deed for the day and deliver it to their doorstep.

There were three homes on our private road, and we lived in the middle one. I was headed for Don and Jeannie's house, the third and last one on the street. When I approached their home, I noticed that, to my left, they had a circular sprinkler turned on in their yard and it was spraying out over the driveway. I slowed, waiting for the counter-clockwise rotation to pass by, and then I pressed firmly on the gas pedal and followed right behind the spray. We slipped past without being hit by a single drop of water.

Ed with daughters, Trina and Wendy

I parked in the driveway, hopped out and tossed the paper onto the front porch and out of the sprinkler's reach. Then I jumped back into the car next to my girls. With Don's car parked in the driveway, there wasn't room to turn around. Looking in my rearview mirror, I studied the sprinkler, trying to figure out its pattern.

I said to my girls, "I feel like taking on a challenge. If I time this right, I think we can get past that sprinkler without getting wet."

Feeling a little cocky about my driving abilities, I didn't even bother to shut the sunroof. I rolled down my driver's side window and poked my head out to give myself a better view as I backed up. I noticed that now the sprinkler was rotating against me. The timing would be even tighter this time. Going backwards was also going to add a degree of difficulty.

In preparation, I put the Cadillac in reverse and kept my foot on the brake. At the right moment, just as the sprinkler whipped past, I hit the accelerator. The car lurched, and we raced backwards. Suddenly, it was clear to me that we weren't going to make it. The water was coming right for us and my window was still open. I reached down with my left hand and hit the power window button. But I had forgotten one important fact: my head was still out the window.

Suddenly, the window slammed into my jaw and forced my head up towards the roof. With my head now wedged in the window, I blindly jabbed at the myriad of power buttons, as the water sprayed me hard in the face, and the Cadillac still raced backwards. Finally, I hit the right button, released my head and slammed on the brakes.

The force of the window motor was tremendous and had me seeing stars. I sat in the middle of the road for a minute trying to recover. I tasted blood in my mouth, and my head was throbbing. Eight-year-old Trina, seated next to me, was crying softly, patting my shoulder and asking if I was all right. Wendy was bent over with her hands over her mouth and her back shaking, and I thought she was upset as well. But when she sat up, I saw she had been silently convulsing with laughter.

"I'm sorry that I'm laughing. I really hope you're okay," she said, "but I can't believe you just rolled your own head up in the window!" Then, my doubled-over eleven-year-old jumped out of the car and ran into the house to tell on me.

I put the Cadillac back in gear and slowly coasted into our driveway. When I got out of the car, Trina held my hand and walked with me towards the house. Connie stepped outside, unsuccessfully concealing a smile, and asked, "Are you going to be okay?"

I nodded, not yet ready to put my jaw back in motion. While Connie went to get me some ice, I sat in my easy chair, rubbing my jawbone. As I rested, I replayed my blunder, and I knew one thing was for certain: I'd never live this one down.

Chapter 32

Close Call

It was September of 1993, and I was playing an early morning racquetball game with my future son-in-law Mark at an athletic club in Woodinville. We started at seven o'clock but, fifteen minutes into the game, I felt unusually winded. I excused myself and stepped out into the hallway to get a drink from the water fountain. I sensed my breathing was shallow, and my face felt sweaty. I assumed I was coming down with a virus.

Mark showed up just after I'd gulped down some water. "What's going on? Are you okay? Actually, you look kind of pale," he said.

"I don't feel very well, and I'm kind of cold. I think I'll just lie down on the floor for a second and rest."

He immediately asked, "Do you have any tingling in your left arm or tightness in your chest?"

To me, Mark seemed overly worried. "I don't know; maybe a little. I'm having some trouble catching my breath, but I'm sure that's just from the game. I'm fine, really, but I do think I might be coming down with the flu. Just let me rest for a minute," I assured him.

Mark's concern rose to a new level when my body began to shiver. I thought the cause was simply the cold floor or a fever from the flu, but he wouldn't buy my excuses.

"I'll be right back," he said, running off.

When he jogged back to me, he admitted, "I asked the receptionist to call an ambulance. I think they should look you over before you go anywhere. You might be having a heart attack."

"I'm okay, really. I'm actually starting to feel a little better now," I said. "I don't need an ambulance. Could you just take me home? I'll pick up my truck later after I've rested at home awhile."

Mark wisely refused.

The fire department was only three blocks away so, within minutes, I heard the sirens. Two medics and a fireman appeared above me: one was on his knees asking me the same questions Mark had asked, another was monitoring my blood pressure and pulse while the third was setting up a gurney.

I started to panic. "I think I just have the flu. I hope you plan on letting me go home."

The fireman looked me in the eye and said, "We need to take you to the hospital to get a more in-depth evaluation. Going home is not an option."

"Mark, please call Connie, and let her know what's happening?" I said as they wheeled me out.

I barely remember the ride to the Evergreen Hospital. We arrived in a flash; the hospital is in Kirkland just four miles away. I wasn't sure what was happening, but, when I reached the hospital, they quickly wheeled me into an emergency room and started rechecking my vital signs. This all seemed unnecessary to me.

Just minutes after arriving at the hospital, I suddenly went into cardiac arrest. I was later told that I flat-lined on the hospital monitor screen, which triggered an emergency alarm. The hospital staff swiftly responded to the code blue and used electric paddles to try to shock my heart back into rhythm. Fortunately for me, it worked on the second try.

Mark had followed the ambulance to the hospital. When he arrived he called Connie at work and also got ahold of Wendy and our new son-in-law Keith at their jobs. Then he called Trina, who was attending the University of Puget Sound in Tacoma. They all jumped in their cars and headed for the hospital.

Unaware of my brush with death, I faded in and out for awhile. The doctor ran a few more tests and then entered my room, explaining, "Unfortunately, you have two blocked arteries. You will need to have surgery right away. Right now your arteries are not stable. But don't worry, we do this procedure all the time."

My head was spinning and I was having a hard time thinking. None of this seemed like it was really happening. In spite of my uncertainty, I reached for the pen and signed the forms. I was being rushed into surgery and my family hadn't arrived yet. What if I didn't make it? I didn't even have a chance for a last "I love you" to Connie and the girls. Scared and alone, I silently prayed, clearly recognizing I was not in control.

The doctor told the nurses to prepare me for surgery. There wasn't a moment to waste.

Before I knew it, I was being delivered to the recovery room on what seemed like a magic carpet. I was in a haze, and I didn't feel a thing. When I opened my eyes and tried to focus, everything was blurry. All I knew was I was alive, and I was infinitely grateful for that.

Soon I was given a room in the intensive care ward. Connie, Keith and the girls had arrived at the hospital and joined Mark. They were all waiting anxiously to see me. I was very tired, and I said little because my brain was still catching up with reality.

The next day, Connie told me what had happened after I was wheeled into the emergency room of the hospital. I was surprised to hear that I had flat-lined. She concluded, "Mark made a very wise decision when he called 911 rather than taking you home. If he had listened to you, you probably wouldn't be here right now."

I was put into ICU, so visitors were limited to family members those first few days. Our immediate family—Wendy, Keith and Mark—came to the hospital right after work each day to visit with me and to keep Connie company. Trina took the rest of the week off from the University with her professors' approval and stayed by Connie's side. We were all very thankful I was going to be okay, especially knowing how close I had come to not making it.

Over the next few days, several friends heard about me and came to sit with Connie and the kids even though they weren't allowed to see me.

On my third day in the hospital, Connie asked if she could bring me anything from home. After thinking for a moment, I asked her to bring me a camera and a Fun Meter.

"Out of everything I could bring you, are you sure that's what you want?" she questioned.

"Yeah, I think it would make this situation a little lighter, don't you? I can use it to show the nurses and doctor how I am doing. Also, I think it would be great to snap a few pictures for memory's sake."

Connie was very surprised; here I was, all wired up to monitors, with a lot of machines connected to me, and all I could think about was a Fun Meter. I guess that's just my personality. I've always tried to make the best out of bad situations.

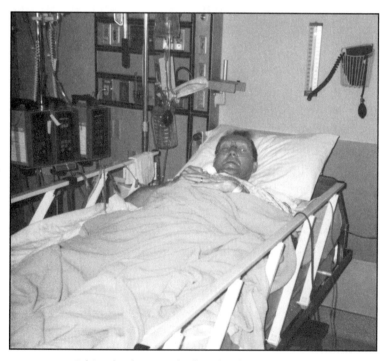

Ed in the hospital after his heart attack

As soon as she brought the Fun Meter to me, I pinned it on my hospital gown and put it on maximum fun. The doctor and the nurses thought it was hilarious. None of them had ever seen a Fun Meter before and certainly not in the hospital. Whenever my nurse stopped by my room, she would look at the Meter to see if the dial was on maximum or minimum fun. I always had it dialed hard to the right, maxed out.

"It looks like it is a good day today," the nurse would say.

By the end of the week, I was back at home with a good prognosis. The doctor asked me if I could lay low and stay away from the pressure of the workplace for awhile.

"Would it be possible for you to find someone at work who can take over your duties for two or three months?" the doctor questioned.

After being home with me for several days, Connie and I talked about our options. She volunteered to step up and manage half days for awhile. We were fortunate to have wonderful managers who went out of their way to relieve the pressure on both of us.

Once I was up and moving around more, she offered to do whatever it took to keep things on track at Lincoln Towing. "You just relax and focus on getting better," she said.

As soon as I had clearance from the doctor, I began exercising and walking daily. Keith and Wendy, now an occupational therapist, lived nearby and made sure I did enough but not too much.

Each day, Connie brought home reports from work. We would discuss what was going on, and she kept me up on all the workplace news. Fortunately, everything seemed to be running smoothly and there were no major hiccups. It was amazing how well she handled all my tasks. I was very impressed.

Thirty days into my at-home recovery, I had a bright idea. "Connie, why don't you become our corporate president instead of vice president? You've proven you can run the show as well as I ever did. If you're officially president, employees are likely to take your new role more seriously. Down the road, when you get tired of being the Top Dog, you can always hand the gavel back to me."

"Are you sure you want to give it up? That's really not necessary," she said, surprised by the idea.

"I'm sure. It's all yours, Mrs. President."

It wasn't all bad vacationing at home on light-duty status. I had a lot of visitors, and, together, we shot the balls on my pool table over and over. I also went on long walks daily with a neighbor who had recently been diagnosed with Parkinson's disease. I could feel myself getting stronger each week. The sweat equity was paying off. On some days, I allowed myself to ponder what retirement might be like.

Coming back to the tow company after several months was a time of adjustment and compromise for both Connie and me. It was apparent that she had taken the company to a new level of professionalism and efficiency. Nothing was falling through the cracks. The to-do list that always sat on my desk was dealt with rather than growing ever longer. Connie found she liked being in charge, much to her surprise.

We sat down to discuss the areas we each would oversee. Since we both had experience in running the whole show with the help of excellent managers, we decided Connie would handle all of the internal areas. She would oversee accounting, office staff and human resources, and work with the managers who handled those departments.

My revised responsibilities included the external areas of the business: buying and selling trucks and equipment, handling the auctions and overseeing the safety program, as well as all of the advertising and marketing decisions. My list was shorter than before my heart attack. I didn't say much, but I felt a little less valuable than before. Perhaps my ego was slightly bruised by seeing how well our company ran without me.

In thanks to my wife for doing an outstanding job, I never asked her to return my old title. During the last seventeen years, she had been happy simply doing the books and being the quiet, behind-the-scenes partner in the management of our business. I knew that she deserved some time in the limelight. In our relationship, I'm the visionary one and she is the person who completes the details. Despite our different gifts, she turned out to be an accomplished president. She even won some business awards along the way.

I can now fully appreciate how this period of stepping back allowed the love of my life to grow and shine. Connie's extraordinary leadership in our company—during and after my recovery—forever deepened my respect and appreciation for her.

And, of course, I'll forever be grateful to Mark for his quick-thinking and actions that gave me a renewed chance at tomorrow.

Mark and Ed

Chapter 33

Opportunity Comes Knocking

It was June of '95, and the summer was off to a nice start. Lincoln Towing and the Wild West Mustang Ranch were running smoothly. Then opportunity knocked a third time.

I picked up the phone and the caller on the other end of the line was John, the manager of the Insurance Auto Auction (IAA) in Auburn. I was acquainted with John because, over the years, I had purchased many wrecked Mustangs for our parts business at his auction facility. He and his wife managed this successful operation together. They had expanded the auction's size by contracting with dozens of insurance companies to sell off their totaled vehicles. They gathered wrecked cars from all over western Washington. Each week an average of three hundred and fifty salvage vehicles were transported to their lot and then sold to auto wrecking yards like our Mustang Ranch.

John's phone call turned into an invitation. "Laurie and I would like to take you and Connie out to lunch. We have an idea we'd like to discuss with you both."

I checked with Connie and said, "We're free on Monday. Just tell us the time and place, and we'll meet you there."

After dinner that same night, Connie said, "Do you have any idea what they want to talk to us about?"

"I'm not sure. John was pretty vague. I guess we'll find out when we get there."

Monday came quickly. Connie and I left the office and headed out to our lunch appointment at a waterfront restaurant in Ballard. We met John and Laurie there and were seated near a window with a fantastic view. The Olympic Mountains appeared larger than life, and I pointed out a Washington State ferry moving across the water.

After discussing our families briefly, the waitress interrupted our conversation to take our lunch order. When she left, John leaned forward.

"We want to run a confidential proposal by you," he said, keeping his voice low. "We currently have a three-year towing contract with a vendor and the contract is about to expire. We'd normally renew the contract, but we've had some serious performance issues with this company. We wanted to know if you two might consider expanding your towing operation into the insurance salvage market."

I looked towards Connie for a reaction and got none, so I proceeded cautiously. "I'm not sure. What are the requirements?"

John elaborated, "Our industry operates with different equipment than what most towing companies use. Instead of picking up cars one at a time, our vendors use large four-car haulers to increase efficiency. They save a lot of time, especially when three or four cars need to be picked up from one location. They also use two-car carriers, especially in bigger cities where getting in and out of body shops can be a tight squeeze."

"How many cars per day are we talking about?"

"On an average day, eighty-five vehicles need to be picked up from around the state and delivered to IAA. During inclement winter weather, that number increases by about 20 percent."

"How much time does the hauling company have to gather each car?" I asked.

"Only three business days. Gathering cars on time is critical because each vehicle is incurring a daily storage fee. If the hauling company doesn't arrive within three days, they are charged a twenty-five-dollar-per-day penalty."

"How many car carriers would we need?" I inquired.

"At least 10 four-car carriers and 5 two-car carriers."

"Wow! That's a lot of equipment," I stammered, silently choking on the upfront costs.

After pondering the equipment hurdle for a moment, I asked, "How is the pricing structured?"

"There is normally a fixed price per zone and an additional mileage charge in remote areas. If you're interested, I'll fax you our rates."

I glanced at Connie briefly and then asked, "If we decide to proceed, where could we find these car carriers at a reasonable price?"

"If you want to buy used equipment, California is usually the best source for multicar carriers," John offered. "It's safe to say the current contractor wouldn't help you get started. But if you decided to do it, you'd be able operate out of the extra office in our building that the current contractor uses. We're only charging three hundred a month for that space."

I was getting more interested as the conversation continued, but, at the same time, I was wondering what Connie was thinking. She had quietly been taking notes throughout the entire exchange.

When we started to gather up our things, Connie spoke up. "How long does this contract last?"

"Three years," Laurie answered.

Connie thought a moment and then said, "That's not going to be long enough to write-off the equipment we'll need to buy. We'd need at least five years."

"We'll check on that for you, but I know our corporate officers generally prefer a shorter term," Laurie responded.

John continued, "I apologize for not approaching you sooner, but Laurie and I just came up with this idea. I know this makes things tight, but the current contract expires in two months. You'd need to be completely ready to go by August fifteenth. Do you think there's any chance you could be ready in that short of a time frame?"

"Possibly, but that does seem mighty short," I replied. "I am interested, but there's a lot to consider. We'll discuss it and get back to you in a few days."

John seemed pleased with my answer.

As soon as we got in the car, I asked Connie, "What do you think about creating a third start-up business?"

I could see the excitement in her eyes, as she answered, "I think it seems like a great opportunity that pairs up nicely with our towing operation. It would certainly keep our drivers busy and also give us a huge block of business. Based on his numbers, their hauling business could add nearly twenty thousand tows a year. But, do you really think we could buy all the car-haulers and hire drivers in two months?"

"I'm not sure. I'll do a little research and see if I can find out how much used equipment is available. Then we'll know if this is even possible." I rubbed my hands together, excited about the prospect of a new challenge.

"Let's go back to the office and meet with our managers," Connie suggested. Pausing a moment, she emphasized, "We'll need their full support on this."

Ed and Connie in front of their corporate headquarters

Mike, the fleet manager, already had his hands full keeping a large fleet of eighty trucks serviced and on the road. I didn't know how he would feel about shouldering a bigger load.

Within an hour all five of us—Mike, Pam, Steve, Connie and me—were sitting in our conference room. The managers listened as Connie and I explained the proposal from IAA. Over the next thirty minutes, we listened to their questions and answered as best as we could. Then, we stressed that this new venture would require a group effort.

Connie said, "We take your input seriously, and we respect your opinions. Ed and I have talked about this, and we've decided that we'd like each of you to vote on this opportunity. On a piece of paper, just write down yes if you want to pursue this and no if you don't. Majority vote will rule. Ed and I won't vote. We know there is still a lot to work out with IAA, but at least this will let us know if we should move forward."

The vote was not unanimous. There were two yes votes and one no vote.

I told them the results and said, "Based on the majority vote, we will go ahead and look into the startup costs. We'll let you know when we make a decision in a few days."

There was one piece of the puzzle I was still concerned about: the profitability of the venture. I assumed there was some profit in the current contract; if not, the other company wouldn't want to renew it. But I had no way of knowing how much. After looking at the rate sheet John had faxed over, I sensed that the margins could be skinny, especially with inflation.

That night, Connie and I talked about what price increase we might dare propose. We studied the numbers and talked about the rate we felt would ensure a fair profit. We were used to working with hourly rates so it took us some extra time to do the difficult cross-comparisons with fixed rates.

Thinking aloud, I said, "Once we give them our numbers, we won't be able to increase our prices unless we build in some price adjustments over the next five years. We'd better guard our profitability up front. In order to protect ourselves, what do you think about asking for a 20 percent increase over the current rates and a 3 percent increase each year after that?"

"I think you should make an appointment with the bank to check on our rates and our loan limits before we commit to anything."

We had been debt-free for several years so it was a tough decision for us to take out a new loan. However, we both knew there were times when there was wisdom in leveraging, and this felt like one of them.

I was able to get an appointment with our banker the next day. After I explained what our equipment needs would be, the manager quickly said, "Our bank would be happy to work with you on an equipment loan."

Now that felt like a breath of fresh air.

We placed a call to John and Laurie to share our concerns and ask for a significant price increase along with the extended contract length we'd already proposed. After praying about it, Connie and I agreed, if they didn't accept our pricing, we would put the brakes on and let the opportunity pass us by.

After we had said our piece, John responded by saying, "I appreciate your offer and the efforts you've made in such a short time. I'll forward your proposal to corporate headquarters and get back to you in two or three days, but you should know that corporate is sensitive about any unplanned price increases. We'll have to see how this all shakes out."

John continued, "If we decide to go forward, I trust you will keep our deal under wraps for at least four weeks. We don't want the current contractor to leave us high and dry. That would cause a huge backlog of wrecked cars that would be difficult and costly to remedy."

The rest of the week felt long as it passed by with no word from John or Laurie. I started to feel disappointed, presuming the silence was not a sign in our favor.

Finally, on Wednesday morning, John called. "I want to apologize for the delay, but I'm very pleased to tell you that IAA has accepted

your terms and rate increases. Surprisingly, they are not counter-
ing on any of the items in your proposal. In fact, they are currently
preparing the extended, five-year legal contract you requested."

I think John may have been even more shocked than we were
by this news.

Time was now our adversary because, after this extended
wait, we had so little of it. Looking in the newspaper, I found a
potential truck. I made a trip to Tacoma and purchased our first
four-car hauler. It was a used, low-mileage truck that I was able
to purchase at a big discount.

Later that same week, I took a second trip to Sacramento to
inspect six trucks that were for sale. I brought Mike along to check
the trucks over thoroughly. We purchased four additional four-car
carriers and drove them up in two separate trips. Days later, we
found out about a handful of two-car carriers that were for sale
in northern California. We were well on our way to amassing our
hauling fleet.

One of the four-car haulers

Connie and our office manager, Steve, made an application for a new business name, Lincoln Transport Service, and took care of all the paperwork needed to start a business in the City of Auburn. All three businesses were carefully tucked under our corporate name, Lincoln Enterprises, Inc.

Finally, the day came for John to notify the current contractor that IAA would not be renewing their contract. Simultaneously, we put the word out that we were hiring experienced two- and four-car carrier drivers, and we set up interviews at our Seattle corporate headquarters. We were flooded with applicants desiring to work for Lincoln Towing's new division.

On August 15, 1995, the first day of our contract, our fleet of car carriers hauled in over eighty wrecked cars for the IAA. The volume each day varied with the number of accidents, and the weather was a big factor in that equation as well. Year in and year out, the pickup orders varied between eighty and one hundred cars per day.

We accomplished the IAA work with twenty car carriers and some extra help from Lincoln Towing's trucks and drivers when needed. Lincoln Auto Wrecking's former five-acre lot now held our company headquarters. This great location was the perfect place for our tow truck drivers to deposit the IAA cars they towed in from the Greater Seattle area. Then the four-car carriers could easily and efficiently pick up the staged cars from this central location

After we completed our first year of the contract, we were very thankful that we had proposed the 20 percent rate increase. It turned out that it was just enough to assure us of our target goal of 15 percent profit.

Lincoln Transport, our third and final startup, added an excellent boost for our business. I felt proud of all of our managers and workers who took on the extra load to make it happen. Our dedicated office staff and drivers made something that seemed so impossible, possible. Special thanks are owed to Mike and his shop crew for keeping all of the one hundred trucks in our fleet on the road during those years.

Shop Manager Mike, on the right, handing new
truck keys to a driver

You never know what surprising developments might be right around the corner in life. I had always thought that I would go out and find the hidden doors of opportunity and bust my way through. But, I have to admit, most of my big opportunities actually walked right up to me and knocked.

Chapter 34

The Popular Pink Toe

When I first decided to build the Toe Truck, in my wildest imagination, I never dreamed it would become so popular with the public.

The Pink Toe turned out to be an advertising gold mine: postcards with the Toe Truck appeared at Seattle visitor locations, coffee-table books highlighting Seattle often included our Toe, and, throughout the years, a number of tour buses made a special stop at the Fairview and Mercer intersection just so tourists could snap photos in front of the unique truck.

When Seattle's *Evening Magazine* began airing in 1986 on KING-5 TV, the local NBC affiliate, the opening of the show featured a cartoon clip of the Pink Toe Truck pulling the Space Needle down the freeway. We were as surprised as anyone to see it pass across the screen each weeknight, since no one had contacted us about using it in the show's intro. But we never complained about that minor detail because who doesn't love free advertising, we thought, especially every weeknight at seven o'clock on a major network like NBC.

Throughout the years, we spent very few advertising dollars because the Pink Toe generated all those advertisements on its own. It became such a strong symbol for our company that sometimes people didn't even remember the name Lincoln Towing; they just remembered the Pink Toe Truck. We didn't mind the confusion, and, once we recognized it, we added a listing in the phone book white pages under the alternate name of Pink Toe Towing.

Over the years, we had so much fun with the Toe Truck. But for all the joy and goodwill it has generated through the decades, there were also a few mishaps.

One summer day, just prior to a parade, the driver who was piloting the truck momentarily forgot about the height of the toes on top. He moved over to accommodate another parade float and slammed the toes into the branches of an overhanging tree.

This was no minor stubbed toe. The branch completely severed the big toe and it fell to the ground, fracturing into a handful of pieces. The driver, mortified by his error, loaded the remnants in the back of the truck and drove slowly back to the office, not relishing the phone call he would have to make to me.

On another day, the Pink Toe was the victim of vandalism as it sat in a fenced-off area in front of our Fairview office. Someone threw a flaming molotov cocktail from a passing car. The burning, gasoline-filled bottle shattered in the truck's bed and the fiberglass body erupted in flames. The fire department was alerted, and they quickly put the fire out, but not before a two-foot section of the left side of the Toe Truck was melted like cheese and blackened from the fire. I figured the vandal was a misguided teenage prankster or, more likely, an enraged impound customer. It saddened me to see the friendly Pink Toe Truck assaulted in that fashion.

Fortunately, all of the damage could be repaired. After patching everything up, the Pink Toe was back in action, delivering smiles to Seattle motorists as they passed on by.

As we saw its popularity skyrocket, we decided to donate the services of the Pink Toe to charities. It seemed to be a consistent hit at charity auctions. We were asked to come to numerous birthday parties for children and give their party guests rides around the neighborhood. Many times the Pink Toe was requested at elementary schools for show and tell. Others wanted it for a special event at their church or civic organization. We started a sign-up list and asked drivers to donate a few hours of their free time to drive the Toe Truck as a service project. Even our managers got involved.

While sitting in my office one day, I received a phone call from a gentleman asking if he could rent the Pink Toe Truck.

"The National Painters Association is having their annual convention in Seattle this year," he explained. "As a fun tradition, each year we pick up our executive director from the airport in a unique vehicle. In Chicago last year, we hired a garbage truck for the job."

I said we would be happy to rent out our truck, as long as we provided the driver. I knew right away that I would be that driver. This sounded like too much fun to pass up.

Four weeks later, at the appointed time, I pulled into the arrival area at SeaTac Airport and was told to hide the truck behind a concrete post, which is harder than it sounds when you are driving a large, bright pink truck with toes on top. The Toe ended up causing quite a stir as I waited for the signal to swoop up to baggage door number fourteen. Onlookers, some with cameras, were smiling and joking among themselves as they pointed at our truck.

Finally, when I saw the signal, I steered the Pink Toe around the post, pulled up next to the "victim," and, with my "ooga" horn, announced the truck's arrival. When he turned around and saw me, he busted up laughing. This guy obviously had a great sense of humor.

After the director climbed aboard, the convention photographer took several pictures, and then we headed off towards the Four Seasons Hotel.

While driving on the I-5 freeway, the photographer rode in another car just ahead of us. As we drove, he poked his head out of the car's window and continued to shoot video for the convention's upcoming entertainment roast.

Our entourage was attracting a lot of attention on the freeway. Cars honked their horns as they zipped past us. A late model

Chevrolet honked twice and then its passenger stuck his bare foot out the right window and waved his toes in the air.

It was all caught on film to be shown later that evening to the convention attendees.

———

At the end of the fourth summer's parade season, I made an executive decision to move the Pink Toe from the fenced area in front of our Fairview office up onto the rooftop. From that point on, during the nine-month parade off-season, the Pink Toe's home was atop our leased one-story building, prominently positioned just above one of the busiest intersections in the state. It was there that the Toe enjoyed its greatest exposure.

The Toe Truck sitting on the roof of the Fairview and Mercer lot

One day Ichabod Caine, a friend and well-known radio personality, called us at home with an interesting request.

"I'm competing in a music video contest against other radio disc jockeys on *Evening Magazine*," he explained. "The contest will be aired on TV and the best and most original theme will win. We drew songs out of a hat, and I got *Pink Cadillac*. My wife came up with the brilliant idea of changing the lyrics to make the song about the Pink Toe Truck. Could you bring your truck to the station on Wednesday for taping?"

Connie answered sadly, "Unfortunately, that's not going to work. It's up on top of the roof, and it's a lot of work to take down. I'm very sorry; we would've loved for you to have used it."

Minutes later after Connie explained what he'd said, a bright light clicked on in my head. Immediately, I called him back with my idea.

That Wednesday afternoon, Ichabod—dressed in a pink scarf and coveralls with *Tow King* written in gold across his back— danced around in the Pink Toe up on top of our roof. Hundreds of passing motorists craned their necks to catch a glimpse of the unusual sight. Accompanied by three backup singers, he sang the very original song, *Pink Toe Truck*, to the tune of *Pink Cadillac*. After the performances aired on KING 5 TV that very next week, Ichabod was declared the winner.

Ichabod Caine and the Ostrum sisters performing on top of the roof by the Pink Toe Truck

As the years passed, a number of radio stations latched onto the idea and asked to broadcast live from our roof in the Pink Toe. They loved the visibility of the location and often requested permission to paint the toenails or decorate the truck for special holidays or promotions. As music filled the intersection, motorists honked their horns and shouted encouragement to the radio personalities in the dolled-up truck. I loved the win-win advertising collaboration created through these special events.

Although I'd originally never imagined using the Toe in that capacity, I knew the Pink Toe Truck on our roof was the best billboard Lincoln Towing could ever have. With the millions people who passed by, this most famous foot became a true Seattle landmark. There's no way to measure the sales impact of the Toe over the years, but I'm confident I've earned back my small investment in the truck thousands of times over.

Painting the toes green for a radio station promo on
St. Patrick's Day

Chapter 35

To Sell or Not To Sell

In 1996, a merger-and-buyout frenzy raged through the national economy. Just when it seemed there was nothing left to consolidate, the towing industry was unexpectedly caught in the fray. The takeover buzz tore through and divided the brotherhood of small, local companies. Many independent towers chose to sell out to the big boys for satisfying chunks of stock and cash. Others wouldn't consider that option, no matter what.

In the spring of 1997, Lincoln Towing was approached. The suitor was RoadOne, a large tow truck manufacturer and recent acquirer of towing companies, located in Chattanooga, Tennessee.

I'd anticipated this phone call for months, but I still wasn't sure how I felt about it.

"We'd like to have an informational meeting with you and your wife," a representative from RoadOne said.

"I'll check with her and get back to you by tomorrow," I told him.

Connie wasn't interested in talking about selling to anyone. But when I said, "Let's at least meet with them and listen to what they have to say," she reluctantly agreed to lunch on Friday.

On Thursday evening, I brought up the next day's lunch meeting and questions we might want to ask.

She said, "I'm sorry but just thinking about this makes my stomach feel unsettled. I've only agreed to listen to what they say because you've asked me to. Our company is consistently profitable, and we have a great team in place. How could we just walk away?"

Despite our disagreement on the issue, the next day, we put on our smiles and presented a united front as we walked into the restaurant.

During lunch, the reps informed us, "We have researched your company, and we are impressed with its reputation and large annual volume of business. We think Lincoln Towing could fit very well into our national operation. If you two have any interest, our management team would like to discuss a potential buyout."

He continued on, "As you probably know, we have been accumulating individual companies across the United States this past year. We believe that a national tow company will have distinct advantages in the marketplace. We are targeting national motor clubs because of their huge customer base; many have told us they would rather deal with one company and one 800 phone number than thousands of separate tow companies. These clubs handle millions of calls every year."

During the last twelve months, I knew these big boys had acquired nearly a hundred and ten tow companies nationwide. RoadOne's representative revealed a lot of information about his national company, but we remained stingy about ours.

His counterpart left us with a final invitation: "If you plan to be at the National Towing Convention in Tennessee this June, a few of our board members will be there. I know they would be very interested to meet both of you and answer any questions you might have."

As Connie and I drove back to work, I said, "I know retirement could be a long way off but, by the time we do want to retire, there probably won't be an opportunity like this. I think we should check it out. I'm very curious what kind of offer our company would fetch, aren't you?"

"I know you're right, but it just doesn't feel good to me. You've worked longer than me, and I understand how you feel. I'm just not there yet." Connie emphasized, "I still love going to work every day."

"I won't force you to sell. If the offer we get doesn't make complete sense to you and me, we can just politely pass."

After two months of discussions at home and several phone calls from RoadOne, Connie reluctantly agreed to go to the convention. During the two weeks before the trip, we didn't discuss the topic. I was hopeful that she might have a change of heart once she was exposed to the big picture.

I knew Connie had softened ever so slightly when she said, "Before we sign up for the trip, we need to speak with the kids. It's important that we ask if either couple has an interest in taking over the company."

We called Wendy and her husband, Keith, who, at that time, were expecting twins. We explained the offer and our willingness to pass it by if they had any interest. Wendy declined politely. She would soon have her hands full as a mother of two, and Keith was happy in his career.

Next, we called Tucson, Arizona, to talk to Trina and her husband, Mark. Our offer was met with an almost identical response. They were honored that we'd asked but not interested.

The fact that the kids had passed on taking over our company was no surprise to me. One of the main roadblocks had just vanished.

I decided to go directly to the meat of the matter. I asked Connie, "What would it take for you to sell?"

"Well, for me, money isn't the biggest issue; I'm most concerned about our employees. But I do realize that we'd be foolish if we didn't think about the future earnings we'd be giving up in a sale. The company is doing very well right now. Keith just did a full-blown Lincoln Towing business appraisal last year for his master's program. I think we should take that number and double it. If they get close to that price range and they address my concerns about the welfare of our employees, I'd be willing to at least entertain an offer."

I smiled. "Wow! You're going to be one tough negotiator. Those boys back east don't know what they're up against."

In June of 1997, Connie and I boarded a United Airlines flight to Chattanooga. I was quietly excited about the possibilities.

Connie still wasn't thrilled about making the trip, but, reluctantly, she had agreed.

By the time the convention was over, we had gathered a lot more information about our suitors. We spent time talking with former tow company owners who had sold to RoadOne. Connie asked them some tough questions, mostly about their employees. Their answers seemed to make her more comfortable. We were impressed by their level of contentment with the sale. In addition, RoadOne's executives were very open and helpful. Adam, the CFO, offered to fly out and visit our firm to answer any further questions.

I said, "I think that's a good idea. What do you think, Connie?"

"On one condition," she stipulated. "When you come, we'd like you to meet with three of our key managers and respond to any questions or concerns they might have."

For a moment, there was dead silence. Then Adam spoke up, "This will be a first. Employee involvement is rare, but if it will help you in your decision, I'll do it."

One week later, Adam came as promised, along with John, RoadOne's CEO. I picked them up at the airport and brought them to our company headquarters. As Connie led a quick tour, I was praying the day would go well.

The back of corporate headquarters for Lincoln Enterprises, Inc

When we told them about our IAA contract, they were excited about our new expansion business. A national account with Insurance Auto Auctions was one of their corporation's goals.

We answered numerous financial questions. Adam and John kept glancing at one another and nodding. We could tell they liked our answers and our operation. They were especially impressed by some of our innovations, such as our electronic gates, state-of-the-art office equipment, and our converted pneumatic bank machine that we used to send and receive paperwork and car keys from the lot up to the office. This last innovation greatly increased efficiency because, after dropping off a vehicle in the lot, the drivers never had to get out of their truck; instead, they were able to quickly head out for the next tow.

When they entered our truck repair facility, they paid us a compliment. "Your shop is impressive, plus you have some of the most modern equipment we've seen. The cleanliness of your whole facility shows your staff really cares about this company."

The mechanic's shop

"The best part for us is it's all paid for," I pointed out.

Connie had arranged a dinner at our home with Pam, Mike, and Steve. The invitation included our daughters, who each held minority stock in the corporation. Trina had flown up for the weekend from Tucson and got a head start on making dinner. Wendy and Keith arrived soon after.

While our family finished up the dinner preparations, Adam and John met with our managers in the living room. Connie assured them, "Ed and I will give you complete privacy. You have the freedom to ask these two gentlemen whatever you'd like."

Forty-five minutes later, the group broke up their meeting. We all sat down to dinner and talked about subjects other than business. Afterwards, we excused our managers so they could get home to their families.

The rest of us gathered in our family room. Wendy, Trina and Keith were finally able to ask questions. Connie and I had also come up with a new list of our own since returning home from Tennessee.

After answering all of our questions, John looked at me, then over to Connie, and asked the big question: "I'm sure you have both thought a lot about this, so what number do you have in mind?"

I wasn't surprised by the negotiation tactic; in fact, I had used it myself. However, I wasn't about to show them my cards so I responded, "We don't have a price. We are waiting to hear your offer."

Adam looked at John and said, "Would you mind if John and I step into your home office to discuss our offer?"

I said, "Certainly, but I just want you to know that we aren't people who play games. If you truly want to buy our business, make sure your offer is your final price, not just a preliminary one."

The two executives left the room for ten minutes to discuss their strategy.

When they came back and took a seat in the family room, Adam handed me a folded sheet of paper with a number written across the middle. We had previously spoken with our kids and asked them not to react regardless of the price. The offer was slowly passed around the room. Not one of us said a word or exhibited any emotion.

Adam and John looked completely baffled by the lack of reaction from any of us.

I made a pre-planned statement: "Thank you, gentlemen. We will think your offer over and get back to you in a few days."

Chapter 36

Deal or No Deal

As Connie, Trina and I drove the executives to the airport later that night, Adam admitted, "Over the last twelve months, we have made hundreds of offers, and this is the first time there was absolutely no reaction. I find this quite unusual."

I smiled privately but still offered no response or explanation.

When we reached the airport entrance, Adam asked, "Connie, can you come to the check-in area with us while I fill out an official letter of intent and sign it? If and when you and Ed are ready, you both can sign the form and mail it in the envelope I will provide."

While John was getting their boarding passes, Adam quickly filled out a document that he had in his briefcase. He handed it to Connie and said, "I hope to hear from you soon."

When Connie returned to the car, we headed home to Woodinville. As I drove, I could still feel a slight tremble in both hands from the nervousness that had surrounded the four hours of business discussions.

As we entered the freeway, Trina broke the ice. "Mom, what did you think of their offer? Wasn't it much higher than you expected?"

Connie wiggled in her seat and responded, "Yes, it was, and I guess I should be happy. But, at this point, I just feel sad. I know that your dad really wants to sell now." She paused, taking a deep breath, "Actually, this whole thing is making me feel sick. Let's not talk about it for the next twenty-four hours. I want to just enjoy tomorrow with you, since you'll be flying out on Sunday."

Over the weekend, I began to consider the ramifications of a no-sale decision. We had already thought through the worst-case scenario: being ready to retire at a later date but not being able to find a buyer. If we passed on this deal and RoadOne bought up other Seattle tow companies, they would no longer be interested. Our company had grown to be the largest in the area so it was not likely that another independent tow company would have the cash to buy us out. Given that set of circumstances, we would simply have to close our doors and sell off all of the trucks and equipment. In that case, we would only get a fraction of the company's true value. It was painful to consider this option, especially when we had a potential buyer with a very generous offer in front of us now.

By mid-morning Monday, I was anxious to discuss the offer with Connie. "Are you willing to take the next step and let me contact our lawyer's office?"

"I guess so. I'd feel more comfortable after being assured by our attorney that this is only a preliminary document and not a binding one."

I called Alan and made an appointment to go over the "intent to sell" document we had not yet signed.

On Wednesday, we arrived at the law firm at Fifth and Columbia. The elevator door opened on the fiftieth floor, and the receptionist buzzed for our lawyer. Alan and another colleague approached us through a side door. He introduced us to Lisa, who handled sales and acquisitions for their firm.

Alan said, "Over the years I have become specialized in wills and estate matters, but Lisa's expertise is contract law. With your permission, I would like to assign her to work on the legal aspects of your business sales contract. I've told her a lot about you both, and she knows about how far we go back. I'm confident she'll take great care of you."

Lisa acknowledged she would process the first stage documents and suggest any changes within twenty-four hours. Almost immediately, we felt comfortable working with her.

After a few phone calls, Lisa said, "If you're in agreement with this revised paperwork, why don't you both come to my office and sign, and I'll send it off to the buyers. All the real work won't begin until their auditors show up."

After adding a slight price adjustment, we signed the document and mailed it to RoadOne. Even though the offer was higher than we'd expected, Dad had trained me—no matter how good the deal—to never accept the first offer on anything. I couldn't help myself; I felt compelled to tack on just a bit more even though I knew our counteroffer might be rejected.

Later that week, we received a call from Adam. He said, "We've received your request for a $250,000 price increase. That's a lot of money. I can guarantee the final price will be somewhere between our price and your price. If that sounds reasonable to you, we'll set the price aside for now and deal with it in the end. We will be sending our accountants to your office to do an audit of your books. They've got a lot of work to do."

"I'll go along with delaying the final price, but, remember, the deal isn't done until we see it and agree to it."

Two weeks later, the CPA arrived from Chattanooga. We knew the audit was going to be an intrusion, but over the years we'd become accustomed to state, county or city auditors looking over the books. He explained, "This process is quite exhaustive because a public company is involved. Please be patient with me; it's going to take close to three weeks for me to complete all of the necessary research."

We set him up in our quiet conference room and gave him whatever information he requested. Connie was exhausted from the extra workload and the stress of trying to keep everything under wraps.

She was thrilled when the audit was finished in ten days. We knew that must a good sign.

A few days later, Adam called. "You've passed the first phase of the due diligence portion. You can expect the preliminary purchase and sale agreement in five business days. Review it, and we'll go over your final concerns in a conference call."

After reviewing the entire document with Lisa, we arranged a call in early August to discuss our final sticking point with Adam.

"Are you ready to sign off on everything?" he asked.

Connie took the lead and replied, "We noticed that some of the employee benefits were missing. I want to be sure our employees don't lose anything in this deal."

Adam responded, "All our other buyouts have the same language, and we can't go back and alter the other hundred agreements. This is part of our standard corporate benefit package."

Like a warrior, Connie stood her ground. When it was clear she wasn't going to budge, Adam finally offered to match Lincoln Towing's superior benefits for the first twelve months.

I smiled in Connie's direction, proud of her selfless crusade.

Now that the terms of the sale were hammered out, Adam told us we could expect a preliminary written agreement by mail.

When the priority envelope from Tennessee arrived, we were overwhelmed by the forty pages of legal documents. We spent hours reading them and taking notes.

Finally I said, "It's easy to tell some lawyer had a heyday with all these pages of legalese. Can I deliver this agreement to Lisa tomorrow, so she can get started evaluating this package?"

"Let me think about it overnight," Connie answered.

"Don't delay this too long," I cautioned her. "Remember my trip to Romania with the youth group. We leave in ten days. I won't be back here to help for three weeks."

"I know. What doesn't get done will have to wait. I sense that they really want our company so let them adjust to our timeline. Remember, I promised Wendy that I would make the bedding for the twins' room while she's on bed rest. Towing isn't the only thing on my mind; our first two grandsons will be here soon."

By Monday morning, Connie came around without any additional push on my part. She agreed that it would make sense to get our attorney started on the paperwork.

I arrived back in Seattle on August twenty-eighth after a great trip. I wished Connie could have been there with me. She might have preferred that I hadn't gone because she had to carry a heavy load while I was away.

On September ninth, we received a call from Wendy and Keith saying that we needed to head to the hospital in Bellevue. Anything business-related would have to wait. Because the babies were breech, Wendy needed a Caesarian section. We arrived just before our first grandchildren, Isaac and Luke, were born. We were waiting in her room when they brought Wendy back from surgery.

After being weighed and measured, Keith carefully lifted Luke and placed him in Connie's arms. Her smile lit up the entire room. Then Keith passed Isaac to me. Nervousness and pride bubbled up inside. I didn't expect the flood of emotions I felt. Until that moment, I don't think either of us realized how much these little guys were going to touch our hearts.

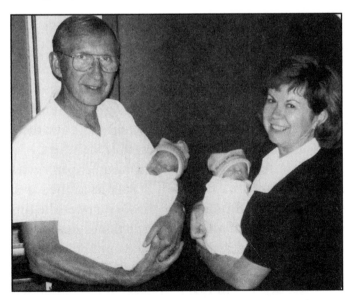

Ed and Connie with newborns Isaac and Luke

Thinking back, I remembered all those years I worked six days a week. Many times I'd come home Saturday afternoon so exhausted from yet another sixty-hour week. You might say my kids got the leftovers of what I had to give. Now, I would have another chance, and this time I wanted to do it right with the grandkids. I looked forward to all of the basketball games, soccer games, track meets and music recitals in my future.

A few weeks later, we received a request from RoadOne for additional copies of documents going back five years. Connie and I arrived at the tow office after church on a Sunday. Only a few people were working, so we quietly rolled the main copy machine down the hall and into the accounting office and closed the door. It took three hours and a ream of paper to photocopy all the requested items. We were both exhausted from the tension of possibly being discovered. The next day we sent the copied documents back to Chattanooga. One more item was checked off the list.

I glanced towards Connie at the breakfast table the next morning. "To me, the sale is looking like a done deal. I'm very happy. I know it's been a little scary, but thanks for taking this giant leap with me."

Finally, we received word that the lawyers on both sides had come to an agreement on all of the technical points. A time was set for the all-important conference call on October thirty-first at two o'clock. Connie and I would be in my office on two separate phones; our attorney, Lisa, would be taking part from her office in downtown Seattle; and Adam, RoadOne's CFO, and their head counsel from Tennessee would be representing the buyers. Members of each group introduced themselves to the other party's attorney.

After a few minutes, Adam said, "It appears all the paperwork is completed, except for one item: the final price. The time has come to nail down that number. To keep things simple, I suggest we take the formal offer we gave you at your home four months ago and your proposed amount of $250,000 more and then split the difference. In other words, we will agree to pay you $125,000 over our original offer."

I took a deep breath. I knew this was the biggest deal I had ever negotiated.

With a steady voice, I responded, "The number we gave you is the price we need to have. As you know, we were not for sale when you approached us. We would be happy continuing to do business as usual. We don't need to sell and, therefore, that number we gave you is what it will take to win us over."

Adam seemed rather surprised. "You mean to tell me that you would walk away from a deal of this size if we don't pay the extra $125,000? We agreed the price would fall between our two numbers. We're stepping out of our comfort zone for you; where is your willingness to bend a little?"

With a sweaty palms and a racing heart, I made my final case. "Well, let me take a moment to tell you about my morning. I drove over to visit my employees at the Wild West Mustang Ranch in Woodinville, and I parked my truck in the customer parking lot. As I pushed opened the driver's door, I noticed a penny on the ground a few feet away. I didn't hesitate; I scooped it up. Dirty or not, I pick up every penny. Actually, I pick them up all the time. This extra money that you think is not very important in the scheme of the whole deal is important to us. As a matter of fact, I still have that penny right here in my pocket."

There was dead silence on the line. I looked over at Connie, seated at the small conference table in my office, and she cracked a smile. Over the phone earpiece, I could hear some whispering in the background. After what seemed like a long delay, Adam was back on the line. "Okay, you have a deal."

I don't remember what we did right after hanging up the phone, but I do remember the phone ringing again just a few moments later. It was our attorney, Lisa, who said, "I couldn't believe what I was hearing. I had to bite my tongue to keep from laughing, knowing your frugality the way I do. You certainly know how to squeeze blood out of a turnip. Remind me to always be on your side of a deal."

Chapter 37

The Big Announcement

Included in our sales agreement was an option to sign a five-year employment contract to stay on as managers and continue to operate the business for RoadOne. Our managers were also offered the same deal. Some agreed to a three-year contract, and others went for the five-year agreement.

"Do you have a desire to stay for a while longer?" I asked Connie. "It might soften the transition for our employees."

"Definitely. I'm not ready for retirement yet," she said energetically.

In the end, we both decided to sign on for the five-year extension. Now, it was time to plan the official announcement to our employees.

We both felt the extra $250,000 we had negotiated into the deal would be fun to give away. After all, we were completely content with RoadOne's original offer.

Connie knew exactly what she wanted to do with her $125,000. Along with the announcement, she had decided to hand out all of her share to our managers and employees. She wanted to reward our dedicated staff.

I decided to spread my entire portion between the charities we regularly supported. Our daughters' minority ownership allowed them to receive a small share as well. We all considered this extra cash a blessing.

On November 1, 1997, the first day Connie and I began operating as non-owners, we both felt like we were walking on air. The sale had been completed, and we still felt like we were in charge.

I spent my first day doing my normal duties and also making sure the lunch room was squeaky clean for our first-ever, all-employee meeting that was set for 7:00 p.m. The sale had been the best-kept secret at Lincoln Enterprises, Inc., and this news would finally be revealed in the big announcement that night.

Connie spent the entire morning and into the early afternoon hand-writing personal thank-you notes to each and every employee.

At around three o'clock, she put on her coat and whispered, "I'm headed for the bank."

Earlier in the day, she had met with our five managers to thank them individually and present them with a check. Now, her mission was to pick up the remaining eighty-five thousand dollars in fifties and hundreds to be given away later that evening.

When Connie returned with several bulging money pouches, she whispered, "The first bank could only give me thirty thousand dollars in cash without shorting their vault. I had to cash checks at two other branches just to get it all."

I felt like a bank robber as we concealed the loot and moved into my private office. We only had two hours to stuff the employees' envelopes with cash; each individual's amount reflected their years of service.

The money bags were spread around the conference table and the cold cash was ready to be counted and divided. We double-checked each amount, matching it against our date-of-hire list. Realizing the process could take longer than the two hours we had left, Connie rounded up Pam and Steve to help finish the task. We all raced against the galloping clock, tucking cards and wads of cash inside each envelope.

Our daughter Wendy and her husband Keith showed up at six o'clock that night, and we discussed our plan with both them and our managers before heading downstairs to the large lunchroom area.

With approximately one hundred and ten employees in attendance, there was standing-room-only for our special meeting. Because we were contractually required to stay open twenty-four hours a day, 365 days a year, ten of our workers had volunteered to remain on the job.

"I want to thank all of you for coming to our meeting," I began. "I also want to take this opportunity to thank all of you for your professionalism and hard work. You have helped make our company a success. Now I would like to turn the meeting over to Connie for an important announcement." I was happy to pass over the microphone.

Connie proceeded to tell the story of how we came to make the decision to sell our company to RoadOne. Shocked looks filled many of the faces in the audience. As she sincerely expressed how difficult that choice had been for us, there was a murmur throughout the room; almost all of our employees were caught off guard.

It was only right that Connie was the one to tell the story, since she was the one who had struggled with the decision the most. I knew our staff would better understand once they heard it from her perspective. At the end of her brief but moving explanation, she told the employees how much we appreciated them and asked for questions. There were only a few. But we knew, once the shock wore off, the days ahead would bring many more.

To soften the blow, she revealed, "Ed and I have signed five-year management contracts, so we will continue to run the business for the new ownership. We know our decision to sell probably surprises most of you, but we needed an exit plan and believe this decision will be good for all of us in the long run."

Connie went on to explain, "When we sold, we bargained for a higher purchase price. Out of gratitude for your dedication and hard work, I've decided to pass on my share of that additional money to each of you."

More surprised looks and then smiles filled the room as she and I, along with our managers, handed out all of the envelopes.

On the drive home, Connie commented, "That was one of the best nights of my life! It was exhilarating to freely give back to our employees, especially when they least expected it."

I smiled, feeling very relieved and content. A new phase in our lives had just begun.

Chapter 38

Throwing In the Towel

Brimming with enthusiasm, we began our new positions with RoadOne. Our jobs felt almost identical at first, and we enjoyed taking on a new challenge together.

Months earlier, Connie's brother, Conrad, had given us some advice, "If you decide to sell, don't stick around. That never works out well. Just take the money and run."

Connie and I didn't anticipate any major problems so we'd decided to go ahead and take the plunge. After all, we were only in our fifties and this short-term contract seemed like the perfect way to finish out our careers. But, later, when we looked back on that shrewd advice, we realized we should have heeded it.

Within months, we were working more hours than we had when we owned the place. Instead of having more time to spend with our children and grandchildren, we suddenly had much less.

The corporate offices were located on the East Coast, three hours ahead of us. By the time we arrived at work each day, we were already bombarded by urgent email messages. We felt like we were behind before we'd even gotten started. It was irritating to have to run almost every decision by the head office. Every day felt very long and frustrating.

It was an especially difficult time for Connie. The corporate headquarters repeatedly sent requests that seemed unnecessary and greatly reduced our administrative efficiency. They also regularly lost documents we sent back to them. Within a few months, we wondered if the corporation was being mismanaged.

After one year, Steve, our human resources and business manager, decided he no longer wanted to work for a national company. His departure put an even greater load on Connie's shoulders.

When we asked for more office personnel to process the increased workload, Corporate responded with a hiring freeze that left us working even longer hours.

To top it off, RoadOne asked me to go to Portland, Oregon, to oversee a struggling company that they had purchased. For many weeks, I had to be out of town from Monday through Thursday. This wasn't what we had signed up for. Babysitting a business in Portland was stealing valuable time from our family.

The biggest sacrifice was missing out on many of the "firsts" with our two young grandsons. When I came up for air on weekends, those little guys were on the top of my priority list.

Once in a while, our daughter Wendy would need help during the week with the twins. Had we been working for ourselves, the requests would have been no problem. But in our new contract positions, we didn't have the luxury of taking hours off in the middle of the week.

On a day in early February of 2000, Wendy was in desperate need of a sitter. I was in town so I decided I could go to her house to cover for her and still stay in touch with the office.

As soon as the three of us were alone, we got busy playing. I galloped through the house, giving lively "horsey rides." I couldn't believe how fast Isaac and Luke were growing; they were nearly two and a half already.

I was expecting a phone call from RoadOne's corporate office sometime before noon. I had hoped to be long gone from Wendy's house before I had to take the call.

At ten o'clock, my cell phone rang. Unfortunately, it was my boss. Evidently, he had decided to call me two hours early. I quickly ducked into the powder room to escape my charges. As I tried to write down verbal instructions on a pad of paper, the bathroom door swung open. There stood two smiling toddlers staring up at me. Waving them off didn't work. Instead, each of the boys grabbed hold of one of my legs. Then, suddenly and loudly, they started to sing a silly song.

Luke and Isaac

Slapping my hand over the receiver, I gave them my meanest stare. Quickly, I grabbed some blocks and cars and dumped them out in front of them. I had to find some way to keep them busy. I really didn't want my boss to know I was babysitting. I ran around the corner, stepped over the childproof gate and trotted up the stairs.

After finishing my twenty-minute phone call in the upstairs bedroom, I ambled back down the stairs. It seemed especially quiet. The powder room door was open, and I thought I heard voices.

I poked my head around the doorframe. There was Luke, standing by the towel rack, offering words of encouragement to his brother. I looked over to see Isaac grab the toilet paper, and, in long pulls, unroll it from the dispenser, depositing all of it into the toilet bowl. When I opened the door further, their two heads whipped around. They instantly froze, their eyes opened wide. Isaac stood like a statue, his guilty hands on the last lengthy string of toilet paper. I had just caught them, red-handed.

"What are you doing?" I asked pointedly.

There was no answer.

Then I said firmly, "Both of you, out of this bathroom."

As if caught with their hands in cookie jar, Luke and Isaac looked down at their feet and moved past me into the hallway. I stepped into the bathroom for a closer look. The toilet paper roll was nearly empty and, what little remained, left a trail of evidence. I sighed at the soggy disaster choking the passageway.

"Boys, you really made a mess," I scolded.

I reached under the sink and grabbed a small wastepaper basket. Grimacing, I slid my hand deep into the toilet and grabbed all that I could. Pulling a handful of wet TP out of the cold, gray water, I made a large, sloppy deposit into the wastebasket. One grab wasn't going to be enough. I glanced at the twins, who were peeking around the corner. They watched intently as I went back in for more.

After two pulls, I decided I had retrieved enough paper and could flush the remainder down the toilet drain. I pushed the handle and the bowl silently filled up and up and up. Instantly, I recognized it wasn't going to stop.

In a panic, I lifted the tank cover and grabbed onto the float, pulling it up just as the water neared the rim. Immediately, the water stopped rising and very slowly began to drain out. I knew it wasn't fixed; I needed a plunger. At one time, I remembered seeing one in the upstairs bathroom.

I developed a plan that required perfect timing. If I let the toilet drain to its lowest level, I should have enough time—after I released the float—to hurdle the baby gate, run up the stairs, grab the plunger and make it back before the bowl overflowed.

"Boys, move out of the doorway," I said. "I have to run and get the plunger. I'll be back in a second." I'm sure they had no idea what I was talking about, but they stepped back a bit.

I charged out of that bathroom, across the hardwood floor, losing time and traction in my slippery socks. I couldn't find the elusive plunger on my first pass so decided to abort the mission. I raced down the stairs and immediately saw water cascading over the toilet bowl's rim and flowing out into the hallway. I splashed into the flooded bathroom and jerked up on the float. Out of breath and standing in an inch of water, I was out of ideas.

The boys stepped back, beyond the flowing river, their eyes growing ever bigger. Fascinated, they watched me stretch my arms to their limit, holding the float with one hand and, with the other, placing hand towels across the threshold of the door. The quickly saturated towels formed a pathetic levee.

Just then, I remembered something. Most toilets have a shut-off valve behind them. I knelt on the wet floor, quickly found the valve and turned it to the right. I let go of the float and was satisfied with the result. I felt like an idiot: I couldn't believe that, in my panic, I'd forgotten about that simple solution.

It was now time to mop up the mess. The little wastebasket once again came in handy. I used it to scoop up some of the water, dumping the contents into the toilet. Then I went in search of some old towels to mop up the remainder of the lake. I couldn't do a thing about the two gallons of water that had escaped down the heat vent.

Ultimately, I found the plunger in the garage and took care of the original problem. As far as punishing the boys was concerned, I knew they were too young to know any better. After all, I was the one who had left two toddlers unsupervised. If anyone deserved a reprimand, I knew that it was me.

After this experience as a relatively new grandpa, I learned never to let little ones out of my sight.

Even though grandpa duty had its challenges, I loved every minute of it and longed for more time to do it. I wished that there was way to throw in the towel a little early on my contract with RoadOne. I was tired of working for someone else.

Chapter 39

Making The News

A big break came our way at the two-and-one-half year mark. RoadOne gave all of its general managers across the United States an opportunity to opt out of their employment contracts. The deal included payment of half of the manager's salary for the duration of his or her contract. It was a move designed to thin the management numbers and cut costs in the long run. Most had a year to go, but we had much more.

I approached Connie with the new offer. It really was too good to refuse, especially with the frustrations of working within the corporate bureaucracy. I jumped at the "Get Out of Jail Free" card, but she had a hard time deciding.

"Come on. Let's do it!" I urged. "We can't pass up a deal that gives us 50 percent pay for thirty months while we spend time with the grandkids or on vacation."

She smiled agreeably, "You're right. It's time. Let's take it."

We notified RoadOne that we would be taking the company up on its offer. A representative called us back as soon as they received our paperwork.

"We didn't want you two to leave. The contract buyout is intended for non-performing markets, and yours is the second strongest."

I told her, "I'm sorry, but it feels like a good time for us to leave. We want to enjoy life while we have our health. This is a strong market, and I am sure that, with the right management, this company will continue to do well."

Five days later, we were signing releases terminating our employment in ninety days.

We notified our staff and let them know that the thirty-first of March, 2000, would be our last day. That gave us a few months to hire and train a new general manager.

We both worked hard those last three months to tie up dozens of loose ends, bid on the City of Seattle impound contract, consult with employees and inform key customers of the transition.

Connie and I joked with each other about what our new life would be like. "Next Friday, we will be out of a job. Are you still okay with that?" I asked.

"I'll be a little sad, but I think I'm finally ready."

On Monday, I decided to contact *The Seattle Times* to see if the paper was willing to include a brief announcement about our retirement in its business section. I thought I would surprise Connie. Throughout the years, I had seen notices in the newspaper about other business owners retiring.

The clerk I got in touch with at *The Seattle Times* said, "The business editor no longer does those types of stories. You may want to try the general editor's office, but I'd say it's a long shot."

I dialed the number I was given and spoke to a reporter who was busy and asked if he could phone me back. Ten minutes later, he called and asked for details about our company, about the Pink Toe and the new buyers.

"I will write a news story that will be ready for Friday morning's paper, but if we have a busy news day on Thursday, your story might get bumped."

"I appreciate the consideration, thank you."

"I'd also like you and your wife to meet our photographer at the Pink Toe's location for a photo shoot tomorrow at noon," the reporter said.

"We'll see you there," I answered.

We arrived at the Fairview location where the Toe Truck was sitting on top of the roof. Despite some uncertainty about getting up on the roof, we climbed up a ladder and into the truck. The photographer took a bundle of pictures.

That Friday, I woke up early. It was hard to believe that this day had finally arrived. I headed out the front door to get the newspaper that was lying at the foot of our steps. I wondered if *The Seattle Times* had included a send-off article, knowing it was likely that other, more pressing news would take priority.

The paper was folded in half, but, even from five feet away, I could see the splash of pink across the front. My heart leaped as I stooped down and gathered up the pages. I unfolded it and there, on the front page, was a huge picture of Connie and me sitting inside the Pink Toe Truck. A full-length story followed.

I ran into the house, waving the paper, and found Connie in the kitchen. We read the article together. I had hoped for a small article or a mention in the business section. I was floored that our retirement was announced as *the* lead article on the front page of *The Seattle Times*. Shockingly our picture and article filled up nearly half of the page.

"Connie, what do you think of this?"

She, too, was stunned. "How in the world did we end up on the front page?"

"I have no idea."

Just then, the phone rang and Connie picked it up. One of our managers, Rich, was on the line. "When do you think you'll be coming into the office? The phones have been ringing off the hook. Ichabod Caine at KMPS radio called and wants you to call him at the station right away. Also, an Associated Press reporter said she would be here in about an hour to interview you both. Did you know you two made front-page news?"

"Yes, we were shocked, and we'll be there as soon as possible."

Connie hung up the phone. "You're supposed to call Ichabod at work, and we're wanted at the office for more interviews. We'd better get going. I really can't believe all of this."

Ed holding up the front-page article

I gave Ichabod a quick call, and he asked about our plans for the Pink Toe Truck. He said his listeners were interested and had been calling the station. I told him we didn't know yet, but we would keep him informed.

We left home and drove to the office in time to meet with the Associated Press reporter. The interview went well. We asked what would happen with the story. Surprisingly, she said it would be available coast to coast.

"When the article goes out, there's no way for us to know how many papers will pick it up," she explained. "But if news editors like the article, they will print the story in their local papers."

We spent the day tidying our offices and packing up the rest of our personal items. We both looked forward to Sunday's retirement party. Rich and the staff had done a great job of planning the outdoor gathering at Lincoln Towing's headquarters.

About one hundred and fifty family, friends, business associates and employees showed up for the festivities. For Connie and me, it was a very special celebration to cap off our working career.

As we waited several days for the Associated Press article to be released, I said to Connie, "I wonder if any other newspapers will pick up our article."

By Monday, we learned that numerous papers across America had run the story about our retirement and that of the Pink Toe. At home, Connie started fielding calls from relatives and friends across the country. "I read about your Pink Toe Truck and your retirement! Congratulations to both you and Ed." We were overwhelmed and humbled by the interest and attention.

A few days later, National Public Radio jumped on the bandwagon. An NPR reporter tracked us down at home and asked if Connie and I would do a radio interview for their national audience.

I quickly agreed.

He explained, "Our broadcasting office is in Washington D.C., but we just need you and Connie to go to the University of Washington campus in Seattle. UWTV's professional broadcast studio can transmit your interview. We've reserved a time slot for both of you at 10:00 a.m. on Thursday. Will that work?"

"We'll be there," I answered.

Still in shock, I turned to Connie. "You won't believe it, but we were just asked to do a live interview on NPR. This is crazy. Who would've thought the Pink Toe Truck would draw so much national attention?"

Thursday came and a technician ushered us into the soundproof recording studio. After sitting down in front of a microphone, they did a sound check and told us to relax. Then they gave us both headphones so we could hear the interviewer at the NPR headquarters in Washington, D.C.

The interviewer called in and chatted with us for a few minutes before the interview actually started. I took a deep breath and tried to relax. When he asked if we were ready, I mumbled, "I think so."

Connie added, "I'm ready too."

The interviewer said, "I would like to start with Connie."

He asked her a few questions, but, after answering, she suggested he speak with me since I was the one who had come up with the Toe Truck idea. I gave my standard answers to all of the questions and, of course, tossed in a little humor. Before I knew it, we were saying thank you and goodbye.

On the way home, Connie asked, "How do you feel that went?"

"That was actually much easier than I'd thought," I said. "I bet a lot of the people out there listening were hearing about the Pink Toe for the very first time."

"What an amazing week," Connie said in wonder. "I still can't believe that our retirement and the future fate of the Toe created such a stir."

I nodded and then said with a smile, "We're only going to retire once in our lifetime; I guess we might as well go out with a bang."

Chapter 40

Here One Day, Gone Tomorrow

Only sixteen months in, we were enjoying retirement more than even I had imagined. Connie and I spent much of our free time with our kids and grandkids and worked just a few hours each week overseeing the Mustang Ranch.

On our last day of work, Connie had surprised me with the best retirement gift a guy could receive: a new Porsche Boxster. With the demands on my time now radically reduced, I cruised around town enjoying the feel of the sun on my back and the wind blowing through my thinning hair.

Ed's retirement gift: a new Porsche Boxster

After just a few months of searching, we fell in love with a house. We quickly purchased it and made the move to our new abode. With a new house and car and finally some time to spare, this retirement gig seemed to be working out just fine.

On August 7, 2001, sixty days after we moved into our new neighborhood, Connie headed out for a short trip to the bank in her Lexus coupe. When she was just a minute from our new home and about ten yards from the stop sign at the arterial, there was a thunderous bang. One second she was driving and the next she found herself turned ninety degrees and parked up on the curb in our neighbors' front yard. She was stunned and didn't know how she had gotten there.

The left front corner of the car was crumpled, the windshield was completely splintered and the hood was crushed downward into the engine compartment. The car looked like it had been in a demolition derby with a monster truck. A haze filled the car from the explosion of both front air bags.

A young lady arrived on the scene, parked her car and ran over to Connie's Lexus.

She spoke through the partially opened window, "Hi, I'm Julie. How badly are you hurt?"

"I don't know. My thumb is throbbing, and I don't know why. What happened?" Connie said, obviously in shock.

"I was following an old blue pickup truck when it started weaving back and forth onto the shoulder. I backed off because the driver seemed completely out of control. Right before your street, the truck veered off the right side of the road, went into the ditch and then crashed into you."

"Is the driver of the truck okay?" Connie asked.

"I don't know. I'll check." Julie said.

When she returned, Connie inquired, "Is he okay?"

"I don't think so," Julie replied.

As Connie bent over to gather her purse and the bank deposit off of the floor, the young lady said, "I don't think you should move around anymore. You may be hurt and not know it. Wait until the medics arrive to check you out."

Connie's car after the accident

Connie picked up her cell phone and called the Mustang Ranch. She said, "I've just been in an accident, can I talk to Ed?"

"Are you okay?"

"I think so . . . "

"I'll give Ed a call and let him know."

The office called me and relayed the message. I phoned Connie, but there was no answer. While driving towards home, our neighbor Robert called to say an ambulance was taking Connie to Evergreen Hospital and I should head that way. Then I immediately called the girls to tell them that Connie had been in accident. Wendy and Trina both rushed to the hospital. Connie had just finished being x-rayed when we all arrived.

At first, it appeared her injuries were minor: just a fractured right thumb and some bruising. They removed the neck brace and backboard, and the nurse told me they were getting ready to release her in about thirty minutes. Then, as they moved her from the gurney, Connie began experiencing severe neck pain for the first time. It shot through the entire right side of her neck. When Wendy saw her face contort in pain, she helped Connie lie back down and immediately requested a second opinion and another scan.

The emergency room doctor came in, heard what had happened and agreed. "To be safe, I want the technician to do a CT scan. We need to find out where the pain is coming from."

When the CT scan results appeared on the monitor, the technician sent an urgent page to the doctor.

She instructed Connie, "Lie still and let us do all the work. We think you may be more injured than was originally thought."

They put a high-tech Aspen neck brace on Connie and wheeled her back to the emergency room where we were waiting.

When the neurosurgeon arrived, he informed us, "Connie has a C-1 vertebrae fracture on the right side of her neck. It is serious. Can you tell me what happened?"

Connie gave the details as best as she could.

"Your type of injury is not what I would expect to see in a car accident. This serious injury most commonly occurs in diving accidents where a person dives into shallow water and hits the bottom with their head. I can't understand how the accident you've described could've caused this type of injury."

The doctor continued, "In addition to her fractured neck, Connie also has a concussion. She'll need to stay in the hospital for a few days so we can monitor her. You know, C-1 fractures can often be fatal." Turning to Connie, he said, "You are a very lucky lady."

When I left the hospital, I was incredibly thankful Connie was going to be okay. Still wondering how this could have happened, I decided to do my own investigation at the tow lot.

When I saw the wrecked truck and our car, I felt a shiver run through my body. The damage was more extensive than I ever imagined. For the first time, I realized how close I had come to losing Connie.

After I finished looking over both vehicles, I was puzzled. Connie's right front tire and frame were bent from hitting something solid. The windshield was smashed downward and the hood was compressed so hard that the engine was almost on the ground. I couldn't imagine how this accident had happened.

The mystery was solved the next day when Julie, the witness, called the hospital to check on Connie.

Connie asked her, "Did you see the actual collision? The medical people are confused by my type of neck injury."

Julie answered, "No, but I saw the pickup truck going over forty miles per hour. It veered off the road into the deep retention ditch, then flew out of the ditch and into the air like it was shot out of a cannon. I didn't know that he'd hit anyone until I reached the corner and saw your car up on the curb and the truck beyond it in the grass. I never actually saw the truck collide with your car because I was a little too far behind."

"Thank you, Julie. You've just solved our mystery. The doctor couldn't imagine how this happened from a car accident that wasn't a rollover. The truck must have come down so hard on my hood that it shot me upwards into my car's roof."

Connie was in the hospital for three days and then released. She was housebound for ten weeks and had to remain in the neck brace for eight more.

Almost losing Connie proved, once again, that life can turn on a dime. I knew I needed to treasure each day just the way it came to us: as a gift.

In the same year, on a sunny day in early November, Mark and I were cleaning out our garage. My little Porsche Boxster was parked, top down, in our driveway, waiting to be washed. We took about an hour lunch break to visit with both Mark and Trina, who had stopped by with their one-year-old son Cole.

When we finished up with the garage, we washed the Boxster and then Mark gave me a hand installing the hardtop for the upcoming winter. I parked my little car in its place in the third stall. It felt good to have the garage clean and my toy tucked away for the winter.

At 7:30 a.m. the next day, I headed out to the Mustang Ranch. When I opened the door from the house into the garage, I instantly noticed that the garage felt colder than usual. Then I saw that the third garage door was wide open and my red convertible was nowhere in sight. Shocked and confused, I walked briskly out to the driveway and scanned the street. Everything looked just as it normally did except my car had simply vanished.

I decided to look around the garage before I called the police. The first place I looked was inside of my work truck. I was shocked to find my neat interior scattered with stuff. My center console appeared to be empty. I raced back into the house and alerted Connie about my missing car and the obvious signs of burglary.

I phoned the King County Police and the dispatcher asked a few basic questions and then advised me. "It will be about two hours before one of our officers can come by."

"I'll be here," I said, feeling a little frustrated and rattled by the situation.

I had no choice but to wait. I didn't want to leave Connie with the problem of my stolen car. She was still in her neck brace and had enough to deal with every day.

When the officer finally arrived, I asked about fingerprints and she explained, "We don't take prints unless there is a suspect. It would be too time-consuming."

I was aware that cars like mine regularly got stolen and shipped out of the country along with freshly forged documents.

When she pulled away in her squad car, I said to Connie, "I'm disappointed. She didn't offer much hope that we'd ever find my car."

Very early Friday morning, almost twenty-four hours later, the phone next to the bed rang and Connie lifted the receiver to her ear, offering a sleepy "hello."

She turned to me and whispered, "It's the King County Sheriff's department." After Connie hung up, she said, "The policeman who called said he had some good news and some bad news. The good news is your stolen car has been found; the bad news is that it was involved in a very serious collision. That's all he could tell me right now. We're supposed to call the Seattle Police Department after nine o'clock and ask for Detective Johnson."

Our first concern was about the people in the accident who might have been hurt or worse. I tossed and turned in bed for about thirty minutes.

At 6:00 a.m., Connie moved into the family room to read. After a bit, she turned on the TV to a local news channel and, right before her eyes, was my red Porsche wrapped around a light pole. She even recognized the license plate.

The news reporter said, "It has been a terrible night for wrecks due to the heavy rainfall and slippery roads after several weeks of dry weather."

As it turned out, my Porsche was so badly wrecked that a utility crew needed to unbolt the light pole from its mounting so that the pole could be pulled up and out through the passenger side of the car. When I called the Seattle detective, I was told my car was in Lincoln Towing's lot.

I called Lincoln Towing and the dispatcher remarked, "Your car looks like a horseshoe."

Ed's car after the accident

The news reported that the passenger was dead at the scene, and the driver had been transported to Harborview Hospital. It was a shame those two young men ruined their lives for what turned out to be a very short joyride. We were thankful that no one else was injured in the crash.

After the dust settled, police reports revealed that both of the young men had been picked up dozens of times for car theft. Their M.O. was to steal cars and then race around town in them until they ran out of gas.

When we thought back to the previous day, we realized that, during the one-hour break for lunch, the crooks must have been in our cul-de-sac to case it for possible cars to steal. They had a perfect opportunity to steal my garage door opener from the Porsche's sun visor. Later, in the pre-dawn hours long after I had tucked my Porsche back into the garage, they must have returned. After simply pressing the garage door opener, they entered and found a spare ring of keys in my truck. With Porsche keys in hand, their getaway was quick and easy.

Fortunately, our car was fully insured and, at the end of the month, I had a check for the original cost of the car.

About two months later, we received an invoice from the City of Seattle saying we owed two thousand dollars for the light pole that was destroyed in the accident. Connie called and explained what had happened to the city clerk and asked her to verify the information with the police. Fortunately, we were let off the hook.

The young car thief received a seven-year prison sentence for vehicular homicide. The police estimated that he was driving my car at speeds of eighty to ninety miles per hour when the car spun out and smashed into the steel pole. The crash was so serious that the pole penetrated the passenger door all the way to the center console, killing the passenger instantly.

Within six months of moving into our home, we were down to one car, but I didn't really mind. After the tumultuous past few months, my primary focus was on helping Connie mend. Cars can be replaced.

Chapter 41

Watch Out

During my post-retirement years, I have spent my Monday mornings with my retired friends Bruce and Charlie, volunteering at a nursing home in Bothell. Bruce is an ordained minister who gives a brief, ten-minute message in the dayroom. For the rest of the hour, we lead the group of seniors in singing hymns.

It is an unlikely job for a guy like me who has been told over the years that he sings off-key. Nevertheless I sing along—just like I do most things in life—with gusto. Most of the seniors are hard of hearing and don't mind a bit.

We always begin our hymn time right after breakfast is served, and sometimes it seems that half the group is sleeping in their wheelchairs before we've finished the second verse. But the show must go on!

Before launching into each requested song, I spend a lot of my time helping the residents find the right page for the next hymn. For these lonely people, a polite hello and a touch on the arm go a long way.

One of the first residents I connected with years ago was Elaine. She habitually sits in the far right-hand corner of the dayroom. She is somewhat soft-spoken but remarkably alert. When we finish our hymn time each week, she always smiles kindly and thanks us for coming.

Another nice lady, Martha, is hard to miss. She is very outgoing and generous with her compliments. Interestingly, she also has a thing for my dress shirts. Without fail, each week she greets me by saying, "Can I feel your shirt?" or "That's a very nice shirt."

She speaks very loudly and is also amazingly forgetful; those two traits make for an interesting combination.

Often, in the middle of a hymn, she forcefully blurts out a question, like "Are you married?" or "What page are we on?" As soon as she yells, I simply trot over to her wheelchair and show her the page or gently break the news to her of my marital status again.

I've learned its best to stand right beside Martha as we all sing so I can respond to her repeated inquiries. Now that I think about it, maybe that's the secret motivation behind her outbursts. But I really don't mind her boisterous mid-hymn interruptions; at least she's awake. Plus, she always adds an element of excitement and surprise to the tame group and definitely keeps me on my toes.

Most of the residents are fragile and in the last phase of their lives. Our little trio simply offers a lighthearted, old-fashioned sing-a-long that we hope will brighten their day.

It's definitely nothing flashy, but it's a good time for all, especially me, as I've soaked in the memories of my deceased mom, dad and grandparents. There's truly no place I'd rather be on Monday mornings.

A few of the residents have offered me special memories to store away for a rainy day. Not long ago, Peter gave me a new story to tell.

Peter is in his early eighties; he is a longtime resident with a variety of medical disabilities. He is also our most regular dayroom attendee. He sings with vigor. His absolute favorite hymn is number eight, "In the Garden." Peter requests that same song every week.

On one particular Monday morning, just after the one-hour hymn time had finished, our little three-man volunteer group picked up the song books. From his wheelchair, Peter motioned me over to his right side. In a soft voice, he said, "What time is it?"

I looked at my watch and said, "It's ten-thirty."

"What time does my watch say?" I looked down as he tried to hold out his arm.

"Peter, your watch says it's three o'clock."

"I'm not too surprised; the time has been jumping around lately."

I remembered having a similar problem with one of my watches just a few weeks earlier. I suddenly had a bright idea.

I asked, "Peter, would you like me to take your watch to the repair shop and get a new battery put in it for you? I could bring it back next Monday when our group returns."

Peter looked surprised, and then he said, "That would be nice."

I carefully slipped the Timex watch off of Peter's pudgy arm and put it in my pocket. I didn't consider the fact that walking out of a nursing home with a patient's watch in my pocket might seem a little suspicious.

The thought did cross my mind, however, that Peter might worry about his watch if he later realized it was missing and didn't remember why. I should have left that thought alone, but, instead, I said, "Peter, how would you like to wear my watch for a week while I'm getting yours repaired?"

He looked at my watch and said, "Yes, I'd like to wear it; it's shiny." The exchange was completed, and I felt good. I'd found a temporary solution that seemed to please Peter.

When I arrived home that day, I told Connie the story about the watch exchange, and she immediately thought it was a bad idea. She pointed out that I could have gotten in big trouble if someone had seen me take off Peter's watch and stuff it in my pocket. She was apprehensive and thought I should have spoken to the supervisor in charge, but now it was too late for that.

After the watch repairman installed the battery on Saturday, the timepiece was ready for Monday's swap.

Monday quickly arrived, and I headed into the nursing home with a spring in my step and Peter's repaired watch in my pocket. I walked down the narrow hallway and turned into the dayroom. I spied Peter at the head table and made a beeline for him. Kneeling down next to his wheelchair, I covertly slid his watch from my pocket.

I smiled and delivered the good news. "Peter, I got your watch repaired, and I have it right here."

He took one look at the watch and abruptly said, "I like the one I'm wearing better."

"Peter, don't you remember?" I asked. "I took your watch to get a new battery put in it. That watch on your wrist is mine; I just loaned it to you so you wouldn't be without one while I got yours fixed."

"This one is shinier," he replied.

I wanted to avoid a scene and get this over with quickly, so I said, "I'm sorry, Peter. I need my watch." I reached down to his wheelchair and, surprisingly, felt like a thief as I slid my own timepiece off his wrist and replaced it with his old but freshly repaired watch.

This was not the happy ending I had envisioned. Peter was upset, and I had a knot in my stomach. Why was this act of kindness now making me feel so lousy? All of a sudden, I was worried I could be in trouble if Peter complained about the watch. What had seemed so right, now felt so wrong; my good deed had taken a sharp turn for the worse.

When I arrived home, I reluctantly told Connie of the complication, and she didn't look too surprised. I knew I was going to eat some crow for awhile.

Hours later, Connie noticed the watch I had placed on the bathroom counter and asked, "Ed, is that the watch you brought home? If it is, it's not your watch."

"What do you mean?" I asked, thinking she was mistaken. Then I walked over, picked it up and looked at the brand. Sure enough, it was a manufacturer I'd never heard of, certainly not a Hamilton, and, on top of that, it was very scratched up. *How had this happened?*

The next day, I returned to the old folks' home and sheepishly confessed my flawed plan and its aftermath to the supervisor. She agreed with my wife, telling me I should've never taken on the responsibility for the broken watch.

She searched Peter's closet and didn't find my Hamilton any-where. According to her, Peter was known to be a "wheeler dealer," and he had recently bragged about selling something for twenty bucks. When she asked him about the deal, things had gotten very foggy, and he suddenly wasn't at all clear about the transaction.

I gave her back the "mystery" watch and said, "I have other watches at home, so I'll be no worse for wear."

I guess I will never know what truly transpired in the watch drama, but I'm pretty sure I have been outflanked by someone more senior than me.

Many months have passed since then, but I still find myself, on Monday mornings, glancing at Peter's left wrist to see if he might be wearing my brand of watch. No luck yet. Although sometimes a good story is worth more than an expensive watch—at least for an avid storyteller like me.

Chapter 42

Unfinished Business

As I looked back over the last several years, I realized we had one important item that was left unfinished. There was still the question of what to do with the Pink Toe Truck. During that crazy week in March 2000 when the media splashed our retirement all over the airwaves, we received numerous inquiries from groups and museums interested in the Pink Toe.

Three local museums—the Museum of History and Industry in Seattle, the future LeMay Car Museum in Tacoma and the History House in the Fremont district of Seattle—each made a bid for the Toe.

Over a period of several months, Connie and I visited each of the museums. We were flattered by their fervent interest in the Pink Toe Truck. We listened to each presentation and afterwards thought that the Museum of History and Industry might be the best choice.

I have to admit that I briefly considered selling it on eBay. I still wonder how high the bidding would have gone. It would have been fun just to see. However, our main goal had always been to keep the Pink Toe in the Greater Seattle area for future generations of our family and Seattleites to enjoy. Besides, Connie wasn't keen on the eBay idea, so I never could have gotten away with it.

Unfortunately, after our initial tour of the interested museums, we failed to follow up because other priorities got in the way: the new house, the grandkids, Connie's accident and the sale of the Mustang Ranch. Four years had raced by and the Toe was still sitting on the roof, rusting in the rain. Even though it was badly in need of repair, Lincoln Towing was happy to squeeze out its last bit of free advertising from the Toe. So without any pressure to make a decision, the Pink Toe just sat.

Finally, in the spring of 2004, we were ready to get back to work on this important decision. Connie and I made an appointment with Leonard Garfield, director of the Museum of History and Industry. We wanted to find out what the museum had planned for the Toe. Our biggest concern was that it would be relegated to a storage area and not put on display.

Ed in front of the Museum of History and Industry

Leonard was up-front with us and said, "The museum would be thrilled to receive the Pink Toe Truck; however, our budget is very limited at the moment. Unless we receive some large donations, we may have to store it in one of our warehouses for a few years until we have the funds to restore it."

This was not what I wanted to hear. Then I had a thought, "What if we made our own arrangements to have the truck restored?

Would you have space to display the Toe in the Museum as soon as it is ready?"

Excitedly, he said, "Absolutely! I'd make sure we'd be ready. I could have my staff do some rearranging and create space in one of our highest traffic areas."

On the drive home, I looked over at Connie, "What do you think?"

She didn't hesitate. "We need to find a new home for the Toe. I vote to get it restored."

I called Mike, the new general manager of Lincoln Towing, and asked if the company would be willing to help us with the Pink Toe Truck's restoration. After talking it over with the company's new owners, he called back a few days later and said, "We would be happy to donate all of the labor if you are willing to cover the parts." Since our former shop manager Mike had a soft spot for the truck, I knew he and his right-hand man Bob would do a quality job.

Within a month, I called my friend Doug, from Mount Vernon Towing Service, who was experienced doing extractions with their cranes. He said he would be happy to help us get the roof-weary Toe Truck down. It was going to require some special handling because the frame was badly rusted. We both agreed on a day and time.

The extraction day arrived and, after sizing things up, Doug planned to pick the Toe up and remove it from the lot side of the building. It would be safer and easier than having to cordon off the busy street.

I nervously held my breath and watched as the Pink Toe Truck was hoisted forty feet in the air in order to clear some wires. Once it was safely on the ground, I could comfortably breathe again. The Toe had definitely seen better days. I stood back as it was loaded onto a trailer and whisked away to Lincoln Towing's repair shop, where it was scheduled for a major "pedicure."

It took about six months for Bob and Mike to work their magic on the truck. The most serious part of the repairs was cutting away the entire rusted floor panel and replacing two feet of the frame member. After many hours of diligent work, the truck was mechanically and structurally restored.

The crane removes the Toe Truck safely from the roof

Now it was finally ready for a brand-new paint job. Bill Pierre Ford volunteered to repaint the Toe in its original bright pink shade at no charge. The toenails had been repainted many times over the years for radio station promotions and needed a lot of attention. A week later, when I picked up the Toe from Bill Pierre Ford, I relived that day twenty-four years earlier when I had first seen the finished Pink Toe Truck in all her glory. I felt like a proud papa once again.

Connie and I were grateful to all of the businesses that donated their time and services to help us restore our one-of-a-kind Toe Truck to its original condition. We were touched by the community effort.

Four years into our retirement, we were finally ready to deliver the Toe to its new home. I called Leonard at the museum to let him know the Pink Toe Truck was ready for delivery. However, he had another idea. He said, "I would like to have the Toe Truck arrive at its new home with a bit of fanfare. I can arrange a small parade from the Seattle Center, through downtown Seattle, ending at the museum."

He asked, "Do you think you could round up some other tow companies around Seattle to join in and make the parade more festive?"

"We'll give it a try."

I asked Connie if she would make some phone calls to see if anyone was interested. All eight of the companies she called promised to send at least one tow truck.

Parade day, February 10, 2005, was one of those rare but amazing Seattle days with the sun shining and the Emerald City showing off all her glory. Lincoln Towing's managers and drivers showed up with six trucks and eight other tow companies were represented. The group congregated at the Seattle Center parking lot. Two Seattle motorcycle policemen were there to lead us all the way through the downtown corridor, up over Capitol Hill and to our final destination at the Museum of History and Industry. We felt honored that so many of our competitors and friends in the industry took time out of their lives to share this special day with us.

The Toe Truck was driven by me with Connie as my copilot. Wendy, Trina and all of our grandchildren sat in the back and waved enthusiastically to the people on the sidewalks. The pedestrians weren't expecting a parade and many had puzzled looks on their faces as we came into view. We collected smiles and waves as we passed by. Clearly, the onlookers were pleasantly surprised by the joyful and lengthy procession led by the Pink Toe Truck.

Local television stations and other media covered the parade. Connie invited our retired managers, Pam and Steve, as well as Joan, who had sculpted the toes. They were all part of the crowd welcoming the Pink Toe Truck as it made its grand entrance at the museum, followed by an entourage of seventeen tow trucks.

The museum staff invited Connie and me to come up to the podium and say a few words before presenting the Pink Toe Truck to Leonard. As Connie stood next to me and thanked our family, friends, employees and colleagues in the industry, I was very aware of the keys in my hand. I squeezed them tightly and the memories of the salesman's sketch, the VW van, the Torchlight acceptance letter and Ed Ellison working his fiberglass magic all spun through my mind. Suddenly, I wasn't sure if I was ready to let go of this silly pink truck with toes that had brought me so much success and joy. When it was my turn to speak, I choked up a bit. I said a few words and then, reluctantly, I extended my arm toward Leonard and handed over one of the biggest gifts, literally and figuratively, I'd ever given away.

Ed and Connie presenting the Pink Toe Truck to
Leonard Garfield at MOHAI

Retirement continues to suit me just fine. I love the time I have with Connie, our kids and our seven grandchildren. I enjoy my volunteer work and having free time to spend with good friends. For me, life is an adventure; I'm always looking forward to whatever is around the next bend in the road. I still do my best to fill my days with laughter, and I love to generate smiles wherever I go.

I've had one new passion and dream during my retirement years and, as usual, I've swung for the fences. If you've read this entire book, you know I'm not one to set dreams on a shelf; that's why, right now, you are holding mine in your hands.

Ed Lincoln

Ed and Connie Lincoln

E d discovered at a young age that he had a head for business. He has pursued many endeavors throughout his life, but his overwhelming love of cars and people has directed his path. He is a man who tackles life with passion, humor and a large dose of hard work. When there is an opportunity that shows promise, he's not likely to turn it down. Over the years, he has started several successful businesses.

Ed is a true entrepreneur and loves to think of creative ways of marketing his businesses. Initially, his Lincoln Towing slogan "We're Pulling for You, Seattle!" pictured a Lincoln tow truck towing the Space Needle and Kingdome as a humorous way of showing his company's willingness to tackle any job. His clean-cut drivers and shiny trucks also helped to put a friendly face of service on an industry that had often been misunderstood.

Ed is best known as the creator of the Pink Toe Truck, a Seattle area icon. Over the years, thousands of people saw the cute and humorous Pink Toe Truck in parades or they drove by its perch on the roof of Lincoln Towing's satellite office at the intersection of Fairview and Mercer, one of Seattle's busiest I-5 off-ramps.

He met his wife, Connie, in 1965, and they married ten months later. In 1970, they had their first daughter, Wendy, and in 1972,

Katrina was born. Both of his daughters and sons-in-law, Keith and Mark, live in the Greater Seattle area. Ed and Connie's greatest joy is spending time with their family, especially their seven beloved grandchildren.

After they sold their business and retired, Ed and Connie decided to donate the Pink Toe Truck to Seattle's Museum of History and Industry. If you visit, you will see that it holds a prominent place there.

Since his retirement, Ed has enjoyed having more free time to give to others. He and Connie serve on the boards of two non-profit organizations: Friends International and Friends of iThemba. Ed also volunteers regularly at his grandchildren's elementary schools and at a rehabilitation center in Bothell, Washington. Those he serves are continually blessed by his compassionate heart and joyful spirit.

www.lifethroughtherearviewmirror.com